First There Is
a Mountain

First There Is a Mountain

A Yoga Romance

Elizabeth Kadetsky

LITTLE, BROWN AND COMPANY
BOSTON • NEW YORK • LONDON

First Edition

Library of Congress Cataloging-in-Publication Data

Kadetsky, Elizabeth.
    First there is a mountain : a yoga romance / by Elizabeth Kadetsky.
      p. cm.
    ISBN 0-316-89096-0
      1. Yoga. 2. Iyengar, B. K. S., 1918–3. Kadetsky, Elizabeth.

  BL1238.52.K33 2004
  294.5'436 — dc21   2003053242

10 9 8 7 6 5 4 3 2 1

Q-MB

Design by Meryl Sussman Levavi/Digitext
Illustration by Peter Bernard

Printed in the United States of America

for Paul

First There Is a Mountain

Prologue

The yogis tell this story:

In South India there once lived a man named Ramanuja. A Brahmin, he lived in the Tamil village of Kanchipuram, where temples sprang from the earth every ten paces, and where, inside, magnificent carvings of the lords Vishnu, Siva, and Brahma stood beside chimeras — man-lions and elephant-boys, sprites with the faces of animals, monsters with the features of demons. While Ramanuja meditated, the figures struck poses: dancing, celebrating, fighting.

Tamil Brahmins lived according to strict codes then. They married among themselves, dressed like their forefathers, and chose foods that contributed to their purity. They avoided tubers and fungi such as garlic, scallions, onions, and mushrooms, as well as red tree sap, "phlegmatic" fruit, and the first milk of a newly calved cow. Pure food easily became impure: one woman's well water could contaminate a neighbor's. People could contaminate too. If even the shadow of a low-caste man fell on a Brahmin, he became polluted; if the shadow fell on his food, that too became polluted. Other things contaminated as well: feet, dirt, meat, leather, corpses.

Like his forefathers, Ramanuja studied the works of South India's eminent philosophers. Their teachings were for Brahmins. Knowledge, like bodies, could also be contaminated.

Ramanuja's lessons followed the work of the great South Indian Sankara. Three hundred years before, in the eighth century, Sankara had taught that God, Brahman, was everywhere. In his commentaries on the ancient Vedas, Sankara argued that Brahman contained spirit as well as all matter. All was Brahman. All was one. Matter, therefore, was not as it appeared but an element of the mystical world. It was maya, illusion.

In Kanchipuram, however, the Brahmins worshiped Vishnu. This, for Ramanuja, led to some questions. Vishnu was not maya. Vishnu was an element of the universal spirit. And yet he was so like a man. In those temple statues, Vishnu dressed as a member of the clan, with armbands and ankle bracelets, a lungi cloth around his waist, a string looping from his left shoulder across his chest and up his back. This sacred thread, worn by all the village Brahmins, symbolized the tether connecting Vishnu's body to the divine — what made him both god and man.

When Ramanuja meditated, he emulated the repose of Vishnu. In this state, he observed matter and spirit cohere into an undifferentiated primordial whole. Like Vishnu, he became one with Brahman. He became like that sacred thread, connected to both ground and sky. Here, Ramanuja felt the divine was a part of him, just as he was a part of the divine.

He didn't feel like maya. He felt like Vishnu. He felt alive.

He posed his doubts to his teacher one day as they perused Sankara's discussions of the Vedas. In one passage, Ramanuja felt that Sankara had gotten it wrong: it described Brahman as the rays of the sun, Ramanuja said. Unlike Sankara's version, Ramanuja's turned the light inward. God was like sunlight, coursing through all animals and objects. Brahman was within. Brahman was like the cord that laced together a row of pearls. Those pearls, clear and white, were not maya; they were holy.

Then Ramanuja began to wonder about his body. It was pure. It too was holy. How could it be maya?

Ramanuja then looked at the images in the temples, man-gods in expressions of reverie: fighting, like warriors, their arms spread wide; seated with their feet curled in, small self-contained circles in which the flow of Brahman spiraled. His body was not a figment, he felt sure; it was no more a figment than the body of Vishnu. It was a receptacle for divinity. It was not an obstacle to be transcended but a vehicle for the expression of God. A clear body, transparent and flushed of impurities, was an instrument echoing with divinity. It was a beautiful white pearl, threaded by holy consciousness.

He felt he had discovered the universe.

This revelation caused Ramanuja to question the very precepts of his clan. For one, if the body was holy, what about the bodies of non-Brahmins? Could they really contaminate you? Tradition held that just as Brahman contained all, his body, Brahma, contained all strata of human society. Ramanuja and his caste, the Brahmins, were the head, for thinking; Kshatriyas were the arms, for fighting; Vaishyas were the legs, for laboring; and Sudras were the feet, for cleaning the muck. It was therefore common knowledge that Sudras, represented as those most dirty appendages, would contaminate you. But if they made up the body of Brahma, weren't they holy too?

One day, Ramanuja met a holy man praying in a temple. The man was a Sudra, but his face radiated divinity. As they prayed, Ramanuja found himself pondering questions of philosophy and religion. A word never passed between the two men, but the next day the Sudra presented Ramanuja with answers to his questions, as if from Vishnu himself.

If holiness coursed through all animals and objects, Ramanuja asked, why should it bypass a Sudra? And yet it violated the taboos to even step in this man's shadow. Worse would be to eat his food. These rules were encoded in the thousand-year-old Laws of Manu. *Ramanuja knew, however, that to eat the man's leftovers would purify his soul. Doing so cost him his marriage.*

Even the Sudra protested. "I am a lowborn Sudra. Good god! How could you serve your servant?"

"Is it the wearing of the sacred thread that makes a man a Brahmin?" asked Ramanuja.

What, really, made a man holy? Certainly not his caste. Certainly not his privileged access to the teachings of his forebears. Certainly not the rites of the cult by Vishnu. Ramanuja soon took these rites: a brand — of Vishnu's conch and Vishnu's discus — in each underarm; a secret mantra; a drawing of Vishnu's feet as an ash U on his forehead. But for Ramanuja, these rites now had new meanings, and he began to teach them.

To place Vishnu's feet on your forehead was to admit that feet, a thing as filthy as Sudras, could not pollute what was first divine.

And the mantra, the exclusive chant connecting Brahmin to Brahman, was not for his caste alone. To demonstrate, he climbed up the tower of a temple and shouted his mantra for everyone to hear — Sudras, women, outcastes.

"Is it better to live in hell," he asked, "than to allow others to live in spiritual darkness?"

This is how Ramanuja turned the world on its head.

Chapter One

In the small Indian city of Pune, in the basement of the Rama-mani Iyengar Memorial Yoga Institute, was a humid sliver-shaped library where cinder-block walls seemed to radiate sweat. Here, an institute librarian, dressed in a sari and with dark eye make-up, pursued her painstaking and apparently lifelong project of cataloging the content of this vault into an antiquated and ever-crashing computer. There were three walls of books — some eight thousand volumes in several ancient and modern Indic languages as well as English, German, French, Italian, and even modern He-brew. This was the yoga master B. K. S. Iyengar's personal library, a random amalgam of yoga texts spanning several centuries and ranging from the classic to the obscure to the kitsch. A handful of Western yoga students, barefoot and dressed, like me, in inex-pensively tailored Indian Punjabi frocks of soft cotton, sparkly adhesive bindis adorning many of our foreheads, diligently examined books at the end of a long cafeteria-style table. Several Indian Hare Krishna devotees from the distant state of Bihar congregated at the other end of the table, wearing ponytails at the crowns of their heads and white cotton wrap outfits. At the center of the long edge of the table sat Iyengar's closest disciple, a Frenchman of Muslim extraction named Faeq Biria, whose dress, comportment, Indian speech inflection, and bright way of communicating with his eyebrows gave him the look of not just a disciple of Iyengar but a smaller and fresher version of the guru himself.

This is where I first heard the tale of Ramanuja. The legendary qualities ascribed to the saint — flexibility, universality, courage, authenticity, a love of the body — were the aspirations of the Iyengar yoga institute. Iyengar and his children could also teach you to stand on your hands, do a split, or lie on the ground for twenty minutes without twitching — but all this in the service of something higher and more noble, and somehow mysteriously connected to this man called Ramanuja.

B. K. S. Iyengar was known now to tens of thousands of American and European yoga aficionados for having transformed an inaccessible and centuries-old collection of Indian philosophies and rituals into a therapeutic melding of meditation and exercise called, in our homes, "Iyengar Yoga." His technique had healed millions and helped secure the place of a mind-body ethic in the modern model of health. He was also revered by Indians as the man who resurrected a dying national tradition by popularizing the practice of asanas, or physical postures, whose beneficial effects on the health and spirit proved the eternal wisdom of ancient India. To both camps, he was a kind of Ramanuja — a populist who brought the esoteric to those who never had legitimate claim to it, and someone who looked beyond caste to fashion a personal vision of the holy.

Classically, yoga is a collection of philosophies sprung from the Vedas, more than three-thousand-year-old Indian holy texts that espouse a quest for liberation from the bonds of the material world through a life of ritual, discipline, and devotion to God. More than two thousand years after the Vedas were written, during the time of Ramanuja, yoga reappeared in South Asia as a series of physical regimens whose practice was meant to link an individual with the divine through the purification of one's "subtle body"— a metaphysical ideal that roughly corresponded to the physical body. In the twentieth century, something called yoga arose in India once again, as a form of sport championed by Indian nationalists. Drawing loosely from a small handful of recently unearthed medieval yoga texts, these revolutionaries sought to create a populist movement rooted in shared, and largely invented, physical choreographies. Rich, open to interpretation, and physically rewarding, this twentieth-century yoga became popular among Westerners and Anglophilic Indians alike. Fifty years later, the work of B. K. S. Iyengar and a handful of other Indians turned it into one more modern craze.

That day at the library, Iyengar himself was seated at an old oak school desk at the mouth of the sliver, peering through owl glasses at a flurry of philosophy texts, letters from his international following of students, and magazine articles about the global spread of yoga. He wore traditional South Indian dress — dhoti, kurta, and forehead markings — though just this morning I'd seen him doing yoga in the shiny green Umbro shorts that were the vogue this year at the World Cup in France.

Ever since my first yoga class fifteen years before, I'd known there was an aging and charismatic Indian with long white eyebrows and a mane growing practically to his knees who ran a yoga school in India, and that he could still balance in a freestanding handstand while touching the soles of his feet to the back of his head. What I'd learned over several months in his company merely rounded out the legend — of a traditional Indian who could navigate the Western mind. Iyengar spoke in Western medical tropes but had neither a formal education nor extensive skills in any Western or even Indian language other than his mother tongue, Tamil, which was rarely spoken here in a city whose own language was Marathi. Iyengar carried a host of other affectations from his ancestral past. Though he was born in the state of Karnataka, the area he called his homeland was a place where no relative had lived for hundreds of years, a town in another state, hundreds of miles from Karnataka.

I'd come to the library today as I did most afternoons. I'd attended a guided morning practice in the studio upstairs, a two-hour workout under the gaze of Iyengar and his offspring. I'd done headstands and twists, backbends and handstands. When I entered the library, still light-headed from the workout and requisite fasting, I touched the floor by Iyengar's feet. He greeted me with a gruff nod of the head, and then I took a seat at the long table across from the Frenchman "Biria," as Iyengar called him.

The room was quiet except for occasional interruptions from the Indian Hare Krishnas. "You want to learn yoga?" one asked me, eyeing the stack of texts on the table at my side. "I can help. But first, please, can I ask you, why do you in the West do yoga?"

I looked at him dumbly.

"Excuse me, can I borrow?" another asked, drawing my books before him and ensconcing himself in my research.

The first gazed at the books again and looked at me ruefully. "A book? Why are you learning from a book?"

"Eh. You," Iyengar grunted. Everyone looked. Biria lifted perceptibly from his seat, kicking his chair so that it rattled the case of books behind him. The guru was addressing me. I sprinted to the metal folding chair beside his desk. He gave me a long look, then gestured to the paperwork cluttering his desk. It was galleys for a new collection of edited speeches, what would become his sixth book. "You see I have my own research." He peered over the frames of his glasses and slicked back his white locks with his palms. "Anyway, you asked what is yoga. Talk to Biria. He knows books. Ask him for the — the — this saint — Ramanuja. You asked. Read Ramanuja."

Biria was on his feet now, having rushed to the exact section of the bookshelf that contained Iyengar's collection on medieval yoga philosophy and located the dozen or so texts on Ramanuja — no easy feat.

"Ramanuja is Guruji's ancestor," Biria said. "This is the same family." Ramanuja, he continued, penned his famous commentaries in the very city the Iyengar family hailed from. The family's traditions all descended from this place: their taboos, their tattoos, their family prayers, their devotion to Vishnu. Ramanuja shared even their dress — down to the white-ash U-shaped impression of Vishnu's footprints they wore on their forehead.

Iyengar was looking down. He nodded and grunted, whether at Biria or at the papers in front of him I couldn't tell. "Eh. Biria. You tell her. Very important this," Iyengar finally called from the front of the room. "Tell her. The pearls."

"Just like Guruji, Ramanuja addresses the body," Biria went on, adding Ramanuja's metaphor of pearls on a string, matter linked by the cohering thread of Brahman. "Sankara didn't believe in the supremacy of the body. He thought it was maya. But if the body is maya, how can you walk? Ramanuja realized the body was an instrument.

"Guruji teaches to bring total awareness to the body," he said. Iyengar was looking at his papers. "The holy dimension of the body comes alive. In triangle pose!" Biria added, now looking at me as if he had unearthed an occult key. He spread his arms as if

13

to demonstrate the stirring of Brahman with his gesture. "The body is like a pearl, awakened by consciousness."

Earlier I'd been trying to balance in handstand so as to ultimately, someday during my lifetime, get the soles of my feet onto the back of my head in the manner of Iyengar. I strained to imagine a connection between this new information and what I'd been practicing in the studio upstairs.

"Feel the divinity in every cell," Iyengar added, mumbling now. "Give her the life."

Biria handed me a yellowed, stained, and frayed edition of a book: *Life of Sri Ramanuja*. It was published in India when books still cost ten cents, and it had a bookplate from Iyengar's first home in Pune. The yogi's handwriting in English looped through the margins like a small child at play. I dutifully brought the book to my seat and read the parable of Ramanuja's life.

When I was done, I gazed at the frontispiece of the book, an illustration of a sculpture of Ramanuja from the South Indian temple where the saint had written his commentaries. The statue wore the mark of Vishnu on his forehead; his feet curled in to his belly. It reminded me of those sculptures that had been so significant for Ramanuja, of Vishnu lying in that state between waking and sleep. I too sometimes believed I embodied a middle ground between earth and ether. I'd felt it this morning, in that moment of free fall in handstand, when I hadn't yet finished rising up but hadn't started to come down yet either. In that instant, nothing was certain, and yet somehow everything was certain.

And then, suddenly, I found myself imagining all the objects and people in the room around me — the Hare Krishnas in their white cotton, the librarian in her sari, the American women with their forehead bindis and kurta pajamas — all of us dancing in the margins of the book. Then, like disembodied pearl ions bouncing off the walls and bookshelves, the people in the room sprang into the air beside Ramanuja and the book about Ramanuja, Iyengar and his collected writings, the three cases of books on yoga, our many competing notions of what exactly yoga might be. We hung there together, suspended in midair in free fall, at a precise moment of buoyancy after we'd risen and before we fell. I wondered if everything in this room — people, books, history, mythology, costumes, tradition — could all interact in a coherent way, if it could all exist at once. And for a split second I was nowhere else; I was inside that thought.

Chapter Two

I learned to meditate long before I got to India. I was seven. We were living with my mother's second husband, during years in which I tried to get as far from my stepfather as possible; I was casting for ways to leave home. Sitting in his old Buick Skylark while he ducked inside the hardware shop to buy widgets and hinges one day, I conducted an experiment. Was it possible to think of nothing, or was it only possible to think of the act of thinking of nothing? I concentrated on this conundrum until I realized that even thinking *only* of the act of thinking of nothing was a feat. If I could maintain my focus on that thought before, during, and after my stepfather returned to the car, I'd performed a successful experiment. As I sat in the car, I understood that with this technique I could manage the things I didn't want to think about. I noticed that if a memory that I found unpleasant seeped into my thoughts, I could head it off by concentrating on forgetting it before it took full shape in my mind. The act of thinking about forgetting that thought was so challenging that before I knew it, I could remember only that I was trying to forget something, but not precisely what it was I was trying to forget. In this way, those memories disappeared. I don't recall what it was I was trying to forget that day.

"What are you doing?" my stepfather asked suspiciously, stepping into the Buick, fingering his widgets.

"Nothing."

"Tell me."

"No."

He drove us to our house, where, in the back of my bedroom, I had an imaginary room. My secret room had velvet walls and no windows. I could hole up here, burrowing into the pillows and carpeting, reading my magical kids' books: *Ozma of Oz; The Emerald City of Oz; Half Magic; The Lion, the Witch and the Wardrobe.* I had an imaginary TV as well, and I could watch sitcom reruns and game shows with no one ever telling me to turn them off, because no one could find me in my refuge. There was no doorway to my hidden place, just a shimmery spot on the wall beside my bed that marked its entryway. To get through it, I had to squint my eyes so I saw double and then shift my focus back and forth between one image and the other. In the space between the two images, I could see through things. This helped me walk through the wall.

At slumber party salons, my girlfriends and I participated in other experiments in magic. In my stepfather's basement workshop, to the sound of a low-growling furnace, we set up in a circle, each of us taking a turn in the center. There, each girl lay down and closed her eyes, trying to empty her head of all thoughts. I remember the girl at my head rubbing my temples to help me unhinge myself from the world of the basement. Then, with one finger from each girl's hand under my body, they chanted in unison, *Light as a feather, stiff as a board, light as a feather, stiff as a board.* I listened until I heard nothing but that chant, over and over. *Light. Stiff.* I imagined my body flattened into a piece of plywood, and then drifting as it became light, fuzzy with feather hairs growing from my sides. And then slowly, each girl supporting me with only spindly index fingers, I began to elevate. This required great sensitivity on the part of the girl at my head, who gave the signal at the precise moment when she felt my body was ready. Then, if all went well, if all the people in the room were in proper communication, if I had entered the proper state of relaxation, my body rose toward the ceiling, the fingers beneath me offering only delicate guidance.

I remember floating. I am sure I floated. I am sure I was doing more than simply resting my weight on the girls' fingers. It was not their strength, but my own particular state of mind that enabled me to levitate. We all knew this because you stayed buoyant in the air until you thought, *I am floating,* and then you plunged — *plunk* — inexplicably, to the floor. The thought — *I am floating* — was the membrane separating the realm where your body obeyed gravity from the realm where you were something other than your body, something that could hover outside of it. The act of tricking your mind allowed you to cross that membrane. And then, like a password at a gate, the utterance of that thought spit you back to the basement. *Plunk,* and you hit the ground. Your eyes popped open, and you remembered the faces of your friends, the objects from the workshop, the hum of the furnace. You were back. *Hello, Colleen Copitelli! Hello, Debbie de Marche! Next!*

In the seventies, these were the parlor games we played, left over from the Surrealists, encouraged by such forces as the Milton Bradley Co. that in all earnestness believed Twister, Monopoly, and Ouija occupied a single universe. In my case, the particular pathologies of my family conspired to make the occult especially central. My mother was keen to know why that Ouija dial kept leaning to a particular letter — *N*; why the tarot cards kept tossing up, say, the figure of the Jack; why she could come up with a very detailed story of a young prince in medieval France when she closed her eyes and conjured a past life for herself. Later, my mother introduced me to the writings of turn-of-the-century vegetarian cults, to the Nature Cure enthusiasts, and to Alistair Crowley. Through my mother's West African boyfriend, we got free instruction on how to manipulate an invisible ball of energy in Tai Chi exercises; another of her brief romances put us in contact with the philosophies of Alexander Lowen, the controversial psychologist who believed that memories resided in the muscles. It was my mother who gave me Carlos Castaneda's tales of otherworldly transport. Around the same time, my sister inducted me into that vast world made accessible through drugs. And so, in high school, there seemed a kind of inevitability to the fact that I got my first real job as an assistant at a foundation for Sufi dervishes.

I didn't know that these experiences were some kind of preparation, but when I made my first descent from the yoga studio to the basement library at Iyengar's school in India, I had the strange feeling I was coming home. On Iyengar's cluttered shelves, I discovered the corpus of Indian mysticism, a trove of testimonials from people unified by their fascination with that ineffable and blissful feeling of being transported. What struck me at first about these authors was not their relation to the divine, but the matter-of-factness with which they discussed the act of flying. For these Indians, the pursuit of this ecstasy was not escapism; it was discovery. When Carlos Castaneda soared above the deserts of New Mexico on Don Juan's magic peyote, he became an absurd symbol of America's spiritual yearning. But for the Indian yogis there were no such contradictions. The benefits of yoga could understandably be confused with the benefits of drugs, even Iyengar understood this. He had told me, for instance, that among his famous students was that spokesman for psychedelia Aldous Huxley. "Was Huxley a good student?" I asked the guru.

"No," he answered abruptly. "After he was coming to me, Huxley found drugs," Iyengar explained, shrugging. "After that, for yoga he had no need."

On another day in the library, a yoga teacher from France handed me Paramahansa Yogananda's *Autobiography of a Yogi.* The edition was the kitsch supermarket paperback from America that I had seen in dozens of yoga studios and used bookstores back home.

"You haven't read it?" the Frenchwoman asked in her thick accent, feigning horror. She wore the Pune chic of Indian cotton Punjabi top and balloon pants, bindi firmly secured on her forehead. "Oh, it's beautiful. It's — it's a romance." I took it from her hand as I might have taken *Gone with the Wind* — guiltily, expecting something titillating and steamy. And maybe, I considered in the back of my mind, Yogananda would explain exactly what was yoga.

He did not. However, the tale of Yogananda's love affair with God was a romance indeed — in the French sense: a *roman,* a tale. He told his life story with the dramatic sensitivity of a *Star Wars* scriptwriter: it was sparkly and full of explosions. Yogananda's primary concern was to convince the reader that the supernatural was possible: his guru could not only send a telepathic message to him from a distant city telling him what time to pick him up at the train station but also amend that message later to communicate whether and how long his train was going to be delayed. Through mind control, Yogananda also instructed, you could nullify the petty irritations of the real world. This he learned from his guru, who, while meditating with his student one afternoon, seemed to Yogananda to be having no problem with the mosquitoes that were savaging the poor apprentice.

"Guruji?" Yogananda finally queried the adept. "There are mosquitoes swarming around my body, and yet you seem to be unbothered. How can this be?" His teacher went on to explain that the mosquitoes weren't actually attacking Yogananda. They only *seemed* to be. If Yogananda could concentrate adequately on the reality that mosquitoes were in fact maya — that if only God existed, there was no such thing as *mosquito* — they would no longer bother him. And, sure enough, as soon as the student ceased to believe in the mosquitoes, they miraculously vanished.

I was riveted. The book transported me to a romantic Indian countryside where the atmosphere was thick with genies, where the primary purpose of air currents was the transmission of heavenly particles. What connection Yogananda's technique of mind control had to what I was learning in the studio upstairs I had no idea. Iyengar taught that yoga involved not an out-of-body state but an inhabiting of your body to the point of hyperawareness. The world was no more an illusion than the body that you walked around in. I'd read in a newsletter published by the school that Iyengar believed the goal of yoga was the very embrace of one's body. "When your body, mind, and soul are harmoniously healthy," Iyengar wrote to his students, "you will bring spiritual glow and dynamic harmony to those around you and to the world — not by withdrawing from the world but by being an electrifying, living organ of the body of humanity."

Yogananda, on the other hand, counseled, "Man is essentially a soul, incorporeal and omnipresent." This idea seemed impossibly quaint — but his tales of magic were winning. Yogananda described in great detail, for instance, how enlightenment came to him at a young age. In the presence of his guru, he found that he often "received" samadhi, or bliss — the ultimate goal, he wrote, of yogic meditation. As in any proper romance, Yogananda saw stars when he realized this state of rapturous union with his love — "a diaphanous luster." "The vast space within me," he described, became "a chamber of light." This was a sensation of such utter euphoria that he was drawn, in the manner of generations of renunciants before him, to seek a life in the perpetual state of ecstatic unification with the beyond.

I already knew something of Yogananda because a boyfriend of mine in California had once taken my mother and me, during one of her visits from New York, on a picnic to the grand ocean-front garden in Malibu that had been Yogananda's American headquarters. Here, Yogananda oversaw a new universal religion called yoga. A visitor's center on the grounds held the same iconic photograph that adorned the book jacket: Yogananda with his long black hair draped across his cotton tunic, a mild and knowing grin on his face. Other photos documented the rise of the mystic in California's social arena beginning in the 1920s, when he amassed a following of wealthy esoterics seeking instruction in meditation and this new eclectic religion. The photo gallery, reproduced on the inner sleeves of the book, was a social register of the cosmopolitan 1920s — Yogananda with Calvin Coolidge, Yogananda with the governor of California, Yogananda with Gandhi, Yogananda with a sparkling entourage of luminaries. Zeliglike, he had a knack for getting himself photographed with the great personages of the post–World War I world.

Whatever Yogananda's relation to headstands, it occurred to me that reading about such characters was neither a bad nor unentertaining use of my time here, and so I lingered at those shelves in Iyengar's library dealing with Indian mysticism. I easily located the urtext, the Bhagavad Gita, a crumbling 1890 edition

that on further examination appeared to be among the earlier translations of the document from Sanskrit, and the first into English.
The Theosophical Society, in New York, had published it. I knew
something of them as well. When I was about twelve, my mother
dragged me to a meeting at their New York headquarters. This
amounted to very little — elegant, older Upper East Side people
with large polished jewels in their brooches sat in folding chairs
as a speaker addressed some topic that failed to capture my attention. My mother sat forward in her chair, her legs elegantly
crossed, her brow knit in concentration, a skeptical but knowing
smile on her lips. She apparently took away something from the
meeting that did not require her to return. I was simply left with
a feeling of a kind of privilege, as if I was in on a secret, when I
passed their offices afterward and knew that here they spoke
about esoteric, obscure things. The building was just five blocks
from our apartment, mysterious and austere with its Deco front,
its facade sparely adorned with small symbols whose meanings I
couldn't exactly place — scales, stars, moons, urns.

Around the time of our visit to the Theosophical Society, my
mother announced to me, on the way to the Bar Mitzvah of her
best friend's son, that I could choose whichever religion I wanted.
She had none — she'd converted to Judaism when she married
my father after a messy breakup with the Catholic Church, but
upon divorcing my father fell into the Protestantism of my stepfather. When she divorced him, she swore off both marriage and religion. She was by temperament a believer, however — hence her
weakness for the séance and similar forms of communion with
Something Out There. Theosophy to me was a part of her spiritual universe, religion in the same intriguing, vague sense as a
game of Ouija.

I later learned that the Theosophists were likewise focused
more on the mysteries of the spiritual than on its actual content.

Theirs was an aesthetic kind of spirituality. In photos, their founder, Madame Blavatsky, was adorned in draped silks and large rings, her jowly personage obscured by misty figments that were either ghosts or swaths of the fabric that covered her tea lamps, in salons oddly reminiscent of the apartment I grew up in. This Theosophy edition of the Gita was, like all the books I'd read here, Iyengar's personal copy, and like most of his copies duly marked in the margins. It seemed odd to me then that Iyengar would have wrestled with a Western rather than an Indian edition of the text. Later, I learned from Gandhi's autobiography that many Indians first encountered the Gita in English. Gandhi didn't read the so-called Indian Bible until the Theosophist Annie Besant, an Irishwoman, handed this same edition to him no less ceremoniously than the Frenchwoman had given me *Autobiography of a Yogi*.

The Gita, though not concerned in the least with the project of fitting your body into the shape of a table or a tortoise or a tree, was a constant point of reference at the yoga institute. The two-thousand-year-old text was, we learned, the handbook on bhakti yoga. Only through devotion to Krishna — a manifestation of Vishnu and, in turn, God — might you attain union with an all-encompassing divinity. By understanding that your actions contribute to an eternal, karmic plan, you might see yourself as one element in God's realm.

But for the Theosophists who provided this translation, the Gita was more a source of enigma and allure. Their introduction heightened the mystique of the religion, speaking of "cosmogenesis" and the "Astral world"; the "immortal Spark" and "mystically begotten" children. Of its author, the editors warned titillatingly, "Who Vyasa is and when he lived is not known." I turned the page eagerly.

What followed was the story of our hero Arjuna locked in

hours of heated debate with the man-god Krishna — told in the flowery, nineteenth-century English of those European spiritualists. I imagined the quirky Russian Blavatsky as she scrutinized the new manuscript in English, sitting at her séance table wearing her amber rings and bracelets. Like Yogananda's, Arjuna's mystical vision was one of blinding threads of colors traveling on airwaves. First, Arjuna witnessed Krishna's man-body decompose into a formless entity of lurid and magical shapes

> with many mouths and eyes and many wonderful appearances, with many divine ornaments, many celestial weapons upraised; adorned with celestial garlands and robes, anointed with celestial ointments and perfumes, full of every marvelous thing, the eternal God whose face is turned in all directions. The glory and amazing splendor of this mighty Being may be likened to the radiance shed by a thousand suns rising together into the heavens.

Reading the Gita, I felt the excitement and comfort I had felt as a girl ensconced in my books about magic — the Oz tales and the Narnia ones. I once again inhabited that story that had been my favorite, *Half Magic,* in which a girl rubbed a coin and got not everything she wanted, exactly, but half of it. I was also aware of Iyengar's presence at the front of the room as I pored through the text. I felt a kind of invisible guidance. With his white hair and gauzy Indian kurta, Iyengar seemed to float in the background as I read, a twinkling white cloud hovering in the space above my shoulder where I might otherwise have placed a reading lamp.

As I continued to excavate Iyengar's impressive cache of Indian spiritual testimonies, I found that every celebrated yogi had his own Arjuna-under-the-spray-of-heavenly-colors story to tell.

Swami Vivekananda, one of Yogananda's forebears, was described in a biography issued by his Indian disciples as entering
the bliss state regularly and from an early age. Years before he
made his celebrated journey to Chicago as the "Hindoo holy man"
at the World's Fair Columbia Exposition in 1893, "he daily experienced a strange vision when he was about to fall asleep. Closing
his eyes, he would see between his eyebrows a ball of light of
changing colours, which would slowly expand and at last burst,
bathing his whole body in a white radiance."

Like Yogananda, Vivekananda came from an upper-class family that pushed him toward things Western — philosophy, logic,
European history. Members of Calcutta's rarefied elite, Vivekananda's parents took great pains to educate their son in the
best English manner available. But Vivekananda continued to have
mystical visions, until one day he saw something that looked to
him like God. On a family outing to the country, the young Vivekananda was watching from his vehicle as it traversed a mountain
cutaway. Then he noticed a large beehive in the cleft of a giant
cliff. "Suddenly his mind was filled with awe and reverence for the
Divine Providence," according to the biography. "He lost outer
consciousness and lay thus in the cart for a long time. Even after
returning to the sense-perceived world he radiated joy." Thereafter, Vivekananda, too, found himself inexorably propelled by a
yearning to return to that state of ecstatic revelation.

Coincidence had it that a mentor at his English school was a
Scotsman who was enchanted by the Transcendentalist writings
of Emerson, influenced by the very Bhagavad Gita. This teacher
knew a local holy man who he believed embodied Emerson's
philosophies better than anyone, Eastern or Western. Ironically
enough, it was at the Scotsman's urging that Vivekananda returned to the provinces to meet his future guru. There, he discovered a man from humble roots. Though a Brahmin, the guru

was so poor he dressed in rags. Vivekananda might have noticed, too, that the guru's eyes seemed to wander, as if pasted too far on either side of his head.

Like Yogananda's teacher, this guru gave little thought to his physical being. "I saw that my body didn't matter," the guru wrote of a period of meditation and self-imposed asceticism excerpted in a hagiography released by his followers. "Birds would perch on my head and peck at the grains of rice that had lodged there during the worship. Snakes would crawl over my motionless body."

Vivekananda became a disciple of this guru, who some years later took a place among the most revered and mythologized of India's modern saints. This guru was Ramakrishna, whose biographers claimed that he, like his disciple, had the habit of falling into involuntary ecstasy without warning. He enjoyed a fireworks of the mind — like "an infinite shoreless sea of light; a sea that was consciousness." At other times he experienced "particles of light like swarms of fireflies" and "bright waves of light like molten silver."

"The boy's face wore a smile of extraordinary beauty, and his gaze was fixed as if in profound meditation," his disciple Christopher Isherwood wrote of him in another biography. As a child, the guru performed the role of the god Krishna in a play. Then, he fell into reverie. "Some men carried him home on their shoulders. But despite all their efforts, he could not be aroused from his ecstatic state until after sunrise of the next day. Certain narrators of this incident even say that he remained outwardly unconscious for three whole days," explained Isherwood.

There were other yogis too. There was Sivananda, whose Divine Life Society in Rishikesh once attracted George Harrison. When Sivananda came of age — one generation after Vivekananda, two generations past Ramakrishna — he too could identify bliss as "balls of white lights, colored lights, sun, stars," as he wrote in his autobiography. "All desires have disappeared," he elaborated. "Now I aspire to nothing but Thy blessed feet. . . . I was lost in ecstasy. I was at once transformed. I was drowned in the Divine Consciousness. In the ocean of bliss."

One afternoon while I was busy being illuminated by this lovely literature of transport, Iyengar grunted something from his desk at the front of the library. I'd been so engrossed in the spectacles I was reading about that it took me a second to remember where I was. The library was quiet today — just the guru; two yoga students, Elena, a Russian, and Gloria, one of my yoga teachers from California; and me. Gloria had initially encouraged me to come to Iyengar's school, and we were now sharing a flat. Outside, it monsooned. All day the weather had fluctuated dramatically between downpour, cataclysm, and calm, each mood reaching us through small leaky apertures cut deep in the concrete. The thick walls and the damp inside gave the space a protected feeling. I felt the same intimacy and quiet of my imaginary room at my stepfather's. I listened to the thrum of the rain; saw the shadowy shelves and their overflowing books. The grunt startled me. *Hi, Elena! Hi, Gloria! Hi, Guruji!* Iyengar indicated the seat beside his. I walked over and sat.

"Hey, do you want to ask a question?" he inquired. Under his glasses, Iyengar's massive aquiline eyebrows were magnified. Elena and Gloria moved quietly to the front of the room. I thought for several seconds. What I'd been reading today seemed very remote from the yoga I was studying here. If Iyengar so revered the body, why did his modern forebears reject it? What relation did fireworks have to handstands? What made *that* yoga, and *this* yoga? I had been content up until now to believe that there was little if any connection. But I decided to try Iyengar nonetheless. "I've been reading about samadhi," I offered, well aware that my question sounded absurd. "What does it have to do with yoga?"

"Yes, Guruji," Elena cut in. "In Russia we have many yoga students who are practicing and practicing. They want to know, 'When will I reach samadhi? How long does it take?'"

I gave Elena a look. How could she see what we did in the studio upstairs as even a distant cousin to the yoga that espoused "liberation"? What we did here seemed unrelated to the bodiless state regaled by Ramakrishna. Physical reality did not fall away in the studio upstairs. It imposed itself, perhaps with an even greater intensity than in normal life. Could samadhi be a goal for yogis at the school?

Just then, the sky cracked, a sound so loud it seemed to come from inside my body. Gloria, Elena, and I all started. Elena seemed pained; she was peering at the guru. He looked amused. "I get lots of letters from Russia. They are jumping to the mystical world very soon," he exclaimed finally. His eyes landed on mine, and I had trouble looking away. "Samadhi means to feel the soul in each and every cell of the body, to feel the self existing in each and every pore of your skin. If you have attained that, you have seen the soul; you have seen the self."

Elena looked at him reverently.

"These students, they think with motivity. I want this; I want that. The mind is caught up in the motion of the future. You are calculating, you are asking, Where does this end? The future is predominant. Not the present." I noticed that his fingers had been brushing against his palms in a quick repetitive gesture. "Your mind is like an engine which is vibrating forward. We have to create a space for the thinking brain to look, to peek into what it has done. Reflection in action!" He paused, his eyes darting between all of ours as he gave the mot juste a moment to settle.

The roar of the rain outside suddenly escalated. It made me

worry, vaguely, about nothing in particular, and everything. Even now, as much as I'd been imbibing the literature of meditation, I had to fight the distractions that Iyengar disparaged. I'd come halfway around the world for this opportunity to discuss matters of concentration and awareness in the sanctuary of the wise man's library. But only half of my brain was engaged. The other half was occupied with what I'd been doing earlier in the day — food and phone calls, shopping and letter writing — and my plan for the rest of it. This, according to the primers spread out on the table behind me, was the bane of yoga. Yogananda described the ever-present background noise of thought as the "whirlpool." He counseled the student to direct all one's concentration on the present: "All thoughts vibrate eternally in the cosmos. The goal of yoga science is to calm the mind that without distortion it may hear the infallible counsel of the Inner Voice."

"Stand up!" Iyengar bellowed suddenly. "Tadasana!" Before I realized it, I had jumped to this pose — the mountain. Gloria and Elena leaped up as well, and we three stood like that. I adjusted my posture just as Iyengar and his deputies taught us to do in class and practice, holding my spine straight, drawing my fingertips downward, and tightening the muscles of my legs. As in those classes, I thought about the angle of my pelvis, the rolling back of my shoulders, a stretching sensation through the vertebrae in the back of my neck. I relaxed the canals in my ears and let them take in the roar of the rain. I softened my eyes. "Don't devour with your eyes," Gloria had told me once.

After sitting for so long, words knotting up in my brain, the simple exertion invigorated my skin, and I felt a tingling all over. How dull I'd felt, a membrane inside my skull squeezing the circumference of my head. I imagined the membrane expanding.

"Bring the mind to the bottom of the feet," Iyengar announced. My bare feet were cold against the slate tile. "Which bottom skin of the foot is broad? Which is narrow? Which touches the floor more; which it does not touch the floor? One toe is up, no? Can you see now?"

Without looking, I could tell that my left foot was angled slightly outward, and I noticed that I could feel less of the texture of the floor with that sole. Under my right foot, I could make out a slick quality, and I noticed that the warmth of the floor extended from my foot, washing up my calf.

"The yogi says as my brain is so warm, so alert, why should not this skin at the bottom of my feet feel the same warmth? The consciousness is active in your brain. Why is the consciousness not active in your foot? When the body stretches, the mind you have stretched. Now sit!"

We popped back into our chairs.

"Now Gloria is sitting. Right, follow?" He pointed to her; she had settled with crossed legs onto the chair, her arms folded in front of her and resting on Iyengar's desk. "Gloria is sitting. At certain places her consciousness is not active because her elbows are entwined. Her consciousness is on the armpit — probably you may not know, but I know because I reflect where is the pressure."

"It's true!" Gloria exclaimed.

"It's true? Ah. Now is your thigh — think of the soul, the self — is consciousness on your thighs?"

"Only on the back because it touches the chair," she answered.

"Now it's on the top. See your quadriceps muscles? What happened? Consciousness came up or not? Can you see now?"

"Yes," she said.

The tops of my feet were warm as well.

"So you see dormancy and awakening in action. So to reach samadhi, this dormancy of the intelligence has to be awakened

31

second to second, moment to moment. That is what these asanas teach, and that is known as reflection. Why should the consciousness be dormant here and active there?"

Iyengar then leaned back in his chair with his arms crossed, nodding his head victoriously. "What is samadhi?" he whispered half to himself, drawing his glasses up on his nose and slicking back his hair as he returned to his flurry of paperwork. He fussed with those papers, snorting now and grunting, and then, as if reverting to a dream state, mumbled more about samadhi, half laughing again. Gloria quietly got up and made her way over to her seat, and then Elena followed. I gathered my books into a pile and, touching the floor by the guru's chair on my way, crept up the stairway and through the lobby until I was gulping the moist air outside.

I felt tranquil, I was thinking as I walked through the rain. Was it possible that simply paying attention to the spread of heat through my limbs and the sensation of air on my skin had given me this feeling of serenity? By the time the rain stopped, I was crossing a nearby park. The sound of rain softened to just the echo of water dripping from trees. Then the squawks of birds got loud. Their calls had begun abruptly, as if by pact the birds kept silent until the rain stopped. Their voices built to a cawing and hooting. This was more deafening than birdsong. The barrage of shouts and cackles became menacing, and it occurred to me that nature was tipping out of balance. Ravens were overtaking the ecosystem. But the cacophony nevertheless exaggerated my peaceful feeling. It was as if to stand beneath this canopy of bird chatter was to exist in a world where reality was sharpened — color more lurid, noises more staccato, the feeling on my skin more sensual. And I tried to decide, Was calm God? Was lulling my nerves to a state of relaxation any less mechanical an accomplishment than jumping into a handstand? Had my stillness caused a reaction in my receptors so that I experienced *more* of everything than there really was? And if so, what was there, really?

In the shelter of his shadowy library, the kinetic Iyengar had temporarily convinced me of something, and inspired me to something. His charm and passion had won me over. But did his speech on bodily awareness really explain what was happening to me now? Was there something more at work, something still connected to yoga, still connected to B. K. S. Iyengar, but also ineffable, more slippery than his words? I didn't know if it was samadhi that I'd sought when I came to India, or samadhi that I'd discovered here beneath the deafening screech of these ravens. I only knew it felt good right here, right now.

Chapter Three

I first encountered yoga when I moved from New York to California to go to college. I went to Santa Cruz, that mecca near San Francisco of feminism, gay culture, acupuncture, homeopathy, naturopathy, kinesthesiology, astrology, Satsang, Zazen, Buddhism, Jainism, Hinduism, Zoroastrianism — anything. The world seemed big.

On the vast wooded campus, there was an expansive eight-sided redwood dojo, where the blue of California's drought-era sky streamed through ceiling-high windows onto a floor made of a single custom-fitted martial-arts mat. This was our rec center. The windows gave on to a meadow, beyond which you could make out overlapping layers of gopher fields terracing their way down to the ocean. Up top, you could spend afternoons learning Tai Chi, massage, Frisbee aerodynamics, or yoga. Because I'd already tried Tai Chi and Frisbee in New York, I enrolled in yoga.

On the first day of the quarter, the teacher came huffing through the gopher field on a bicycle. She was about four feet tall, with a dense and firm little body, pink skin, a button nose, and sunflower-yellow hair cut close to her head. She introduced herself — Julie Kimball — and described her guru: Mr. Iyengar. Of Pune. A genius.

Julie led us through a series of simple poses, reciting their names in Sanskrit. I liked the way her words fit together. They were not scattered and chaotic like the messy-haired hippies and meditators you met in Santa Cruz, but neat and coherent, like a piece of Romantic poetry with the repeating end rhyme "-asana." Her composition employed inventive similes and metaphorical language applied to body parts. "Never grip the abdomen!" "Hold the belly in the pit of your pelvis like an egg yolk resting in its shell!" "Drive the tailbone in!" "Open the backs of the legs!" "Let your head drop to the floor like a piece of ripe fruit!" "Lift the kneecaps!"

I liked this yoga, because it demanded something of my mind and, therefore, did not seem flaky, and because Julie's teaching suggested that mastery lay partly in memorizing words in another language — a skill I was better adapted for than anything remotely athletic. The information came fast and furious, and I liked that too. It required a concentration that made it impossible to think about things that were bothering me.

"Lift the kneecaps!" Julie shouted today from her powerful little body. I found her kneecaps line particularly mystifying, especially because she kept repeating it, heightening its currency by promising that if we didn't heed it, we'd wind up with dislocated or otherwise mangled patellae. I imagined palming one kneecap in each hand, gripping each by its edges, and then prying them loose, holding out patellae in my palms as offerings: two lotus-shaped bones, globular masses of flesh congealing around swaying ligaments. Two lifted kneecaps.

"Come look," Julie said, sighing.

We sat in a semicircle as Julie took a yogic version of military posture. She seemed merely to be standing still. But in her very stillness, she said, was the embodiment of the mountain. Solid. Strong. Singular. Watching her, I too felt motionless.

"In the beginning of all yoga," she said, staring at a spot on the window behind us, "there is tadasana — mountain pose. In mountain pose, you feel like a mountain. The human form in the posture of a mountain is dense, rooted, the heels and toe-balls descending into the earth — like the millions of shoots from a thickly growing patch of postdiluvian dandelions — the crown of the head ascending like a redwood, the diaphragm flat and wide, like a vast savanna." The similes rushed forth. "In the mountain, the knees are firm. If you learn to keep your knees strong in this pose, you'll never hurt them. Look." She tensed her quadriceps muscles, and the skin of each kneecap wrinkled toward its center like a little smiley face puckering into a kiss. Her kneecaps moved several centimeters up her legs.

She went on to explain that how one carried one's body not only reflected but also influenced one's mood. When you're defensive, your shoulders hunch, she lectured. When you're proud, your chest puffs. If those of us of the shoulder-hunching persuasion puffed our chests, we would feel more confident. By relaxing their shoulders, the puffers would grow more humble. Physical features not only revealed mood but created it, she continued: knitted brows, pursed lips, clenched jaws. By unknitting, unpursing, unclenching, you gained relief from worry, judgment, anger. By the same logic, she counseled, eye drops called forth the sadness of crying. Her wisdom seemed apt. By inhaling deeply into the chest that I more typically held protectively curled, I experienced an exhilarating feeling of confidence.

I continued studying with Julie in classes that offered no philosophy, never a mention of Vishnu, never an explanation of how the medievals believed the body to be a seething battlefield, grounds for war between the holy and the impure. Yoga class was a place to torque our bodies into shapes with Sanskrit names, into triangles, fish, herons, pigeons, planks, trees, wombs. When we finally became those shapes, we were something other than ourselves. I felt my body click into a shape, as if for each asana there was a Platonic model in the heavens. Table, rod, chair, crow, lotus. That was when I could squint my eyes and recognize not myself but a pose in the mirror. My body became a medium through which the universe flowed, a chink in the divine. In this way, yoga felt liberating; it distracted us from our preoccupations, suggested we were more than what we were. When we took on the outline of a banyan or a tortoise, we could believe that we were connected to a deep history, that we belonged to a vast universe.

The best reason I could give myself as to why I stuck with Julie's classes was that they made me feel pure. Practicing yoga postures during the day gave my body an airy quality, as if rays of light could shine directly through me. The clarity got muddled by the next day, so I did the postures again, pushing through the jumble. Yoga, like vegetarianism, which I'd subscribed to since I was fourteen, purified your body, unstuck those things that clogged you up inside. With yoga, I felt ethereal and untouched. Julie taught us breathing exercises as well. These, she said, "cleared away the furniture." Like wind, they swept old leaves from your tree branches.

One day, Julie told us do as many backbends as we could, one after another, at our own pace. We stood on the mat in the dojo and, with our palms supporting our sacrums, arched our heads backward to look at the windows behind us. Then we did handstands, resting our feet against the pillars and, with another student spotting, slowly walked our feet down until we hit the ground on all fours in a backbend. Alternately, we stood with our backs to the pillars, arched back to touch them, and walked our hands to the floor. Then we lay on our backs and pushed up — more backbends. Another backbend, dozens of backbends. We excavated yoga's every invention for coming into a backbend: urdhva dhanurasana — upward bow. Julie described the upward-facing bow of urdhva dhanurasana as the frame for an arrow. "You're an archer," she gushed. "Touch the sky."

By the time I'd done thirty, I was exhilarated, my heart racing. I lifted up to a backbend from the floor, flopped down, and popped straight back up. I stood with my arms in the air, arched back so far that my hands dropped to the ground, then pulled myself up to do it again. The more backbends I did, the more I felt I could do them forever, as if each backbend worked according to an algorithm to give me the will to continue. I was giddy and breathless, happy and crazed. I'd lost awareness of the room around me. I was flushed with a feeling of well-being. My heart was beating quickly, my mind racing as I was struck by thrill and wonder at a surge of excited thoughts about life in college: I could drop science and study art! Read up on lost languages at the library! Research the psychological applications of exercise!

Unfortunately, I could not always count on yoga to inspire this euphoria. On another day, the sun was low, and Julie took us out of the dojo and onto the rec center meadow, where we did poses barefoot, standing on grass as dry and yellow as straw. There was a massive coastal live oak that shaded the dojo, the kind with sinewy boughs extending parallel to the ground in lengths greater than the tree's height. She joked that it was our bodhi tree, and that because Buddha found enlightenment under a bodhi, we too might discover something elusive. The tree was also another prop, useful for handstands, leaning, pulling, and hanging of all sorts.

Julie devised an elaborate traction system with a strap and sturdy ropes from which to suspend ourselves from the live oak. "Rope sirsasana," she announced — rope headstand. We took turns hanging with our hips supported by the ropes — our legs in the air and our knees bent outward to hold ourselves in place — our torsos and arms dangling toward the scrub. "Good. Turn upside down," Julie counseled. "Forget what you thought you knew." When it was my turn, Julie held me steady as I stood on a rock to secure the rope in the proper location behind my sacrum, and then I fell backward, catching the rope with my legs and coming to position upside down. I exhaled, letting my spine extend as my ribs stretched toward the ground.

I was a tall girl — lanky and gangly — and the droopiness of my back had long been exacerbated by my tendency toward slouching. For a second, I felt my back get longer than it had ever been. In the next second, my mind flashed to an image of myself as an awkward young girl. At that moment, the rope at my sacrum pulled against my lengthening spine, and then there was a tug in a place somewhere deep in my upper back, between my spine and my right shoulder blade. Something hot welled in the back of my chest, and I would have cried if my throat hadn't caught. I flipped out of the pose, flushed and queasy.

For the rest of the class, I was aware of that locus inside my shoulder blade, and when I noticed it, I felt a stabbing at my chest. The spot in my back didn't exactly hurt; it just nagged, reminding me there was something there to remember, as if I'd exposed a fast frame of my past too quickly for it to take full form. There was something deep in my flesh, tucked behind my shoulder blade, a sliver of memory like glass.

Julie now instructed us to sit on the ground with our legs straight in front of us. She told us to lean forward and rest our heads on pillows. With my head down, I felt suffocated. The pose was excruciating. It was called paschimottanasana — pose of the West — she explained, but sometimes it was also called ugrasana — powerful pose. I could not understand how a pose that made me feel so weak, so *spineless,* could be thought of as "formidable." Julie described the pose as a gesture of surrender, a submitting to fate. My fate right now was to endure the density of sensation in my body. I noticed that ache in my back and a similar one deep in my chest, something raw and vulnerable. There were also pains in the back of my neck, my spine, my legs. My hamstring grabbed. I exhaled. The muscle released for a second, then clenched again in reflex.

We stayed one minute, two minutes, three. Slowly the pose became bearable, as if there were a switch in my brain that, like my hamstring, came unstuck during instant-long but ever-lengthening respites. I observed my thoughts from a distance ebbing around the simple issue of whether I could stay: *I can't stand it; I am coming up. No, I can bear it another second. But not another. Okay, one more second, that's it. Okay, one more.* A multiplier had kicked in to make the thought that I could endure the pose overtake the thought that I couldn't. As it became easier to resist the urge to bolt from both pose and class, I understood that whatever I was afraid of had no power if I didn't try to push it away. Everything, really, was fine.

And then the pain began to dissolve to a feeling that was no less prominent but somehow more manageable, less in my muscles than in my chest now, less like grief than plain sadness.

After, we lay in savasana — corpse pose — in which we sprawled on the floor impersonating dead bodies. I'd experienced such relief when the forward bend ended that I now felt euphoric. It was as if I'd emerged from the end of a long journey, from craggy desert to plains — lush, flat, firm. Julie whispered instructions for relaxing each appendage, each joint, each swath of skin and length of muscle. "Make the journey from mountain to corpse." I drifted off.

And soon, I felt my body breaking down into particulate matter that looked like earth, and then I was rising up, molecule by molecule, fusing into the air, floating in pieces, all coherence to me lost. I believed I was levitating — and then I had the thought: *I am levitating.* And *plunk,* I plunged to the floor. I was awake now, but I thought I had seen something, a place that may have scared me once but now no longer did. When I left class, I thought again about the pain in my shoulder. It was still there, like a bookmark.

Chapter Four

I made the decision to go to India to see Iyengar during the L.A. fires. This was the year that finally put the lie to the maxim that California had no seasons. By then, I had been living in California on and off for ten years, long enough to internalize the rhythms to the region's shifts. Drought led to earthquake led to fires led to floods. Our proximity to Latin America also gave us the season of war. And so I traveled to Mexico as a freelance journalist covering the insurrection in Chiapas. In one afternoon, I moved from the site of carnage at an abandoned Mexican jailhouse to news on the TelePrompTers at our Mexican hotel that a massive earthquake had shaken my then home of L.A. I flew back to L.A., where over the next week, the temperature rose something like a dozen degrees a day. Then the Santa Ana winds came, ionizing the air with small particles that made everyone alternately depressed, energized, and ultimately just restless. This only heightened the effect of the pollution from the freeways, which seemed to me to further stimulate everyone's anxiety.

I was driving on the freeway one afternoon, trying to determine whether the panicky feeling in my chest was caused by pollution or something more idiosyncratic and psychological, when the pointillist bits that more generally made the air a flat shade of gray slowly began to grow more visible. They were expanding, until the air was not gray so much as a speckled canvas of black flakes against white. Over the course of that afternoon, those small flakes swelled. By the time I got home, my front steps were covered in a carpet of soft charcoal, and the sky was raining large flat disks that landed on your head and arms and left impressions reminiscent of the nuclear suntans burnished on victims of Hiroshima. Off to the west was an ominous red glow. L.A. burned like that for four days.

Inside, I too was burning. There was something in my chest, what felt like grief and pain at the same time. I was unsettled deep inside, in my veins, in my limbs, in the fibers lacing around my ribs and connecting to my lungs.

Contrary to the idea that yoga's popularity in L.A. owed to the deeply bred and rampant vanity, I believed that yoga was suited to L.A. because it was a system of purification and relaxation that worked on two fronts to undo the nefarious effects of smog. A buildup of toxins, my teachers at the Iyengar Yoga Institute of L.A. suggested, could be combated with ten- or fifteen-minute interludes in headstands and shoulder stands. These served to spur the circulation of lymph through your nodes, creating a cleansing effect while also easing whatever urban tension might have built up since the last time you did the poses. This explanation was so relevant to my experience of the city that the teachers at the yoga institute seemed like prophets to me, and I began spending as much of my free time as possible taking in their wisdom. I eventually signed up with Gloria and a handful of others to undergo training to become a teacher. Gloria suggested I write to Iyengar in India to learn yoga from its source, and I did. That afternoon when I tiptoed up my steps, leaving footprints in the carpet of ash, I received my response.

It was an invitation to come to India for two months, in the form of an aerogram from the small Indian city of Pune, a sliver of blue parchment with an arabesquelike signature in the script of an institute secretary named Pandurang Rao. The crudely printed Indian postage stamps had the hallowed look of ancient seals. Their script, in Roman and Devanagari letters, evoked something sacred and wise.

The aerogram had a literal message as well. Demand to visit the Iyengar institute in India was high these days, and I'd have to wait several years before they could make a place for me.

I waited. During those years, I enrolled in graduate school while continuing to practice and teach Iyengar yoga. On a trip home to New York, I called the New York City Iyengar institute to inquire about classes.

"Today?" the person on the line asked.

"Yes."

She paused. Her pause suggested she was guarding some secret society, its exact nature unclear to me and into whose ranks I was for some reason unwelcome.

"There's a Level Two class at ten A.M., a Level Three at noon, and at three, Guruji's coming to dedicate the studio."

"Who?"

"Guruji," she said carefully. There was more silence.

"Mr. Iyengar?"

She paused before uttering yes.

"This is *the* Mr. Iyengar? Not his cousin or somebody? From India? Pune, India?"

"Guruji," she said weightily.

The environmental contamination I'd escaped in L.A. had followed me to New York on this trip. It was the most foul day of the year — mid-August, about a hundred degrees and sticky. The soot from taxicabs and subways stuck to your skin like sugar. The air felt soggy, like walking through a sponge. New York was irritable, only furthering my theory that bad air worked on the psyche in a physical way. It was a dubious activity to even venture outdoors.

I nevertheless made my way to the studio, an unmarked eighth-floor loft on a Midtown side street. Several dozen Americans, many in Indian dress, sat on the wood floor waiting quietly. I sat with them until finally a flash of white appeared at the doorway. I recognized Iyengar from pictures I had seen of his yoga demonstrations, in which he twisted into contortions while wearing shiny shorts. This Iyengar looked smaller inside his loose-fitting garb. Even as he strode through the parting sea of devotees, I was struck by how hefty his belly seemed in the photos and yet how weightlessly he seemed to move. He installed himself at the top of a tall dais sitting cross-legged. His hand gestures were jumpy, his fingers flying to his head again and again to tame his silver mane. His eyes flashed from face to face. One time, they met mine. They made me feel warm, as if there were a furnace inside of me. But then his eyes darted to the next face, kinetically, feeding off the nervousness on the street outside. There, high-pitched melodies cycled on broken car alarms, taxi drivers leaned on horns, pedestrians took out frustrations in shouting matches.

The guru seemed as sensitive to the urban irritants as I was. "People say the cities in my country are the most polluted cities in the world," he complained in his difficult accent. "But New

York City is worse than even Calcutta." A yogi must perform breathing exercises first thing in the morning, I had read in one of his instruction books. At first I'd taken this as holy if mysterious counsel that had to do with the auspicious quality of the sunrise hours. But as I read on, I learned that in such highly polluted cities as Calcutta, it was only during the early morning that you could breathe a suitable level of oxygen with your air.

I had always understood this kind of a concern for the sanctity of the human body as related to the fact that yogis tended to be vegetarians. So after Iyengar performed his short speech and a dedication in Sanskrit, I was not at all surprised that the celebration meal, specially prepared with Iyengar's favorite foods, was vegetarian.

I had become a vegetarian mostly because I never liked the way meat made me feel. It was heavy and goopy, and even as a child I imagined its oils congealing beneath my skin to create a thick layer of noxious gelatin. Sitting at the dinner table with my mother and sister, I used to make sure the garbage was within easy reach so I could deposit forkfuls of meat when my mother wasn't looking. My hunger strikes persisted through the years with my stepfather, when I refused to eat steak or meat loaf or hamburgers. Back then, I spent several evenings sitting alone at the dinner table into the late night in defiance of my stepfather's order that I remain at the table until I was done. By the time I was fourteen, my stepfather long gone, my mother herself gave in. At my urging, we made a vegetarian pact, much to the disgruntlement of my sister. "What does your mother think of this?" my father asked suspiciously from Boston, only to receive the worst possible report.

Today, the substance of the Indian buffet confused me. My desire to create a clear and uncluttered feeling in my body had led me to cut out other things from my diet that, like meat, seemed to thicken my insides, to muddle my clarity. This was what yoga worked against. But the buffet today was laden with sweet, gelatinous, fatty things: dairy, sugar, refined carbohydrates. Rice pudding. Curries with globules of oil floating on top. I watched Iyengar eat heartily. I imagined the food sinking into his big belly. I saw it undulating on its way there, sprouting bacteria as it swam. Clearly, if there was some equation that connected vegetarianism, purity, and yoga, it had little to do with my own ideas about nutrition.

My encounter with the holy man nevertheless inspired me to prepare for my journey in earnest. My teachers at the L.A. institute instructed me that, indeed, the twin topics of contamination and cleanliness preoccupied travelers and hosts alike in India, particularly the orthodox Brahmin Iyengar family.

"India is filthy," one yoga teacher told me point-blank. The country was parasite-infested and dangerous, a nation of rats and ringworm and poisoned water. "I hate it," she added blandly. "Put me on the plane, drive me to the hotel, don't tell me where I am. I go to see Guruji."

India was also smelly. Pier Paolo Pasolini titled his India memoir *The Scent of India,* though a more accurate rendering of the Italian might have been *the stench* — "that odor which, little by little, becomes an almost living physical entity," he wrote. A generation later, Günter Grass was most impressed by the visceral quality of the filthiness. It seemed to assault his body "like flotsam, thrown in with everything and everybody, skin rubbing skin, sweat mixing with sweat." Shrouded forms of people sleeping were strewn everywhere, "lying like litter."

Because many of their protégés had received invitations to make the voyage to Pune, my American yoga instructors hosted informational sessions to better orient us. We learned of Indian commonplaces such as the belief that feet were foul. Shoes were dirty and never to be worn inside. For a reminder, we needed only to look as far as the doorway behind the speaker at the yoga studio, where a forest of shoes lay before a scaffoldinglike structure. Dirtier than even shoes were the soles of the feet, which one must diligently keep to oneself. We'd be expected to sit on the floor quite a bit — for ceremonies, speeches, music performances. This was good reason to practice sitting comfortably in lotus or some cross-legged position, because you couldn't point your feet toward the person on the dais. To do so would be to commit a mortal insult.

Food was above all symbolic. According to Ayurveda, India's native medical system, from medieval times "clean" food was believed to purify psyche as well as body. "Unclean" foods promoted an accumulation of not only physical toxins but mental worries.

To guard the cleanliness of one's food, one must keep the left hand hidden at all times, the teacher added. To learn by demonstration, that evening after class a group of us went to a nearby Hare Krishna restaurant. Our teachers instructed us to eat so that our left hands never so much as glanced against our food. We attempted to balance flatbread in the crooks of our right thumbs and forefingers, to retrieve spoonsize portions of chana masala in the fold of the bread. After flatbread touched lips, and right fingers with it, we then put aside all qualms about dipping those same fingers back into the communal dish to scoop out more. Our left hands, they advised, must remain firmly under our seats.

Most of us already knew about and largely subscribed to Hinduism's vegetarian ethic, but we now discovered its particularities. Meat, my teacher explained, was not unhealthy in the literal sense. It defiled you spiritually, tainting you with the act of violence implicit in the journey from life to dinner. Ahimsa, or nonviolence, proscribed against all killing, including for food. The strength of this belief was illustrated by an anecdote Gandhi recounted in his autobiography. His wife, Kasturbai, was perched on the brink of death, delirious. When her doctor recommended a cure of beef bouillon, her life was in her husband's hands. Gandhi resolved that she would rather die than dirty her insides with the stuff of killing.

I was excited to travel to a place where I wouldn't have to explain my preference against meat. When I got home that night, though, I was troubled. I couldn't understand why yogis didn't see meat the way I did: it kept you from flying; it weighed you down when you tried to jump to a handstand. I checked my copy of Iyengar's famous manual, *Light on Yoga,* and there found that the guru, like me, seemed to have a less symbolic idea about eating. His only mention of food concerned its absence. "Asanas should preferably be done on an empty stomach," he wrote.

He'd come to this conclusion after having practically starved as a young man in depression-era India, often surviving on just water and tea for days. It was under these circumstances that Iyengar had his first encounter with divinity. "My body was at rest," he wrote of the experience. "My soul was calm. I had no sense of awareness of things around me. All my thoughts, actions, body and ego were completely forgotten. I was only conscious of that moment of rapture."

If meat sullied the body, fasting purified it, he reasoned at this time. Performing asanas was an offering to the Lord, and doing so on an empty stomach cleared the body, leaving space for the divine.

It was unclear to me exactly how my predilection toward lightness aligned with Iyengar's idea of the body as an empty vessel, but I felt I was on to something. I too made a connection between fasting — feeling *light* — and preparing myself for the sweep of epiphany. There seemed to be a link. He called his subject "*light*" on yoga, after all.

Chapter Five

I first became aware that I suffered from depressions when I was in college. Julie, my yoga teacher, was encouraging me to be sensitive to what I experienced in my body, and when I looked there, I found emotions. After I'd hung in the live oak that day, I came home and noticed the raw pain still growing in my chest. I lay down on my bed and felt the uncertainty of my life in California like boiling water pouring over me. That semester, California's winter ended abruptly, bringing intense heat and perilous news about a water shortage. They were times of a blue sky so crystalline I thought it might crack. The sunny days demanded an optimism I couldn't match. Behind the brilliance of the sunshine was the hidden message of drought, of dry crops and animals dying off, of strange pollens and an ecosystem out of balance. Outside my window that afternoon, the sky darkened to the most insistent blue I'd seen. The gorgeous weather refused to break. I could feel nature's imbalance in my flesh. I wanted to touch these emotions, to penetrate them as I would probe a muscle. Sometimes, the pain in my chest accompanied a feeling of desperation, as if there was something I needed to do, only I didn't know what.

Over several years, the pain in my heart traveled to other parts of my body. My hip. By the time I lived in L.A., ache in my hip felt like grief in my hip. I wanted to attack my hip as I'd wanted to attack the pangs in my chest. One day in a yoga class at the L.A. institute, the teacher, Manouso, instructed us to do a forward bend. If it was easy, he said, we could intensify the stretch by taking large wooden blocks beyond the soles of our feet. It was simple enough for me to lay my forehead on my shins with my legs straight, so I grabbed a block that essentially extended the length of my legs six inches. Manouso walked past, observed me, nodded, and added another block; I was now grasping onto feet that might have belonged to a person a foot taller than I was.

The pain in my hip soared. By stretching harder, I could ratchet it up so precipitously that the only thing I knew was pain. I was composed of it, built of grief. After a few minutes, the ache took on more subtle and differentiated characteristics — nausea, fatigue, sting. All kinds of pain, layered like sediment. It was the closest thing to relief I knew. At the end of class, just like in Julie's class a decade before, by the time we lay in corpse pose, it had vanished.

But when I got home that day, something was different. The pain had metamorphosed from an ethereal memory into a real and tangible presence within me. When I woke up the next day, the presence was larger, stronger. I decided then that I needed something more violent than this feel-good Indian meditation. Yoga had once worked to counter this pain. Now I needed to penetrate my body more deeply, to encounter this thing at its root.

I went to an orthopedist. He took X rays of my back and then placed them on his light board. I stood back and squinted. My spine looked straight, bent only with the calligraphic sweep of a French curve. It was the spine of a feather, graceful and vibrant. But when I unsquinted my eyes, my spine revealed crags and angles; a slight jutting to the right between my shoulder blades where I'd felt the torquing on the live oak in Santa Cruz; a thickening of the bone in the vertebrae of my lower back; a bend where my spine plunged to meet pelvis at sacrum.

The doctor directed his pointer to the X ray. "Could be arthritis," he said quizzically, shrugging. He pointed to a spot on my sacrum where the bone was a deep white. This, he said, signified calcification. "But you're too young. It's a good spine, actually."

I looked more closely at the spot where he pointed, and then touched the corresponding indentation on my body. The imperfections were palpable. I felt pain there, where the X ray showed white. The doctor had given me a secret view into my insides, what I'd never been meant to see. Now I wanted to work inside my body with some kind of tool. When I felt the ache in my hip at home later, I saw it sitting inside the milky bone at the base of my spine, crouching like a small person.

My doctor suggested, on the other hand, exercise. This would increase endorphins, he promised, which in turn worked analgesically to dull the pain.

So I began running. Indeed, with the runner's high came relief. Oblivion to the pain person inside me. In addition to doing yoga, I was now running daily. It wasn't long before I found that if I missed running one day, the pain crept back to its many dwellings inside me: more pain in more places. I came to feel parts of my body that I'd previously only taken on faith existed.

It was a synergistic effect that caused my weight to drop. Running took off weight. I was growing increasingly sensitive in all parts of my body — inside and outside. Food began to irritate my digestive tract. I ate less, got thinner. I had no idea I was in the grips of a strange disease. From there it took only a simple intuitive leap to discover that if I wanted to get within striking distance of the pain in my bones, I needed only reduce the flesh that covered them. This was, perhaps, the moment when the mystical under-tones I'd ascribed to my quest for health and wholeness came to overtake my quest for integrity in my body. I entered a shape-shifter's fantasy, a dream I could invent my body.

Around this time, I went to one of Manouso's yoga classes. Yoga was at two. I had run in the morning. After, I'd felt the en-dorphin buzz of the runner's high. I rode that high through the blood-sugar drop of a skipped lunch, so that when I got to class on the requisite empty stomach, I was famished. The hunger inside me felt like a bird, soft and alive, so weightless it might fly. The hunger gave the world a different cast. I felt ethereal. Luminous shapes shimmered around the edges of the purple gym mats that lined the floor. The universe had a sparkly, tingly effervescence. This was a numinous, radiant world, alluring and dangerous.

I was also tired. I nodded hello to the yoga students I knew but avoided conversation, sitting on my mat to stretch until Manouso arrived. When my thighbones touched the ground, I no-ticed that the flesh at my hips and sides had diminished from even the day before. As there was less and less of me, I was grow-ing to dislike what was left. The skin pushing against my tights and tank top reminded me of my body. I lay down and hunted up my skin for places where flesh gathered. I pinched the back of my thigh, hard, until it hurt, and still harder, until it was numb. I won-dered if I could pare down my body to the point where, some-day, there would be no place left for the pain to hide.

Soon Manouso was at the front of the room, instructing us to do a sun salutation: stand with arms raised in tadasana — moun-tain — inhale; hands to feet — uttanasana — exhale; look up, inhale; jump feet back — chaturanga dandasana — exhale; lift up, inhale. From the great height of my head, I observed my body move from position to position, the actions executed as if by external force. I felt separate from the rest of the class, hovering above and watching. My body seemed to be operating outside of my will. There was a freedom in being able to mold myself into any shape I wanted, I was thinking. Body as topiary.

I completed the sequence and jumped back to the original posture — mountain. In the space directly in front of where my feet landed, I saw Manouso's feet. Manouso was facing me, standing very close. As I lifted my head, I noticed that the ribs on his ribbed T-shirt were shimmering so that they made moiré patterns. I felt dizzy. Manouso peered at me angrily.

"What did you eat for dinner yesterday?"

"Vegetables, tofu," I answered abruptly, startled. I recalled having eaten quite a bit.

He looked at my eyes, and then he grabbed me by the shoulders. He shook me. My limbs shuddered. I imagined them like the edges of feather threads as they trembled in wind. *Light as a feather.* I watched Manouso's moiré pattern. I gaped at him.

"That's not enough!" he said. Then he shouted my name. "Elizabeth!"

Suddenly I was in a different place entirely. The sound of my name called me back from something very distant. I felt my body take shape again, as if it had ceased, for a while, to be solid: *Elizabeth*.

Manouso did not, however, succeed in shaking me back completely. That weekend, I threw my friends a dinner party. Would they, like Manouso, see the pain in my body? To me, my pain was palpable. Now my body drew a picture of that pain.

For my party, I prepared a dish from every category in *The*

New Vegetarian Epicure and invited everyone I knew. I started on a Thursday. A mole simmered in my cast-iron Dutch oven for thirty hours. When the guests arrived on Friday night, there were braised *nopales;* four different homemade salsas made from twenty different species of chili pepper. There were oyster mushrooms, portabellas, shiitakes; nans, rotis, parathas. My guests sat in a big circle on the floor, and I watched them eat. The food was good, they said. "Elizabeth! The food is amazing!"

"Thank you!"

"You *made* the mole? How did you *make* the mole?"

"I made it! From a recipe!"

I didn't eat. I'd been cooking for thirty hours — too long to be hungry, too long, even, to be tired. I was exhilarated. After food, we danced. At 2 A.M., my friend Simon carried a mole-encrusted dinner plate to the kitchen as if to wash it, and I stopped him: "Don't help!" At 3 A.M., Simon departed, the last of the straggling guests in tow. The apartment was quiet. I surveyed the expanse of empty wine bottles; of plates, in little stacks, like cold pancakes; of crumbs on wood floor and plastic cups tipped on sides; of dishes picked clean and a food table stained red from wine splashes and brown from salsa and green from the skins of braised cactus.

Suddenly I was hungry. All that food, and I hadn't had a morsel since breakfast on Thursday, almost two days before. I washed a dinner plate and took it to the buffet, where I piled it with roasted green beans, salad greens, three categories of salsa, brown rice, then slathered the whole thing with the homemade mole. I ate slowly. The food was good.

At 4 A.M., I was still not tired. I gathered the plates and stacked them on a single countertop, then collected the empty bottles in a corner of the floor. I rinsed the plates, washed them; swept the floor, sponged the table, rinsed the bottles and carried them to the recycling bin, dumped the garbage, rearranged the furniture back onto the wooden dance floor — not before cuing more music and dancing. I felt the food in my stomach and wished it gone. I put the dishes in their cabinets. My studio was spotless. I took it in. It was lovely.

At 5 A.M., the first light cast pink onto the bougainvillea and stucco outside. I was still not tired, and my stomach was too full of food now for me to sleep. I took off my dress and slipped on jean shorts. They hung at my hips. It was a reassuring sensation, my body compact inside loose denim. It was thrilling to observe my weight drop. I put on a bra, a T-shirt, sneakers with no socks. I went outside and began walking quickly, wishing for the full feeling to go away, wishing for motion to overtake sensation.

I walked to Sunset Boulevard, hiked past silent seedy strip malls along the mile to Echo Park, then turned north into the hills. I walked until the street turned scrabbly and gave way to the fire roads of Elysian Park. The roads slimmed to footpaths through dense foliage. As daylight collected into morning, a pack of trainees from the Police Academy came jogging in formation and passed me.

I kept walking brusquely, and then broke into a run. I climbed to the crest of the park, where you could look upon the spectacular vista of downtown Los Angeles. I stopped. The landscape was crisp and blue, but I knew that the sky would soon turn dark with pollution. The longer I stood still, the more the image of grayness overtook me. I grasped for the picture of beauty but could not maintain it. I started running again, and only then could I fix the gorgeous vista in my head. I kept running, ran loops around the park. To stop for just a second would be to see the ashen thing inside me, to have to watch it, like the sky above, turn yet darker.

*   *   *

It wasn't long after when I wrote my plea to Pune. I had reached a crossroads. On one side was a track where I could run circles for the rest of my life as my problems worked themselves deeper inside my flesh. Or there was a path to Iyengar in India. Neither the endpoint nor the way to get there was evident. But there was something about that man's frenetic finger movements, something telling me that in India I could find my guide.

I also had a dream that week. I was in a Casbah, shadowy with Gothic archways. Someone grabbed me by the hand and led me somewhere. "You can ask your question," the person told me. We came to an open area, and there I saw Geeta Iyengar, the guru's daughter, whom I recognized from pictures. She was wearing a white cotton sari that gave her an angelic bearing. Her full face was beatific as she beamed at a crowd of admiring questioners. Her body was soft and round. The person deposited me in front of the yoga teacher. Geeta gazed at me. I didn't say anything, but she knew my question nonetheless. "Go find your teacher," she said.

Chapter Six

More than four years later, I got on a plane in Los Angeles believing I would find my teacher. The trip to India would take two days. I hewed closely to my instincts and refused food the entire journey. Today, I was ostensibly healthy. But I still craved hunger, was still a junkie for the visual starbursts of a skipped meal. Hunger could protect me, I believed in some way, like a shield.

I had my first coffee as the flight departed Los Angeles. Iyengar wrote in *Light on Yoga* that while yoga must be performed after a fast, "a cup of tea or coffee, cocoa or milk may be taken." It had always seemed funny to me that Iyengar never proscribed coffee — in L.A., everyone knew that coffee stained your teeth, depleted your vitamin C, disturbed your sleep cycle, and, of course, jangled your nerves. But as I fasted and felt the giddy effects of the caffeine on the first leg of my flight, Iyengar's advice made all the sense in the world. The yogi wanted to keep his stomach empty of solids — the injunction was purely physical. It had nothing to do with the particular qualities of the substances inside him. In this way, he left room for God; God took up physical space. I too wanted to keep my body clear. I wanted to create as uncluttered a transition as possible between L.A. and India. I wanted to keep outside of me anything that lay between. I wanted to be empty when I met my teacher.

Unfortunately, a dozen coffees coupled with two days of traveling left me feeling not so much empty as polluted. When my plane opened onto the Bombay tarmac, I had a headache in every cell. Bombay smelled exactly as bad as its reputation. There were many things floating on the air currents, things I couldn't recognize and things I could: roasting meat, soot, fire, shit. On the street, the smells were even stronger. I traveled by cab through the last minutes of late night to Bombay's central train station, where after a short wait I would catch the train to Pune. Five hours and the mountainous Western Ghats of India stood between me and Iyengar.

It was the height of monsoon season. Water puddled everywhere. I stood on the train platform, watching a thick gray cloud gather above the far edge of the railway terminus. I had arrived in India prepared — for Iyengar and his poses; for Sanskrit nomenclature and mythic resonances; for filth, purity, feet, left hands. But I'd learned nothing to explain how this land of yoga had produced the squalor and poverty that stretched before me.

Across from the train platform was a rough sidewalk lined with vendors' carts made from scrap wood. Sheets of soggy cardboard flapped above the carts from connectors made of old twine, lengths of wire, twist ties. Dawn light broke through the monsoon sky, revealing people sleeping under wraps on carts and rubbled pavement.

Soon a gust of wind, wet and rich with tree smells, swept

over the platform. Bird sounds got loud; squawks and screeches accompanied the frantic beating of wings. Herons with long yellow necks landed on the tracks and then flapped up into the air. The noises seemed invented to try nerves. Short sharp horns blasted. A hawker advertised his foods with a sibilant and alliterative song. It echoed shrilly in my head. I tried to hear in its threads the devotional chants we recited in yoga classes, but I couldn't find the rhythm. The wind carried a tremendous heat, hot as a blow-dryer, like a Santa Ana. In L.A., the winds' nervous energy was fabled for making people do things they were never wired to do: men murdered wives; authors found themselves shopping in supermarkets dressed in nothing but bikinis. "Every voice seems a scream. It is the season of suicide and divorce and prickly dread, wherever the wind blows," was how Joan Didion described it.

The winds aroused the sleepers. The shrouded figures began to move slowly on the carts and pavement. Rain began to patter, drawing whole families from under covers. Blinking children emerged and squatted naked over puddles. Lithe women with black skin in water-streaked, brightly colored saris moved to street-side cook pots; the landscape transformed into a sea of scarlet and emerald and magenta and mud. Vendors set up wares — papayas and bananas and cauliflower and cooked things, everything dripping water at its edges.

Finally, the spicy smell of fried food overtook the stench of sewage and earth. I was hungry. I felt light-headed, floaty. I smelled fresh bread and traced it to a young boy and girl huddled over a dry metal cylinder. I wheeled my luggage off the platform and walked through craggy pavement and puddles to the stand, moving quickly to dodge the water and waking humans. An ounce of dirt hosts 28 million bacteria, I'd read in *Harper's* before I came. The same dirt, wet, hosts 28 *billion:* 28 billion bacteria swimming in the wet spot on my suitcase. I walked faster. These people were the fabled untouchables of India's streets, that caste whose touch and food and shadow were once thought to pollute. I tried to banish the thought, but it was easy to imagine that the people had lifted from the filth of the sewers.

The boy and girl were balling up dough globes and flattening them into the dry drum. I held up two fingers to ask the boy for two chapatis. He palmed two globes and flattened them into patties in the pan and, when they were cooked, rolled the breads in pink newsprint. He charged me two rupees, the equivalent of three cents. The newspaper was moist and fragrant. I ripped a small hemisphere from the chapati's edge. It tasted like rich clay.

As I chewed, a small wet thing caught my hand. I jerked it away. There was a girl. She was about five, wrapped in a tattered dress cut from emerald sari cloth; mud streaked her bare feet and legs. Her right arm ended at a stub just above her elbow. Her feet rested at the edge of a puddle the color of sienna. She moved her one hand away from my wrist and up to her mouth, her eyes stabbing toward mine. Behind her, the eyes of several dozen hungry Indians under the age of seven turned circumspectly toward us. I gave the girl some rupees, the eyes of the strangers moving closer.

The girl was unsatisfied and repeated an insistent gesture, her fingers hitting at her mouth, then pointed at my roll of steaming Hindi newspaper. "Chapati," she said. *Chapati,* of course. I handed her the chapatis, a cramp in my stomach killing my hunger anyway. I edged back to the train platform, handing out rupees as I slunk back, the children following until rail guards stopped them.

Back on the platform, my train had pulled in. I rolled my luggage along its length to locate my compartment. Amid a roar of shouting and throwing at the rear of the train, bags and boxes careened toward the train doors, vying with hundreds of passengers attempting to board. A sign on the carriage said SECOND CLASS. Farther along the platform, signs on windows designated the cars SECOND-CLASS SLEEPERS. Here, the commotion was tempered. Next came SECOND-CLASS AIR-CONDITIONED, then SECOND-CLASS SLEEPER AIR-CONDITIONED, the chaos lessening and the crowds thinning outside each successive car. I imagined each category as one of India's four castes, chugging across the landscape in self-contained hemispheres fashioned from train cars.

On a list on a window at the front of the train I found my reservation. A family of well-to-do Indians and several men with briefcases and loafers lingered on the platform. The family members looked serene, exhibiting none of the anticipation and panic of those at the rear. The adult son, a handsome if pudgy young man in a Dartmouth sweatshirt, Adidas pants, and Reeboks, talked on a cell phone. The sister wore a saffron sari of a silk so lustrous it showed not a wrinkle, from the bottom of which peeked elegant pumps dyed the exact same hue. A rope of black braid ran down her back, tied at the end with a swatch of silk from the same sari cloth. She reminded me of girls I knew when I used to visit my father in Boston. *We "summer" on the Cape,* they used to say. The edge of the woman's sari hung in a long scarf slung over her left shoulder, but its end lay in a puddle of iridescent water. A wet stain crept up the scarf like a rising pestilence. Finally, she peered over her shoulder with a haughty arch of the upper back and lifted the silk from the puddle. Then she flicked its excess water toward the track and scowled at its tassels, casting off the creep of Indian dirt. Then she flung the cloth so that it was suspended precisely two inches above the puddle.

My seat was in a sleeping compartment featuring flat sleeping bunks, air-conditioning, and hazed windows. This seemed wrong, as I was wet, cold, and awake. Only one man shared the compartment, a middle-aged Indian in loafers who was studiously examining the contents of his briefcase. A porter popped in his head and handed trays to each of us. I scrutinized mine uncertainly.

My cabin mate looked at me and assumed a similar sneer. "Vegetarian," he noted.

I lifted the aluminum wrapping and indeed found a piping gelatinous meal that appeared to lack meat. Chana masala, rice, chapatis. I sniffed it, not sure it could resurrect my hunger.

"You are American?" my cabin mate ventured.

I nodded, trying to determine the oil content of my chapatis. They were not smooth and dry like the chapatis on the street.

"California?" he added.

I nodded. I was preoccupied with whether I could perform the one-handed chapati-and-chana-masala maneuver on a moving train, though I was still not committed to the act of eating.

"And I imagine you are vegetarian?" he continued.

I nodded again, wondering what to make of this mystic.

"You see, I thought so. Because I happen to live in California as well." He went on to explain that he was an engineer who had just flown in from his home of the last ten years, Sunnyvale, California, and was now visiting his family in South India. In his lilting Indian-English accent, he added that he'd chosen this class of car because he liked the darkened windows, which gave our compartment and its flat bed-seats the surreal yellowish tint of a darkroom. He said he preferred to sleep through the landscape, that he wasn't ready yet to look closely at his native India.

"And you, what brings you halfway around the world?" he asked with a mocking grin.

"Iyengar yoga," I offered.

"Iyengar. Yes, I know the name. The Iyengar family comes from the same state as mine. Tamil Nadu. This name, Iyengar, it is, like mine, a Brahmin name. In Tamil Nadu," he said, "there are two strains of Brahmins. The Iyers and the Iyengars. I am an Iyer."

He winked, suggesting that his name meant everything — that his lineage connected him to the sages and scribes who for all India's history had occupied the top tier in the caste hierarchy — but also proposing that, paradoxically, he was now far too modern to put stock in such clannish identifications. "My family chose not to use the name," he added with even more pride. "My last name now is Singh. Keeping the old caste name is a way of advertising your family, that you come from the priestly race, that you are from an old strain of Indian royalty. We've ripped off the sacred thread." He said it with an air of importance.

The sacred thread was associated exclusively with Brahmins, but I'd never known exactly what it meant. In fact, I didn't actually know, precisely, what a Brahmin was, and only vaguely that Iyengar was one. I knew that he wore the thread. It appeared in the photos of even the most elaborate postures in *Light on Yoga*. The sling rested loosely over Iyengar's left shoulder, crossing his chest between his nipples, circling to his back at the waist, and looping again around his neck. In the upside-down poses, it fell haphazardly toward the floor. I'd never given much thought, though, to the meaning of the word *Brahmin*. A Brahmin was from India's highest and most cultured class, a Boston Brahmin only from India.

As I considered the man's words, I thought about how my grandmother used the term. She was a Boston Jew with Protestant airs and little patience for the rigors of her Orthodox upbringing. She'd told me about how she used to sneak bacon grease into her matzo-ball soup such that her mother — who kept kosher until the day she died — declared it the best matzo-ball soup this side of Grodno. Despite her mixed feelings about her Jewish roots, my grandmother often spoke in snide terms about the Boston Brahmins — those elitists who thought the Jews inferior and denied them membership in their country clubs. When my grandmother talked about Boston's WASPs, it always seemed to me that she did so with equal parts scorn and respect. I wondered now about the significance of our own rituals in this context. On the one hand, our Jewish rituals made us strong. But on the other, they made those elegant and handsome WASPs inaccessible. I always got the feeling that my grandmother believed, on some level, that if we could all talk like Cary Grant, if we could wave our gloves in the air like Katharine Hepburn, then Boston's glamour would coat us too. We could glide through the world with that cultured patina.

My grandmother's ambivalence was especially complicated when applied to her grandchildren. She didn't really consider my sister and me Jews. Our mother, though a convert for the sake of her marriage to my father, was forever regarded by her Jewish in-laws as a shiksa — albeit a beautiful and charming one. After the divorce, I became for a whole clan of Boston Jews the doppel-gänger for the French beauty my father let get away. "You're not Jewish," my grandmother would tease me. I never knew how to take it, as insult or compliment.

Where, I wondered now, did India's Boston Brahmins "summer"? Did non-Brahmins feel the same complicated draw to them? Were these Brahmins oppressive too, their rituals exclusive and arcane, the Indian equivalent of croquet and Harvard–Yale games? Just then, the porter peeked his head back in and, without pausing to ask, extracted both of our untouched trays. Food. Was refusing food a way to keep us separate?

Iyengar was certainly a product of his exclusive upbringing. In the photos in *Light on Yoga* he looks like an emissary from an exotic tribe. Many of these images were taken from an album the yogi put together in the 1950s, when he was just thirty-three, a thick-lipped, dark-skinned, slick-haired Gary Cooper of a yogi.

One of the poses, simhasana, had always stuck in my mind when I tried to imagine where Iyengar came from. The pose was named for the god Narasimha, an incarnation of Vishnu in which he was part man, part lion. It was also the asana that won Iyengar his sobriquet, the Lion of Pune — a description, however lovingly bestowed, of the yogi's infamous temper. Iyengar was known for being fierce and fiery, proud and fearsome and animallike, a feral king. I had always found this photo the most startling and strange in the guidebook, sleeved though it was among hundreds of images of the man twisting into flying, crouching, arching, balancing impersonations of moods, deities, and circuslike wonders.

In simhasana, Iyengar was a contortion of feet wrapping into middle, his face morphed into the horrific cross-eyed expression of an enraged monster, its mouth agape, its tongue bayoneting forward. Here he acted out the myth of Narasimha, in which Vishnu proved the existence of a boundless and universal God by revealing his divine form. His transformation was as awe-inspiring as the metamorphosis of Krishna into the multilimbed discus-throwing warrior in the Bhagavad Gita. In the legend of Narasimha, Vishnu turned himself into a chimera that was part lion, part human, part god. Breathing fire, he made mincemeat of a demon who had challenged the existence of God. Iyengar, it was said, dealt with detractors with a similar lack of restraint.

The metamorphosis of Iyengar into simhasana made him fearsome, but it also made me wonder how he came to present such a ritualistic image to the modern and Western readership of *Light on Yoga*. In the photo, he wore the string, giving the sleeve the look of a document from an anthropologist's field book. It occurred to me now that Iyengar embodied the very essence of Brahmin here: regal and otherworldly; part animal, part god; an anachronistic relic from an India ruled by sages. Not a Boston Brahmin, but an ancient and Eastern one.

"We've traded in the sacred thread for our computers and our Ph.D.s," I heard my seatmate saying, now sounding almost wistful. "This Iyengar, what does he do?"

I told him about the yoga institute in Pune — how despite a lengthy waiting list, it attracted nearly a thousand Western visitors a year, how Iyengar was the single most important influence on the practice of yoga in the United States, how Indian and foreign students learned the mind-body healing techniques of the master side by side according to a strict pedagogy that was half exercise workout, half meditation.

He looked at me ironically. "I have never done yoga," he confessed.

"Why not?"

"It is not something you would do," he responded. "Frankly, no one I know has ever done yoga. They think it is old and quaint, something your grandfather might have done. When I was young, I never knew anyone who did yoga. It is not something that interests the Indian people. If you are someone who works in the professional sector, if you have the time for this kind of study or recreation, you want to do the Western things, hiking and jogging. You go to the gym." He gestured toward the cabin with the young Indian man in sweats.

"Yoga's popular in the West, though," I offered.

"Yes," he said. "And so it will come to India." He sighed. "All things come here backwards. And now, I must sleep." He lifted his loafers onto the vinyl seat and lowered the shade over his yellowed window, casting the compartment in a deeper shade of jaundice.

I looked long at his loafers on the seat but finally kicked off my own sneakers before laying my feet on my bunk. Then I drifted to sleep to the rhythm of train gears and crashing monsoon bursts. The hum of the downpour and the circular drone of the engine started to sound like the words to familiar songs, and I thought about how the mind tries to make things familiar when everything is really foreign, and how I was in a place connected to nothing I had ever really known, how all the knowing would come in the future, and I thought that the music in my head felt like a kind of home.

And then I wondered if there was anything else truly worth searching for.

Chapter Seven

Where Iyengar actually came from, and how exactly he progressed from provincial Brahmin to a man who had presented medical theories of the body on three continents, was a topic of much discussion, confusion, and obfuscation in and around the library in Pune. There were many myths about the man, and many falsehoods. Marveling at Iyengar's ability to communicate complicated ideas in broken English, one student insisted to me that the guru's first language was Marathi, the language of Pune. Iyengar made himself understood most grammatically and purely in that, according to the student. A Marathi speaker, meanwhile, commented on Iyengar's inability to articulate his thoughts well in that language but assured me that Sanskrit was his chosen mode of expression: in this he was as fluent as a medieval priest. A Sanskrit Ph.D. from the States, however, told me that after reading Iyengar's translations from the Sanskrit, he concluded that Iyengar had never actually studied the language extensively, but that his Hindi appeared solid. In Hindi he could converse fluently, one presumed, with Indians from all reaches of his homeland. The truth was that Iyengar was the master of no language in particular other than his ancestral Tamil, which he spoke only with members of his family. However, since his relatives were, on the whole, a generation younger than Iyengar and had been born in Pune, they didn't speak Tamil all that well themselves. Iyengar, in fact, was a man who had earned his accomplishments by communicating most essentially with his body.

Bellur Krishnamachar Sunderraja Iyengar was born in 1918. The influenza pandemic that year took by some reports nearly 20 percent of the Indian population, accounting for nearly a quarter of deaths from the disease worldwide. For a strapped and burgeoning Indian populace, this plague set the tone for decades of poverty to come, and presaged, for one future yogi, a childhood marked by indigence, poor health, and desperate choices.

The previous generation had seen the publication of the first widely circulated Bhagavad Gita in English and the proclamation by Swami Vivekananda of a new universal religion at the World Parliament of Religions in Chicago. Eleven years before Iyengar's birth, the Irish Theosophist Annie Besant delivered a series of lectures with titles such as "Yoga Is a Science" and "Samadhi" in Benares. During the year Iyengar was born, the swamis who would define the image of India in the West for the century to come were on the brink of worldwide popularity: Vivekananda was fifty-five; Yogananda was twenty-five; Sivananda was thirty-one; Kuvalayananda, presiding at a school of physical yoga in Bombay, was thirty-five; and Aurobindo, who was creating a new society out of an ashram in Pondicherry, was forty-six. At the moment of Iyengar's birth, India may have suffered from poor health, but it was in the midst of an encounter with the West that seemed to promise a cure: prosperity, intellectual rejuvenation, and spiritual resurrection.

Iyengar's mother was among influenza's victims. She survived her bout with the disease, but in childbirth passed it to Iyengar, her eleventh child. "I was born a weak child," Iyengar writes in his autobiography. "My head used to hang down and I had to lift it with an effort. For almost ten years I had seasonal malaria. I had tuberculosis and an attack of typhoid for twenty-one days. A parasitic life affected not only my body but my mind also. At times I felt like committing suicide. I never played in my childhood nor had books to read."

He was to be one of thirteen siblings, ten of whom survived childhood. His early years were punctuated by misfortune. His father died when he was nine. By the time he was fourteen, he'd survived not only malaria but also a bicycle accident that left him unconscious on the way to his graduating exams, undermining an already lackluster academic career.

Like the swamis of his day, Iyengar was born a Hindu, but the Hinduism he learned at home was what Vivekananda derisively called a "kitchen religion"— a collection of rituals and modes of worship with little direct relationship to an experience of the divine. The Iyengar family's parochial Hinduism followed the orthodoxies of custom to the point where his mother believed that to drink from a tap would be to pollute herself by sharing water with another clan. "I was brought up to live in a certain environment," Iyengar told me, bristling at the term *Hindu*. "It was only a grooming, not a system."

Iyengar's clan, however, was Brahmin. Although Iyengar was poor, he descended from the landed aristocracy. His family came from a small town in Tamil Nadu State in South India, where to be Brahmin was to be a descendant of the sage Ramanuja. By tradition and by constitution, they were followers of this sage's teachings, a philosophy and set of observances known as Srivaisnavism. In South India, Srivaisnavites were the very cream of the Brahmin crop. If India was rigidly divided into four hierarchical castes, each of those castes was further subdivided into additional hierarchies. Srivaisnavites occupied the top tier of the top tier.

Nonetheless, the effects of the worldwide economic depression and the death of Iyengar's father together conspired to impoverish his family. In India, having only a mother was the functional equivalent of being an orphan. "He *was* an orphan," an acquaintance from that time assured me, though it was technically not true.

Before he died, Iyengar's father did his family the service of marrying off his six oldest children. The youngest four were left to fend for themselves. Three of them scattered to live among older siblings, leaving only the future yogi, Sunderraja, casting about for a home.

As luck would have it, only a year before his death, Iyengar's father had made an excellent marriage between Sunderraja's older sister Namagiri and a much older and esteemed cousin. The cousin was Tiruvanamalai Krishnamacharya, a name that spoke the details of his ancestral past. His connection to the family was close. While the Iyengar family lived in Bangalore and Krishnamacharya in Mysore, about a hundred miles away, all traced their genealogy to two towns in Tamil Nadu that were associated with their common heir, Ramanuja. Like Ramanuja, all males in both families went through a ceremony when they came of age in which they acquired the five sacred rites of Vishnu — armpit tattoos, a secret mantra, the sacred thread, forehead paint in the shape of Vishnu's feet, and a small chunk of black fossil stone on which to focus their prayers.

In another time and place, however, certain differences between the two branches of the family might have prevented the marriage. The problem lay in the fact that though both families came from the state of Tamil Nadu, the Krishnamacharya family came from the town of Kanchipuram, while the Iyengar family came from Srirangam. Kanchipuram was Ramanuja's birthplace, but Srirangam was home to the temple where in later years he led his populist movement and penned his revolutionary commentaries. Each town was the headquarters for a rival cult of Ramanuja dating to a philosophical split in the thirteenth century. In the seven hundred years since, the two strains had internalized certain conflicts such that it was now less than kosher to marry across those lines. To bridge the divide required a leap across barriers both linguistic and practical. Members of the Krishnamacharya clan, known as U-Srivaisnavites — or Vatakalais, meaning "from the north"— communicated in the Telugu language and worshiped in Sanskrit. Members of the Iyengar clan, the Y-Srivaisnavites — or Tenkalais, from the south — did both in Tamil. While these distinctions had little bearing on the day-to-day life of the Iyengars and the Krishnamacharyas, the philosophical underpinnings of the split had deep resonances that would later come to bear in the two yogis' teachings. The rift pitted those who favored the more elevated associations of Sanskrit culture against those who followed a more populist philosophy that revered not only the indigenous language but also the local gods. Krishnamacharya subscribed to the former, Iyengar the latter. Which was truer to Ramanuja's reformist ideology was a point of fierce debate.

The U-Srivaisnavites and the Y-Srivaisnavites looked different as well, though an outsider might never notice the difference. All wore forehead markings depicting Vishnu's feet, made from a substance prepared according to a painstaking recipe that mixed the ash of burned and fried cow dung with turmeric. But Krishnamacharya wore the marking in the shape of a U, representing only one of the lord's feet; the Iyengars in the shape of a Y, representing two feet. This accounted for their U and Y designations.

Despite these distinctions, Krishnamacharya graced the Iyengar family with a regal wedding. "Namagiri's groom came to the house on an elephant," one relative told me. "What does this mean? It means he was a rich person. Not all his brothers-in-law were as well educated as Krishnamacharya. He had all these degrees, he was a philosopher, and he was the most educated person. That was his pride. He wanted to show it: 'I am the most educated one in the family.'"

Krishnamacharya's prestige owed to his standing with an entirely unrelated strain of Indian royalty, the Indian princes. Their genealogy never intersected the Srivaisnavites', for they were not Brahmins, or priests, but Kshatriyas — warriors. In small fiefdoms, these princes ruled India as proxies for the British Raj. Krishnamacharya was employed by one of those princes, a Hindu Kshatriya who was the maharaja of the kingdom of Mysore.

Krishnamacharya was a contemporary of those swamis who were now introducing teachings from the ancient Vedas to a wider public. In seeking to cure India of its weakness for "kitchen" rituals, Vivekananda and other popularizers had set about preaching the philosophy of the Vedas, what was once the exclusive purview of Brahmins. Their movement, known as Neo-Vedanta, won acolytes in the West as well as among India's lower castes, people taken in by the fact that unlike traditional priests, even Vivekananda himself was not a Brahmin but a Kshatriya.

Like Krishnamacharya, these swamis had links to the Kshatriya leaders of princely states. Over his career, Vivekananda received support from the Maharaja of Baroda, while his disciple Sivananda founded his Divine Life Society with help from the Maharaja of Tehri. Yogananda relied on the Maharaja of Kasimbazar. These Indian princes helped along Neo-Vedanta to the extent that the routes between their palaces formed a kind of Underground Railroad on which educated Brahmins could travel and disseminate their learning.

Krishnamacharya, now Iyengar's brother-in-law, was not firmly in support of the classless pretensions of this movement, but he nonetheless spent the early part of his career moving on this palace circuit, appearing at Sanskrit colleges created by patron maharajas in virtually every princely state on the map: Lahore, Baroda, Benares, Jaipur, Hyderabad, Patiala. He offered counsel, gave speeches, and parsed intricate matters of Vedantic punditry not debated with such intricacy since the times of Sankara. He was, it was said, among the most elegant manipulators of Sanskrit logic of his generation. It wasn't long before the Maharaja of Mysore installed him on salary at his private Sanskrit college.

There, Krishnamacharya brought up a circle of young Brahmins. He developed a reputation for relentless drilling on the fine points of esoteric arguments, impatience at the slightest hint of incomprehension, and violent outbursts at errors. When he administered tests, most of his pupils failed. Once, the maharaja asked him to explain why so many students couldn't pass his exams, but then immediately retracted the question. "Never mind," he reportedly said. "We'll have you do something else. We're starting something new."

Not long afterward, in the early 1930s, Krishnamacharya came to stay with the Iyengar in-laws in Bangalore while on a call for the maharaja. He was on his way to Pune — then still spelled the British way, Poona — to see a well-known swami named Kuvalayananda. In Bangalore, the destitute Iyengar family made an appeal to their rich cousin and in-law. They asked him to adopt the young Iyengar and take him on as a student. The older cousin surveyed the fifteen-year-old. He was sickly, skinny, a poor student, and depressive. To everyone's surprise, Krishnamacharya accepted.

The "something new" in Mysore was a school where martial athletics would be taught to the maharaja's warrior son and nephews. Krishnamacharya needed to seed his school with pupils and assistants who could provide the necessary patina of priestly Brahminism. By doing this, he could mold the school into a legitimate purveyor of an Indian practice with priestly and Brahminical roots — yoga.

Unlike his Neo-Vedantist contemporaries, Krishnamacharya did not consider yoga and the parsing of Vedantic philosophy in Sanskrit to be one and the same. Vedantic philosophy belonged in books. Yoga, on the other hand, was a mystical craft. Whatever the distinctions, neither was appropriate for the masses.

Krishnamacharya had first encountered physical yoga as a boy. His father taught him some poses and also instructed him that his lineage could be traced back to a saint named Nathamuni, who was believed to have lived in the ninth century. This sage was thought to be the grandfather of Ramanuja's own teacher, and was regarded by many as a founder of medieval yoga and the author of an important treatise on its practice called the *Yoga Rahasya* (Yoga Alchemy). Because of a series of fateful errors, Nathamuni's book had been lost a thousand years before, and many feared the wisdom of yoga had been lost with it.

But at the age of sixteen, Krishnamacharya had a dream. Nathamuni came to him. In the dream, the sage gave him instructions to locate a distant Vishnu temple. On waking, Krishnamacharya followed the directions from his dream to a small stone shrine in the shape of a box buried into hard sandstone hillside. The roots of several gnarled cypress trees wrapped around the box so that they seemed to be reaching out of the ground to devour it. By the side of the shrine, according to literature produced by his son's ashram, Krishnamacharya saw

> an old man seated under a tamarind tree and asked him where he could see Nathamuni. The old man moved his head indicating a particular direction. He set out till he reached a mango grove by the side of the river Tamraparani. He was very tired and had not eaten anything all day and as a result, he fell unconscious. A trance gripped him and he found himself in the presence of three sages. He prostrated before them and requested to be instructed in the Yoga Rahasya. Nathamuni, who appeared to be seated between the other two sages, began reciting the verses. Krishnamacharya found his voice to be very musical. A few hours later he opened his eyes and looked around and found the sages no longer there. The mango grove had also disappeared. He returned to the temple and found the old man seated in the very same place. When he went closer, the old man asked if he had received the instructions of the Yoga Rahasya and told him to go inside the temple and offer his prayers. When Krishnamacharya came out of the temple, the old man had disappeared. It was then that he realised that the old man resembled the sage seated in the middle. He had received the Yoga Rahasya directly from its author, his ancestor Nathamuni.

Divine coincidence continued to shape Krishnamacharya's life path. Later, as a young pundit, he traveled as princely emissary to the Himalayan town of Simla, which then served as the summer seat of the British crown. There, according to the tale, he helped the British viceroy overcome a bout of diabetes by teaching him yoga postures he'd learned from his father. One day, he screwed up the courage to make a request. He wanted a visa to Tibet.

Tibet was close, and Krishnamacharya was by now enchanted with legends of sacred caves deep in the mountains where one could encounter the lost techniques of Hatha yoga. According to a trove of mystical literature, much of it newly resurrected by the Theosophists and other Western acolytes, these techniques had been lost since medieval times but were preserved by certain swamis in isolated caves deep in the mountains near Kailash. "What has become mere tradition in India is still living and visible in the ancient monasteries of that isolated land of mysteries," wrote one of those who made the journey, a Greek named Theos Bernard, who was pursuing a doctorate in philosophy at Columbia University. "Hatha yoga is not taught indiscriminately to everyone," he elaborated, heightening Hatha yoga's mystery by refusing to name either his teacher or the monastery where he learned it. "It is believed," he wrote, quoting the newly disinterred medieval yoga manual, *Hatha Yoga Pradipika,* "that 'a yogi, desirous of success, should keep the knowledge of Hatha Yoga secret; for it becomes potent by concealing, and impotent by exposing.'"

Another Western ingenue, Paul Brunton, similarly stressed the enigmatic cachet of his subject when he wrote that he "traveled through scorching days and sleepless nights" to locate these yogis. They "are now but a mere handful in the very country of their origin," he wrote in a book titled, aptly enough, *Search in Secret India.* "They are exceedingly rare, are fond of hiding their true attainment from the public, and prefer to pose as ignoramuses. In India, in Tibet and in China, they get rid of the Western traveler who may happen to blunder in upon their privacy by maintaining a studied appearance of insignificance and ignorance. Perhaps they would see some sense in Emerson's abrupt phrase: 'To be great is to be misunderstood.'"

Others disputed the notion that these elusive figments existed. Swami Dayananda, a Neo-Vedantist intent upon demystifying Hinduism and uniting all the castes under the banner of a single, Vedantic set of beliefs, claimed to have traveled far and wide through the Himalayas himself. His nine-year journey, he claimed, yielded not a scrap of evidence that these traditions had persisted.

But perhaps Krishnamacharya would have better luck. Visa in hand, he took off in search of caves in a land where it was said that below-freezing temperatures and the practice of certain mind-body feats had the effect of slowing the body's metabolic functions. These factors could enable a yogi to enjoy a life expectancy of more than two hundred years. Starting with only vague directions and a mystical sense that he was bound for enlightenment, Krishnamacharya, with government funds and leather garments gifted to him by the viceroy, trekked for twenty-one days. He crossed the Himalayas out of India, across Nepal, and into Tibet — 211 miles.

A series of visions led him to an expanse of Vedic ruins at a lake called Mansarovar. There he discovered caves whose entries had been crafted with spectacular granite carvings of Hindu deities. Inside one was a very tall hermit with a long beard; he was wearing wooden shoes and was close to two hundred and thirty years old. Krishnamacharya told him that he had recovered the lost *Yoga Rahasya*. The yogi told him he already knew the technique; he would teach him. Seven years later, Krishnamacharya returned to the Sanskrit lecture circuit in India a yogi as well as a pundit.

At the new yoga school in Mysore, Krishnamacharya imparted bits of that wisdom from Tibet in the form of vigorous yoga asanas named for animals, places, and Hindu gods. He connected those shapes in choreographed sequences that involved leaping from pose to pose. Each choreography, the teacher said, was a salutation to the sun, connecting you to God through mystical shapes and symmetrical patterns of movement.

Krishnamacharya's temper had not abated. At the yoga school, he reserved it not so much for the maharaja's Kshatriya relations as for the members of his own clan, the Brahmins. Iyengar's new position at the school thus proved a frying-pan-to-fire promotion. His days consisted of more toil than tutoring. He did chores in the morning before walking to school in town three miles away. After school, his new guardian insisted he walk the three miles back home to drop off books before returning to apprentice at the yoga school. In his autobiography, Iyengar recalls stealing money to appease hunger pangs, doing poorly in his lessons because of physical weakness and depression, and receiving frequent beatings. "I grew nervous even to stand or sit in [Krishnamacharya's] presence. He would hit us on our backs and his hits were like iron rods. We were unable to forget these imprints for a long time."

"He once slapped me in the early morning," Iyengar also told me. "I said, 'For what?'

"He said, 'You are questioning me,' and he slapped me again.

"I walked ten miles to the river to commit suicide. He came and found me. He was proud. He didn't want people leaving. He pushed me to the car and took me home."

Another Brahmin student from that time, now seventy-five, remembered frequent beatings as well. "If I did correctly, he never beat me, but if I did anything wrong, he used to beat me and say, 'Do correctly!'" the former student told me. "He wanted perfection only. He beat us all. After he hit you, you would have the impression of each of his five fingers on your face."

Girls were not spared. "He used his wrist," Jayalakshmi Shamanna, one of Iyengar's sisters, told me. "For that reason, we all used to say, 'Guruji has a very strong wrist.' Some days he would get so angry he would say, 'Today, all of you are going to fast.' No water. Nothing. It was a punishment."

Like her brother, Jayalakshmi spent part of her youth living with the Krishnamacharya family. She described her trials with the tyrannical mentor one afternoon over coffee in her one-room flat. As she spoke from her seat at the edge of a twin bed, a niece brought a silver tray of cups surrounded by bland British biscuits and a pot of coffee, thick and aromatic in the South Indian style. Coffee, Jayalakshmi was saying, was very important to her mentor, and he took great pains to instruct her in its preparation. This was particularly the case following her betrothal. "I had prepared a silver tumbler of coffee," she elaborated. "But after I set it down in front of him, there was a small drop of coffee on the table next to it. He started to say, 'If you go like this to your in-laws' house —' Then he lost his temper. 'You are getting married now, and if you do this same thing in front of your husband what will happen?' he shouted. He threw the coffee tumbler on me. A silver tumbler is sharp," she added, considering. "You can cut anything on it." She fingered her left scalp, working her nails through her gray-black hair until they stopped at something. "This is the scar." I peered through the hairs to the scalp and there saw the thick gash that was the mark of her mentor.

Iyengar too bore the mark of Krishnamacharya's rage. Learning less as student than as on-the-spot performer in demonstrations, Iyengar appeared on the floor only when called to illustrate poses for the many eminent guests of the maharaja. One day during Iyengar's first year, his instructor announced that the maharaja was bringing an important spiritual master. Krishnamacharya had never mentioned spirituality. Like the Iyengar family's, Krishnamacharya's practice of Hinduism consisted of carrying out countless devotions. No act, however small, had a place outside these rituals. Breakfast consisted of offerings, or prasad, placed before a statue of the Lord Vishnu and eaten as leftovers afterward. Asana had become an ablution as well, incorporated into the master's life and instruction alongside a litany of religious habits.

The esteemed visitor was otherwise. He traveled India delivering speeches about this popular new spirituality called Vedanta. This had little in common with the asanas that Krishnamacharya had learned in Tibet, nor was it what he'd taught in the Sanskrit college. The eminence nevertheless called it yoga.

Iyengar had never heard of the man, but he soon learned that he was a representative from the movement spearheaded by Swami Vivekananda. He was Paramahansa Yogananda, from a place called California. On the day of his arrival, the students gathered with their teacher in the yoga hall. It was in a small palace a few blocks from the spectacular central confines of the maharaja. The children were in the habit of watching the grand palace each evening as it lit up with a thousand small bulbs, gleaming like a kingdom in the sky. Even at the smaller palace, stained glass, boars' heads, and carved rosewood lined the hallways, where mosaic floors and lapis archways led through a labyrinth of chambers to a gymnasium. Tall plaster pillars punctuated the hall; carved figures from the pantheon of Hindu gods looked down from lintels. Ropes and other mysterious equipment dangled from the walls.

Today their teacher looked formidable, dressed in a loose cotton wrap tied into shorts around his hips, his head shaved except for a small ponytail at the crown, long arms resting beside a developed torso. His face was composed into a stern and concentrated grin and bedecked in South Indian face paint.

Though a contemporary and a fellow mystic, Yogananda looked like a descendant from another breed entirely. His body was loose and soft, his robes rounded and flowing, and lustrous hair peeked from under his elegant turban. Unlike Krishna-macharya's, his countenance was nurturing and warm.

As the young Iyengar scrutinized the yogi from California, Krishnamacharya ordered Iyengar to perform Hanumanasana, a yoga pose named for the flying monkey-god Hanuman. The pose was a favorite of the maharaja because Hanuman represented to India's Kshatriya warriors the religious dimensions of military duty — in the Ramayana, Hanuman was Lord Rama's general. The pose may have looked like a balletic split to someone uninitiated in the language of asana, but those present knew it depicted Hanuman's gesture as he leaped across the Indian Ocean to rescue Rama's wife, Sita, from evil forces on the isle of Lanka.

Iyengar balked. "I said, 'I don't know the asana.' I had never done it earlier and I never knew it either," he writes.

His teacher was impassive. "Place one leg forward and one leg backward and sit on the floor with straight legs," Krishna-macharya commanded.

Iyengar pleaded that his underwear was too tight. "I couldn't say 'no' to Guruji in front of respectable guests."

The guru persisted. He sent another performer for a pair of scissors, and then "cut off the cloth from both ends, and said, 'Now, do it!'

"I could not escape. I had to do it, and I did. In turn, I tore the hamstring muscles on account of which I could not walk for the next two years."

Yogananda was by all appearances oblivious to the disagree-ment — carried out in Tamil. On the contrary, he was overcome with awe on watching the young contortionist. "His eyes fell on me," writes Iyengar, "and he asked me whether I would accom-pany him to America." Iyengar felt the first stirrings of a spiritual calling. But his guardian refused to let him go.

That same year, the maharaja presented emissaries from another breed of popular culture altogether — science. They were two French doctors who had also heard the stories circulating about the mystic techniques of Tibet. Pursuing the same sources as Krishnamacharya and those Western esoterics who had plumbed the Himalayas for its secret and sacred Hindu teachings, they came to India in search of certain mind-body mystics whose metabolic self-control was said to defy reason. They traveled India for two months, collecting three hundred meters of electrocardiograph negatives taken from forty-one different sessions with yogis. Through the Maharaja of Baroda they found Swami Sivananda. Then they heard about Krishnamacharya, and they came to Mysore to document the supposedly miraculous skills he'd carried from Tibet.

The doctors, Thérèse Brosse and Charles Laubry, arrived with a black box, wire, cord, knobs, and suction cups. The teacher, students, and host assembled in the hall as before. The guests politely observed the spider-bodied young boys wrap themselves into the menagerie of twisted shapes: Vishnu in his tortoise aspect and Vishnu in his eagle aspect; the warrior god Virabhadra and the serpent god Ananta; the archer Kartikeya and the fish god Marichi; cocks; crocodiles; cranes; frogs.

But today, the star performer was Krishnamacharya. Patiently awaiting their moment, the scientists strapped the yogi to their electrocardiograph box, connecting it to points on his body with wires and electrodes. His students then watched in amazement as Krishnamacharya proceeded to demonstrate a secret and sacred technique from Tibet that seemed as alien to their frenetic jumpings as the beatific glow of the swami from California. "On the last day," Iyengar writes, "the doctors were recording Guruji's heartbeat and pulsations on the machine when it stopped and the lights also went off. For some time as there were no activities recorded the doctors announced that Guruji was dead. Soon thereafter, the machine started re-recording and the doctors in amazement told us that Guruji was alive."

The doctors published their discoveries in the French medical journal *La Presse Médicale* in 1936. The yogi, whose feats they documented with photographs and electrocardiograph charts, had drawn out single breaths to last as long as five minutes; lessened muscular tension by holding his breath; and, through meditation, shifted the rhythm of his pulse. Most spectacularly, to all appearances, he stopped his heart. The authors detected a "pulse imperceptible to the dial, while the machine weakly recorded an inhalation." The implications were large. Modern science, they concluded, was "confronted with a 'human' physiology that is something other than a simple animal physiology. The will seems to act as a pharmaco-dynamic control. Our superior faculties," they stated grandiosely, "carry an infinite power."

The encounter burst open Iyengar's world as well. Like the visit from the swami, it pulled him from his mentor. The gap between what the doctors gleaned from the master and what the master taught to his quarry was large. The science of these Western visitors was as spectacularly suggestive of inaccessible worlds as the divine bearing of the yogi Yogananda. Krishnamacharya was training Iyengar in a yoga of "physical culture," something associated more closely with wrestling and gymnastics. The secrets of Tibet had been withheld. Their spiritual core was not evident. To a disappointed young Iyengar, yoga seemed something he could pursue with the "mercenary" intent of making a living. Among his brothers were a tailor and a rail clerk. With his lackluster education, even these alternatives seemed out of reach. "I could not get a job anywhere in the world," Iyengar told me. He grimly awaited his future, putting to rest his dream of a mysterious world, aglow with science and spirit.

And sure enough, a wealthy patron soon asked Krishnamacharya to send a teacher to Poona. Since the performance for Yogananda, Iyengar had progressed to star pupil. The teacher chose him to go.

"First I hesitated," Iyengar writes. "I said, 'How can I go when I know nothing. What can I teach when you have not taught me?'"

The master was wild. "Go!" he said.

Chapter Eight

When I got to Pune over a half-century later, I wondered if its newness to me now had something in common with its newness to the young yogi when he first arrived. Did Pune via L.A. have the same particular quality of rawness and ugliness as Pune — or Poona — did then, when viewed from the perspective of a grand regal court where a prince and his knighted pundit once practiced a sport called yoga?

At the train station, I climbed into a three-wheeled yellow-black motor ricksha that was barely larger than my suitcase. The driver's leather sandals rested on the platform beside the gas pedal; barefoot, he curled his left foot on top of his thigh in a kind of lotus posture and rested his right at the single pedal. His hair was scruffy and his chin grizzled, causing me to suspect he'd just gotten up from a night's rest on the ricksha's narrow bench. He swiveled back and gazed at me, observing the way my luggage nearly displaced me. "Yoga?" he asked, shrugging.

I nodded yes.

He started the engine with a manual lever. It sounded like a coffee grinder. Riding these rickshas, a yoga teacher from the States had told me encouragingly, is "like being in Disneyland."

"Country?" the driver demanded.

"America," I admitted.

"Very rich country!"

I nodded, peering through his misted windshield. Rain legged down the glass, which he swabbed periodically with a single wiper controlled by a hand-operated knob above the handlebars. "Iyengar yoga?" he asked.

"Yes."

"I myself am knowing yoga," he said.

"Iyengar yoga?" I asked.

He twisted his neck to look at me over his seat back again so that the road sped by without his looking. Then he turned to the street and spat out a stream of wine-dark liquid, revealing coffee-colored teeth. "Yes. Iyengar very famous man. Iyengar I know," he added importantly.

The ricksha cut off the main street, and in a short instant the black exhaust and engine clatter from the city gave way to loamy, wet tree smells and bird chants. We were in a neighborhood now, where raw granite slabs interlocked between thick strips of mortar in a careful pattern to create a sidewalk, the first I'd seen in India. Poinciana trees lined the block, littering the street with orange-colored petals. Fruit and vegetable sellers congregated at one corner. Nearby, a vendor pushed a cart covered with empty bottles and scavenged metal, and chanted a hawker's cry like the one I'd heard in Bombay. Up ahead, four cows lay in the street, their tails swatting flies. For the first time, the driver slowed his breakneck pace. He skirted past the cows on the left, reaching his hand to graze the neck of one with his finger.

Shortly, we turned onto a block even more posh than the last, where the driver stopped in front of a pyramidal white stucco structure set in a large lot. "Yoga institute," he announced. The building was shrouded by bougainvillea, fuchsia, and iris, the colors lurid. Several Westerners and a few well-coifed Indians walked down the driveway and opened the gate to the street: an Indian woman in a thickly woven sari and dark eye makeup, a young man in sweats and loafers. Their eyes grazed over the driver until they landed on me, lingered for a second, and then moved on.

"Now, you come to study with your people," the driver said, nodding toward the students. His expression was heavy.

I nodded back, meekly handing him the fare he asked for. Earlier in the ride, he'd told me his monthly income; if he was telling the truth, my fare amounted to a quarter of it. "You said you studied yoga," I began. "Did you take classes?"

"It is so much busy that is yoga," he answered obliquely. "The man who is having ample time, he goes. But the man who has no spare time, no. And even so it is the intensity. The yoga it is hard work. We Indians, we don't see the importance. In America you see it. Here, we don't know what we have."

"But you started yoga. Why did you take it to begin with?"

"Yoga, I do yoga every day," he answered vaguely. "This is my yoga." He gestured to nothing. "And this," he added, now pointing to his ricksha. "This is my yoga. My life. In India we don't say this is my yoga, my yoga is here, my life is there." He gesticulated more wildly now. "My yoga, it is everywhere."

"Why don't you come to Iyengar anyway? You say you met him." I'd read in a magazine put out by the institute that the school offered classes to Indians at a hundredth the price charged to foreigners. Iyengar was committed to reaching out to a larger segment of Indian society than the upper-class clientele at the school, the article claimed.

The driver looked at me quizzically, as if the English he spoke and the English I spoke had little in common. But then, to my surprise, he stepped out of his ricksha and cocked his head toward the entry. We wrestled my bag from the ricksha together and then struggled over who would wheel it up the driveway. I prevailed. I noticed that standing, he was several heads shorter than I was, and even more wiry. As I started to walk, he kept behind. I slowed, but then he slowed too.

At the doorway was the requisite forest of shoes — Indian sandals and Birkenstocks and ladies' pumps — and then a foyer where even more shoes lay neatly inside a framework of cubbies. DON'T FORGET: WHERE DID I PUT MY SHOES? an avuncular sign asked. Past the foyer was a hallway lined with certificates from various official and pseudo-official Indian and foreign committees and political bodies. In several languages, these commemorated Iyengar as "doctor" of yoga, "minister" of yoga, "yoga raja." Beyond, photos of Iyengar at various stages of life demonstrated much of the animal kingdom — lion, locust, scorpion, pigeon, heron, turtle, fish, cow. I lingered before one photo, in which he balanced on one leg on a ledge, an image of the Taj Mahal in the background. I knew from *Light on Yoga* that the pose was Natarajasana, named for Siva in his manifestation as the god of dance. Iyengar's second leg reached from behind as in a dancer's arabesque, and he held the foot of that leg with an arm stretched from above his head, the other arm pointing forward. The geometries of his body echoed the shapes of the magnificent monument behind him. He and the building together made a strange and systematic arrangement of lines. The angles had an almost hypnotizing effect, and it was hard to pull my eyes away. The ricksha driver stood behind me patiently, his eyes pointing down.

Past the foyer was a large lobby. A man emerged from an inner doorway chattering on a cordless phone in an Indian language. Without looking up, he sat at a desk and plunked down the phone. I walked over, the driver following so that when I stopped he was just behind me and to my side. The man at the desk didn't look up. I dug my hand in my pocket, fingering the thin blue paper with the seal and arabesque-like signature that was my invitation. I peered at the writing. "Do you know where I might find Pandurang Rao?" I asked the top of the man's head.

I held up my aerogram. It was now several years old, and as it dangled there, I noticed that it was crumpled and worn and pathetic-looking, like something someone might have held up at Ellis Island thinking it meant more than it really did and realizing, in a single moment of truth, that it was not actually proof of entitlement in some society or a ticket to a new and better life, but simply a much-fingered piece of paper invested only with hope.

"Pandu," he replied, fixing large dark eyes on me and reaching out to grasp my hand. He let his eyes glide over the driver and land back on his desk, as if he'd seen neither of us.

I pushed my letter onto the desk.

"Wait. You. Just. Wait." Now his eyes rested on the driver, though Pandu was addressing me. I explained that I had come from the States, and that the man wanted to inquire about classes. Pandu brushed at the air without looking up. "Er. Not. Just." Pandu's phone rang, at which point he got up and once again began pacing and talking. Then he disappeared back through the doorway whence he'd come. The driver and I stood alone, contemplating the new quiet.

Then suddenly, the driver became animated, bowing toward

me and slinking backward, talking fast in a language I didn't know. He slunk all the way to the foyer and doorway backward, like a crab. *Crab pose,* I thought as I heard his bare feet scrape into his sandals on the pavement outside.

Alone now, I crept back to the foyer and followed the line of photos and certificates up a spiral stairway. Up top was a yoga studio in the dizzying shape of a seven-sided semicircle, with windowed walls and a marble platform placed according to lines that radiated from the center point of the diameter line. Like that photo before the Taj Mahal, the precise geometries suggested a sacred logic to the arrangement of the room. The floors were made of a slick slate, the pieces cut in triangular slabs so that their seams made radial lines emanating from the platform out to the walls. Photos from *Light on Yoga* were plastered along the tops of the walls; the mural too seemed to be making the point that yoga was a system of shapes, each one contributing a certain meaning in the context of a larger arrangement of symbols, like a letter in a word.

The Sanskrit word for the system of physical yoga that developed during the Middle Ages — *hatha* — was drawn from two Sanskrit letters: *ha* and *tha.* Each Sanskrit letter was invested with a symbolic significance as well as a sound. *Ha* meant "sun," *tha* "moon," though the word *hatha* meant "will." The term *hatha* thus evoked a unification of opposites as well as the act of forcing those opposites together. Around the room, several people lay or stood on yoga mats in a range of poses, and it struck me that here, too, there was a language you could read. The beautiful pose was the pose that lost the personality of the person performing it, like the word *hatha* taking on multiple definitions, while suggesting the embedded meanings of its individual syllables.

As I stood gazing at the silent tableau, Pandu burst past me and rushed through the studio, barking into his cordless. He was unnoticed by the diligent yogis. Then the entryway came to life behind him with a flash of white and a stream of some Indian tongue. It was Iyengar. He looked like he had when I'd seen him in New York, only a little messier, a little smaller, his clothes a little grimier. He wore a long muddy-white silk tunic over a lungi skirt; his hair was bright and silver-white, his hands a flurry of musicianlike movements. Motion overtook the space around him. Everything seemed to whirl, as if the guru, like that hot wind on the train platform, had shifted the charges on the ions in the room. Those students who a second earlier had been fixed in position like the figures in a pastoral painting now flew toward the guru to kneel and touch the ground. Then they whisked back to resume their postures, motionless, as if they'd never been interrupted.

The guru's eyes landed on mine. My arms lay uncertainly at my sides. He seemed to be waiting for me to prostrate, but I didn't exactly know how, or know that I wanted to. Iyengar's eyes drifted from mine as he moved to a spot in the corner of the studio. The students ignored him as he removed his traditional dress to reveal shiny shorts, the sacred thread looping across his barrel chest and belly. He tossed his head, and his hair, reasonably tame a second earlier, became unruly. Then he wedged himself between a pillar and a window wall, contorting himself into a forward bend held in place by an elaborate pulley system of straps that were bandaged above and below his knees, hitched to a window grating, and then looped over the arches of his feet. Next, he unstrapped himself and began to move through several logic-defying physical arrangements, occasionally breaking into gruff prepositionless pointers yelled to students from across the space: "Kneecap!" or "Leg not straight!"

Eventually the one-word grunts extended into a monologue delivered first into the open space and then to several students who had rushed to his side to listen. "You see!" he exclaimed, pointing to an Indian woman who looked crooked in a headstand. "This woman complains her hip is paining. You can see why? You don't see?" He took a mocking stance with his hands on his hips and scanned our faces. We all looked at the woman blankly. I had no idea what he was talking about. "Fourth finger!" Iyengar yelled. He pushed his big toe into her clasped hand, causing the woman to teeter, then straighten. "Hip better now or not better?" he demanded.

"Yes, yes," her upside-down head offered.

"You see. Fourth finger affects hip!"

Iyengar again shook out his hair and walked away from the crowd. Then he climbed onto the platform and walked to the wall, where he placed his palms on the floor. His head down, he made a husky exhaling sound as he kicked a single leg toward the wall. It didn't reach, but slammed back to the floor. Iyengar snorted and bristled. He repositioned his hands and, exhaling louder, kicked up the leg unsuccessfully once more. On the third attempt, his exhalation had the deep machine pitch of a truck skidding out of a muddy ditch. His chest visibly contracted several inches. Stubbornly, both legs lifted, and his heels came to rest against the wall in a handstand. After several minutes, he came down, breathing heavily, and walked to the center of the studio. There, he lay himself face up on the slate floor so that the crown of his head angled toward the midpoint of the platform. His body followed the centerline of the room. His feet and arms splayed out symmetrically toward the windows, echoing the radiating lines of the slate slabs on the floor. With his eyes closed, his chest lifting up and then down, he looked like the man in the center of the da Vinci mandala. He was more iconic than human, his iridescent shorts shimmering, his hair seeming to breathe.

"Iyengar sees everything." A voice broke into my thoughts. It was an Indian woman with pale white skin and a long braid reaching to her hips. I'd noticed her twisted into lion pose earlier. She was whispering to me.

I nodded.

"He's like Patañjali, the founder of yoga," she went on. "You know the story of how yoga almost got lost?"

I shook my head.

"Patañjali was a cobra with a thousand heads," she continued. "He was ashamed of the way he looked, that he was ugly, so he taught his students from behind a screen. He could see everything because he had a thousand heads, of course, but he made his students promise never to pull back the screen to reveal the way he looked." She assumed an ironic expression. "One day, a student got very curious and crept up to the screen to reveal the teacher, but before he got there, Patañjali saw him. He leaped out in a rage and devoured everyone in sight. One student was absent that day, though, and he came the next day. Patañjali passed down his teachings to that student alone. Iyengar is his heir. Guruji is like Patañjali. He has eyes all over his body, to the tips of his toes."

Her story made me wonder where Iyengar really came from. What if he really did descend from gods and chimeras? What if he practiced magic? Where did a person like that go when he died? Then, suddenly, fifteen minutes after he'd lain down, the yogi stood. The woman who'd told me the Patañjali story walked over and pointed out that his body had left a slick impression of sweat on the slate floor. Iyengar sat on the platform, and the woman sat beside him, and both nodded, staring at the way the light reflected off the image. Iyengar grinned, tucking his hair behind his ears as the woman and I and several other students gathered around to quietly regard the floor.

"I have seen my own skeleton," the guru said, laughing darkly.

Chapter Nine

Iyengar arrived in Poona in 1938. He was unprepared for the political foment that awaited him. In Mysore, under the wing of the maharaja, Iyengar and his mentor could remain in blithe oblivion to the changes taking place around them. As E. M. Forster wrote of his stay in another of India's princely kingdoms, "Politically — though not socially — we are still living in the fourteenth century. . . . There is no anti-English feeling. It is Gandhi whom they dread and hate."

Elsewhere, India was in turmoil. Vivekananda had passed on, but his disciples kept alive his vision of a universal religion, now dispatched to create a casteless, pan-Indian Hindu society. Those swamis who had reached out to the West two generations before were now ensconced in an equally earth-shaking movement — the project to wrest India from its colonial past by instilling self-confidence and a new notion of Indian identity. "Our country was enslaved for centuries," Iyengar told me later. "One after the other they were invading the country: first the [forced] conversions [to Islam], then the [British] monarchy one hundred and fifty years ago. They started ruling the place, dictating the terms. The culture had to be kept aside. They made the country completely poor so they could offer jobs to make us serve them. Only now that we have independence do you see the Indian culture slowly rising up. Now we have the self-confidence."

As a spiritual project came to overlap a political one, the country's political leaders also came to communicate their messages in increasingly spiritual terminology. Upon his release from jail in 1910 for conspiring against the British, the freedom-fighter-turned-ascetic Aurobindo Ghose came to promote a philosophy of spiritual liberation. In Gujarat in 1930, Gandhi had staged his first march to protest British taxation of the salt industry. He had now set up ashrams, in Gujarat and in the hills outside Poona, where he tested his vision of economic self-sufficiency as the first line of defense against British imperialism. Here he built up cottage industries and imposed strict experimental diets, hoping also to realize the idea that the personal was political: the liberation of the continent was connected to the liberation of the soul. And just as small communities might influence national economies, the body might be an instrument of political will. Like those ancient and newly published Indian yoga texts, Gandhi employed the metaphor that liberation could be achieved through the purification of the body.

Gandhi's experiments in "embodied political reform," in the words of the anthropologist Joseph Alter, played into a new thinking in which the spiritual, the physical, and the political were increasingly intertwined. Kuvalayananda, another freedom fighter turned swami, had moved his yoga ashram to a hill town outside Poona called Lonavla. Here, residents tested various ways of cleansing their bodies through asana, breathing, and ablutions.

At the same time, the maharaja in Aundh, a postage stamp–size kingdom on the western outskirts of Poona, was promoting physical yoga as not just exercise but an expression of India's regal past. He argued that the daily practice of surya namaskars, or sun salutations, could transpose India's ancient glory into a burgeoning new society. It would, he wrote in a manifesto titled *Surya Namaskars,* "imbue you with a spirit of self-sacrifice for the good of your community, your country and your king." The maharaja instituted his vision on a small scale by requiring daily sun salutations in the kingdom's schools. He sought to create a "State at Exercises," which his publication demonstrated with photos of columns of teenage boys doing yoga drills in paramilitary-like formation.

Poona was at the vortex of a zeitgeist. It was also the home of V. D. Savarkar, the founder of a militant Hindu nationalist organization called the Hindu Mahasabha, which added elements of European fascism and ideas of racial purity to the mix. Like the Aundh maharaja, the Mahasabha and a sister organization, the Rashtriya Swayamsevak Sangh, or the RSS, sought to elevate Hindu culture as a symbol of national identity by encouraging the practice of yoga postures. In morning assemblies, young trainees dressed in khakis carried long sticks, or lathis, as they performed asanas, calisthenics drills, and ritual devotions to gods. In one account of a meeting from the 1920s, men recited oaths to the goddess Kali with the Bhagavad Gita in one hand, a revolver in the other.

When Iyengar arrived, Poona was also the home of one follower of Savarkar's who would become notorious a decade later: Nathuram Godse, the Hindu militant who assassinated Gandhi.

Iyengar walked into this milieu a naïf. He was struggling with his own attempts to reconcile the slipperiness of the spiritual with the demands of the material. He was split between pragmatism and providence, career and calling. Was yoga a career path? Was his journey a spiritual one?

A dream helped him understand his mission. In the dream, he was hammering a nail into his wall when a cobra fell out of the hole and, like Patañjali, fanned into innumerable heads. Iyengar turned to the other wall, where he had affixed a picture of his family's patron god, Vishnu. Just as Arjuna once beheld the many-limbed and terrifying figment of Krishna transformed, Iyengar saw a huge eagle gazing at him intently. It was Vishnu's incarnation as the eagle god Garuda. Iyengar tried to stand strong. "Feeling panicky, I prayed to the Lord to save me, as on one side there was the cobra and on the other side there was the eagle," he writes. Then, he was rewarded with "a brilliant light, ten times brighter than the Sun"— the radiance witnessed by so many mystics. Caught between cobra and eagle, Iyengar was in some ways like his country at that moment, rationalizing the many dualities: the draw of the West against the quest for an authentic India; the promise of the past complicated by the challenges of the future; the rejection of caste against a new vision of Hinduism. Yoga seemed to offer salvation for both country and yogi. Iyengar slipped from danger that day by making a pact before the terrifying gods Vishnu and Patañjali. He chose yoga: not just as profession, but as passion.

This presented its own challenges. Unlike the rarefied environment in Mysore, in Poona Iyengar's physical-spiritual craft was, at times, viewed with incomprehension and even hostility. During his first month in Poona, he had too few paise to buy soap; his wardrobe consisted of two cotton dhotis, one of which he used as a towel. He spent one paisa on a razor blade that he used, dry, to shave just two times in that month. "There were occasions when I had a plate of rice once in two or three days. The rest of the time I had to fill my belly with tea or with tap water," he writes. It would be many years before Iyengar had the distance to see his own fate as connected to his country's.

"In the 1930s, when I started teaching yoga, you can imagine the load on my back, what kind of words people were speaking," he told me. "Now you say, 'I'm a yoga teacher,' people say, 'Okay.' It was not like that. They were ridiculing. Yoga, my friend, nobody had an interest in. In the days that I was struggling, I had to go crawl to get the public to believe that this is something."

Iyengar had his first encounter with Poona's militants while working for Krishnamacharya's patron. He was teaching a class for starvation wages at a local athletics college where his colleagues were trained in martial gymnastics and wrestling. These Indian traditions carried their own devotional associations, but Iyengar's allegiance to the British-backed maharaja put off his peers. One night, they vandalized his studio, burning his props. "What an emotional pressure I had. People said that you know nothing. Even in public performance, people said it's nothing. That's when people started, he's a physical culturist, it's physical yoga," Iyengar told me.

But since his vow, the yogi had applied himself to asana and breathing with new devotion. He waited to see where it led. One day, he lay in savasana after his practice. Then he discovered rapture. The encounter convinced him that you could touch a spark of divinity by performing yoga postures, but not by jumping frenetically from pose to pose as he had learned from Krishnamacharya. The soul received inspiration when the body was still, enduring pain until, through concentration, the pain grew to look like a holy white beacon in the dome of the mind.

At this time, Iyengar was dependent on not just the Maharaja of Mysore but the entire culture of Kshatriya-Brahmin patronage that had made his mentor's career possible. In 1938, while Gandhi was fasting for independence, the Maharaja of Mysore dug into his British purse to gift Iyengar an unheard-of bequest of two thousand feet of film. The yogi employed it to shoot a spectacular reel of himself leaping kinetically from asana to asana in the style of his mentor. Dressed only in a loincloth and sacred thread, and painted with elaborate Brahmin face markings, he balanced on fingertips so that he seemed to be flying and twisted in and out of shapes like a length of rubber band with a motor inside. This film enabled Iyengar to win friends among viceregal British appointees in Bombay and neighbor princes from across the state, who now made special stops in Poona to hold court with the yogi.

But plush times were coming to an end. Iyengar recognized the need to build alliances in his new home, and began papering the offices of local eminences with news of his accomplishments. He got a response from the nationalist Aundh maharaja, the man who claimed to have invented the sun salutation. The ruler took up the yogi on an invitation to visit a yoga class. Iyengar let his students' new skills speak for his prowess. Today, Iyengar's files still contained the visitor's enthusiastic sixty-year-old thank-you note, carefully guarded under a tab labeled "VIPs."

Through similar circles, Iyengar made contact with a nationalist activist who shortly became his sole source of support. Because of this man's membership in Savarkar's radical Hindu Mahasabha, Iyengar met a handful of future clients tied to the budding nationalist movement. Iyengar crossed their path at his moment of greatest desperation. With independence in 1947, the India of the rajas came to an end. Nehru's Congress Party cut most of the funds once earmarked for Iyengar's former patron in Mysore. In 1950, Krishnamacharya's Palace Yoga Shala in Mysore shut down for lack of money — a move that left Iyengar stunned and hurt to this day. "It's not surprising. It's pathetic!" he told me acidly almost a half-century later. "In olden days, Yogis were looked after by the Maharajas and so it was easy to propagate without remuneration," one letter in his files elaborated, responding to a Romanian who requested free tuition to visit the school. "Today even the best of the yogis has sweat and earn for his living. Hence, it is not possible for me to spend from my hard-earned income to teach people outside India just because they are interested."

But by the time the Mysore school closed, Iyengar had lain the groundwork for survival in a new order. He soon finagled demonstrations before the new prime minister, Jawaharlal Nehru, a yoga aficionado who attributed his survival in jail to his regular practice of asanas, as well as for Russian prime minister Nikita Khrushchev and a communist military delegation from China. The Chinese, wrote Iyengar, "were thrilled to see the agility and strength and remarked that such training was needed in guerrilla warfare."

Iyengar continued to keep himself afloat through such contacts, and as these brought him closer to India's power structure, he increasingly came to rationalize the inherent contradiction between warfare and yoga's central tenet of ahimsa, or nonviolence. Soon, the National Defense Academy hired the yogi to train academy conscripts. Effusing about their new alliance, Iyengar's new champion at the NDA, Major General Enaith Habibullah, acknowledged to the yogi in a letter that "yoga was originally instituted by sages for sages who led a sedentary sort of life." Habibullah went on to brush off the sacred dimensions of the craft — "the fact that they could not practice exercises in a violent and athletic manner because of the very nature of their calling."

Iyengar, a lifelong vegetarian and adherent to nonviolence in all forms, put a sanguine spin on his own role. "The internal contentment and peace derived by the method of Yoga training is a weapon to establish world peace as it creates healthy understanding between people of different nations and generates feelings of tolerance," he assured himself.

At Iyengar's institute in Pune, I took classes and practiced four hours a day, hoping to create that white beacon inside myself. Iyengar was always present, twisted like braided bread into some advanced posture at the back of the studio. He situated himself between pillar and window, strapped himself onto yoga furniture, and meditated. As I became familiar with the rhythms of his yoga practice, I began to notice how often and easily he was able to fall into that bodiless concentration he wrote about. He broke the concentration just as easily, wriggling from his constraints to make impromptu presentations on points of such physiognomic intricacy as, say, how to straighten a leg.

One day, a small group of us gathered in the studio to behold a demonstration on a subject along the lines of "how placement of clavicle affects breathing in shoulder stand." We were mostly Westerners that day — Americans, Germans, French, British. Iyengar spoke in his thick accent and idiosyncratic grammar, which by now we understood.

For me, the school had become a cloister far removed from the Indian miasma outside. The complicated fractures and alliances that had shaped Iyengar's early career were also not evident to the foreign eye. Today, Iyengar enjoyed the reputation of a self-created man who had gotten along as maverick and outsider. He presented himself as a person who had been slighted by power, his ambitions buoyed along by sheer dint of his passion. How Iyengar interacted with the larger world of Indian politics and history was obscure. On the contrary, such questions seemed to fall away in the peaceful studio, where sounds from the hectic streets drifted into the airy space through orange poinciana and neem boughs, their leaves dangling over outdoor changing balconies.

But Iyengar's talk happened soon after the Indian government revealed it had developed the capability to launch a nuclear bomb. Testing would soon begin. The American government had issued a stern demand that India desist, lest it provoke war with Pakistan and precipitate carnage throughout Asia, if not a third world war. Out of nowhere, an American student brought it up. "Guruji," he asked mildly, "what do you think of the bomb?"

Iyengar turned from his demo model — a young Brit balancing in shoulder stand. The guru's hair looked wild, his eyes fierce. He glowered at the American, saying nothing. "You Americans are arrogant," he finally barked. "Who is America to tell India what to do?" He continued to glare, then raised his fists to his hips and spread his legs. The rage in Iyengar's eyes was palpable; I imagined Krishna taking shape inside them, transmogrifying into that terrible deity armored with discus and breastplates. Iyengar exhaled long, then inhaled. Here was the Lion of Pune breathing fire. Then he spit out his words — "You do not rule us!" They had the duly decimating effect on his protégé.

The guru ended the demonstration abruptly, and within minutes had returned to his intricate bondage inside straps and ropes, between pillar and window.

We stood, stunned. And then we returned to our private practices in our requisite corners of the studio.

Even without Iyengar's ad hoc lessons, morning practice was not a time for solitude. As on most days, Iyengar's daughter Geeta was in the right-hand corner of the studio in some supine asana — she was not known for her active yoga practice. There, she lectured to a coterie of faithful, sometimes picking up a thread from the yoga class she'd taught the day before. Her followers included a handful of Western women who had relocated to Pune to ingest Geeta's wisdom on yoga for reproductive health. Sitting in similarly restorative postures, they called across the space, discussing Geeta's mission to immortalize her father's words in text, her upcoming travel schedule to the West, and errors made in the blundering testimony of yoga students attempting to distill the nuance of some recent workshop or lecture.

Prashant, Iyengar's only son, also had his devoted followers. Unlike Geeta's, they were mostly Indians, who gathered with him in the far left of the studio. There, Prashant hung upside down for twenty or thirty minutes at a time in either a headstand- or backbendlike configuration, supported by a sturdy loop of rope suspended from the ceiling. By his side stood his devotees, conversing in a jumble of Marathi and Hindi about local politics, Indian music, and Prashant's latest thinking on the Vedas.

Through this mix wove Pandu, talking into his cordless phone while walking it to either Iyengar or Geeta or Prashant, who dutifully responded to telephone inquiries from the equanimitous repose of yoga asana.

Students tended to identify themselves with one of the three teachers and stick exclusively to that teacher's chosen domain — Geeta's at the right side of the studio, Prashant's at the left, and Iyengar's, in the afternoons, in the library downstairs. I had noticed that only a few students traversed the boundaries between them. These students tended to be Indian, and one of them was the pale-skinned woman who had told me the myth of Patañjali. She participated in library hours religiously but also conversed regularly with Prashant, about Indian current affairs, and with Geeta, about how to disseminate the wisdom of Iyengar's technique to Indian women. She also held court with Iyengar, about his favorite subject, hatching new ideas to propagate the world-wide spread of yoga.

Today, this woman was sitting toward the edge of Geeta's domain, arranging herself into a resting posture over a set of bolster pillows. I did my own posture nearby, something without the pillows, positioning myself so that I was about midway between Geeta's realm and Prashant's. Iyengar was off in the back of the studio somewhere, deep in meditation.

"Excuse me, would you hand me that, please?" the woman said, gesturing to a strap. She was incapacitated by pulleys that she was in the process of tying into an elaborate string pattern not so different from Iyengar's. When I approached her with the strap, she gave me a long look. She was striking with her jet-black hair, her dark eyes set deep into white-white skin so that they seemed to leap out of her face. Her nose, with a small shiny stud, was angular and beaklike, giving her the look of a delicate animal. "Guruji gets angry sometimes with these students you see," she said quietly, gesturing for me to sit beside her as she secured the final strap around her thighs and tugged. "You see, yoga is an Indian subject, and sometimes it makes him angry that so many of the people who are devoted to him are from the West."

I answered that I could understand his frustration given that Western students did outnumber Indians here, especially during the practice time that was the domain of the most serious and advanced of his followers.

"Indians are just now coming around to recognize that they are the only true heirs to yoga," she responded, pulling her long braid from under her torso and wrapping it across her chest. "You see, yoga is something that Indians understand genetically in a way no one from any other country ever could."

I nodded. It was true that some of the Indians in class seemed to have an easier time doing certain poses, like squatting while keeping their heels on the ground. According to one popular the-ory, this owed to the use of the Eastern squat toilet, though I had been a guest in enough upper-class Indian homes by now to know that these days using a squat toilet was primarily a practice of the poor, as were such one-time Indian traditions that might aid yoga practice as sitting on the floor for meals or sleeping on a wooden plank.

"You see, yoga came from India so many thousands of years ago, so that even in our culture today, even however much we are Westernized, we still have the flexible hips because it is in our culture to sit on the floor," she added. She spoke in a flawless British-inflected Indian-English. "We still do the poses every day just as part of the way that we stand or sit. At the train you'll see the poor man waiting on the platform. How does he wait? Never on a bench. Rows of these men you see, squatting. Or from the window of the train, you pass the fields, and the workers are bending over with the legs straight. He is working the fields, but he is doing uttanasana. It feels natural for us to take the postures. We understand them in our bodies from generations and genera-tions past."

I later learned that this young woman, Nivedita, was among Iyengar's most esteemed students and an important benefactress to the school. The exchange went both ways. Nivedita credited Iyengar with saving her life. Upon discovering my skills as a writer, Geeta, through Gloria, had enlisted me to edit several tes-timonials from yoga students paying tribute to Iyengar's miracu-lous ability to heal them. These were being assembled for a commemorative volume to be published sometime after Iyengar's eightieth birthday, six months away.

One of these paeans was Nivedita's. In turgid and convoluted British English, she told the story of how, after a dance injury, she'd gone from being a spoiled daughter of an upper-class Indian household to understanding the universality of suffering. She credited Iyengar with doing what dozens of high-priced doctors couldn't: diagnosing her with a herniated disk in her lower spine and treating it by forcing her to overcome her weakness and fear, internalized during her privileged childhood, in painful asanas that brought therapeutic changes to her spine.

I also learned that Nivedita was the daughter of an important figure in the central government, Murli Manohar Joshi. Joshi was much in the news these days. Now the human resource development minister in India's ruling Hindu nationalist Bharatiya Janata Party, or the BJP, he was known for his extreme position within the nationalist coalition and had been prosecuted for his role in inciting anti-Muslim violence in 1992. That violence resulted from a contested Hindu-Muslim pilgrimage site: a centuries-old mosque in Ayodhya-occupied land that the Hindu nationalist RSS, of which Joshi was a longtime member, claimed to be the site of Lord Rama's birth. The RSS mobilized ten thousand Hindus, who stoned the mosque until it fell to the ground, prompting riots that led to, by some accounts, as many as twelve hundred deaths. After the event, Joshi and a handful of political leaders were arrested and held in jail for one month, and for the third time in its seventy-five-year history, the RSS was banned.

Joshi had since graduated to a legitimate position within the new BJP government, and he was using that position to "Indianize" the country's educational system. He was now attempting to institute a "Saffronized" syllabus — what one prominent educational group lambasted as "designed to promote bigotry and religious fanaticism." A pilot syllabus was already in place in fourteen thousand private schools: much of its curriculum pertained to the "essentials of Indian culture." These "essentials" included historically revisionist assertions about the prominence of Hindus in world history — from their discovery of the solar system to their seminal influence on Jesus Christ, Homer, Herodotus, Plato, and the Native Americans. The curriculum offered large doses of Sanskrit, Ayurveda, Vedic mathematics, and yoga. Secular opponents claimed that it encouraged religious intolerance and racial strife by writing the subcontinent's Muslims — historically 25 percent of the population — out of India's past. Not surprisingly, Joshi was also among the leaders of his country's nuclear program.

Iyengar claimed Joshi as a longtime friend, ever since the militant's daughter sought out the miracle healer. Though I never saw Joshi at the school, Nivedita acted as his proxy. Her parents had sent her to live with an aunt in Pune after doctors failed to cure her back pain. Iyengar's files showed that she had since carried the first of nearly five hundred thousand rupees, or ten thousand dollars, in campaign donations from the Iyengar institute to the BJP's ruling prime minister, Atal Vajpayee. Her correspondence with the school was always on Joshi's official letterhead and was often signed with the title "d/o Murli Manohar Joshi, HRT and S & T Minister of India"— meaning his daughter. She had also orchestrated an intimate meeting between the guru and the prime minister in Iyengar's library and had arranged for her father to speak at countless institute functions.

After I witnessed Iyengar's outburst in the yoga studio, I was especially curious about how the guru reconciled his spiritual calling with the political contingencies of India's rulers. No matter their fondness for the bomb, the leaders of today's nationalist government were certainly eager to co-opt the popular yogi. But I wanted to know how Iyengar had nurtured the relationship as well. Did he wholeheartedly embrace certain remnants from the nationalist project, in forms others had reviled as stridently anti-Muslim and connected to the Ayodhya violence — for instance, Joshi's school syllabus? Did Joshi's RSS have a presence at the school today? Was my tuition contributing to these causes?

One day while perusing the library's section on Hindu nationalism, I discovered a typewritten manuscript with a wealth of detail about the history of the RSS. It had apparently been produced from within. Two things caught my eye about the manuscript. First, on the title page, a handwritten inscription referred to the RSS not as its usual Rashtriya Swayamsevak Sangh — Association of National Volunteers — but as the Ramanuja Siddhanta Sabha. This inscription referred to the Pune office of the organization, which had donated the manuscript to Iyengar's library. This organization was apparently not only a local RSS headquarters but also, for some reason that was not at all clear to me, a social club for members of the small and exclusive subcaste Iyengar hailed from — Tamil Srivaisnavites displaced to Pune, who, like Iyengar, claimed a lineage to Ramanuja. It was an oddly specific correlation to Iyengar himself. Second, the title page was personally addressed to Iyengar. "To our Guruji," it read. It was an enigmatically intimate address.

Holding the book one afternoon in his library, I asked Iyengar what he thought of the RSS.

"They have a very bad name is all," the guru answered vaguely. He went back to his papers.

What about his alliance with Murli Manohar Joshi? I pressed. Didn't Joshi have a dubious role in promoting chauvinism against Muslims? And was the bomb a good thing, really, from the point of view of ahimsa?

Iyengar looked at me openly. The rage of his outburst about the bomb earlier in the week had vanished. He shook his head. "America is arrogant," he said. "Who is America to tell India, 'You, you cannot have'? We have a neighbor which would like to use a bomb against us. Pakistan is our enemy. They are hating and threatening us. In the absence of peace, there should be security," he reasoned.

I uttered some American cliché about two wrongs.

He paused and looked at me. "My friend," he admitted finally, "I should not answer, because I am a yoga practitioner. We depend on nonviolence."

He was still looking at me candidly, so I brought up Joshi again. Iyengar had often written that yoga offered a way to world peace. "Even though we all come from different cultural backgrounds, yoga has tied us together and has conveyed to lots of people through our togetherness that it is meant for the whole of humanity," he'd written recently. Wasn't Joshi promoting conflict and violence? He'd been indicted for his role in the stoning of the mosque at Ayodhya, after all.

Iyengar gazed at me meaningfully. Just as working for the army served his ends, his look seemed to say his alliance with the government also ultimately benefited humanity. Yoga was always redemptive. "They want to bring back the ethical disciplines, the spiritual disciplines and all, including yoga," he said, shrugging. Commandeering the school syllabus was not a crime in that light: "The educational system should be guided. It's good. Because the one who practices yoga, naturally their mental frame changes. You introduce yoga, you get special oxygenated energy to brace their bodies, so they can think in a fresh manner. They will see afresh. If you practice yoga, animosity will be less, thinking will be different, the mind will be different."

At that point, Iyengar turned in his chair, slowly stood up, and pulled several file folders from large collapsible manila boxes on the shelves just behind him. The boxes, he explained, held the portion of Joshi's syllabus introducing yoga into public schools. I was startled. This meant that Iyengar had authored this segment of Joshi's Saffronized school syllabus. So he did not just support the government program, but was among its architects. Not unlike the Maharaja of Aundh's a half century before, Iyengar's lessons incorporated final exams in yoga, daily lectures on yoga philosophy, and a repertoire of yoga postures challenging students to the highest level of the physical craft. With a sparkly grin, Iyengar added that in Bombay, the first of these pilot student bodies had just completed exams — and students had passed. "You guide them places," he said.

When I left the library that afternoon, I was charmed, touched even, as I often felt after my encounters with Iyengar. But still, I was troubled that there seemed to be a fundamental contradiction at play. In the grand juggling game that was the complicated world of yoga and the school in Pune, I had begun to imagine that all of yoga's constituent parts might seem to contradict one another but could ultimately be reconciled. But here I found only conflict — between the racism and violence-mongering of groups like the RSS and yoga's rhetoric of universality and nonviolence. It also bothered me that in places like L.A., yoga aficionados were content to idealize yoga's quaint Hindu imagery without troubling themselves to contemplate the roots, its connections to dark strains in India's past. The romance of these acolytes struck me as merely the flip side of the patronizing tone of the yoga teacher who'd told me she hated India, that it was less than intrinsic to yoga. Iyengar was, in a small way, like that teacher, it seemed to me now — someone who both idealized and reviled his foreign counterparts. Whether one came from East or West, there seemed to be an essential superficiality that allowed for this kind of dual resentment and romance. To me yoga had always been about going deeper. This contradiction bothered me too.

Understanding Iyengar's connection to the local Ramanuja society, aka the RSS, seemed key to teasing apart these ambiguities. The association showed that Iyengar's family background somehow intersected with the national project; this link, perhaps, might shed light on how spirituality, caste, genealogy, and politics all somehow interacted in this country and at this institute.

So one day I mentioned the RSS-Ramanuja manuscript to Pandu. He looked at me long. The RSS had been a banned organization many times, his look seemed to say. He nodded. "You know Nandu?" he asked.

I knew him. Nandu was a longtime practitioner at the institute, one of Prashant's faithful. Just then, several things clicked about this student that I hadn't bothered to notice previously. Unlike the majority of Indian students who wore either sweat pants or balloon shorts with funny elastic bands secured at the upper thighs, Nandu always came to the studio dressed in a beige Izod and khaki shorts. This resembled the uniform of the RSS. Nandu was also a member of the circle of Indians who liked to discuss things Indian in Prashant's corner of the studio, and when Nandu was present, those things turned to politics.

Shortly after I spoke to Pandu, I approached Nandu. I asked if he could tell me anything about the RSS here in Pune.

"You want to visit?" he asked. "You're interested?"

I was surprised by the offer; his lack of candor flustered me. "I was just wondering about their connection to Iyengar," I responded. "If he has any connection."

"Connection?" Nandu said. He scratched his head. "Talk to Savita," he went on. "She was part of it." Savita was one of Iyengar's five daughters. She lived in Bangalore, about twelve hours from Pune. "Or you can go to a meeting." Nandu then wrote the address of the local RSS headquarters on a loose slip of paper.

I pressed on clumsily. "Are you a member?"

He looked at me, lolling his tongue in his cheek. "No, no. No."

I stuttered. "I mean, you know, will I see you at the meeting?"

Nandu's eyes were looking away now. "No, no. I mean, you

know, maybe in the past. Once or twice." He looked at me again, smiling pleasantly.

I went to the place Nandu had led me, half expecting to see people with revolvers in one hand, Bhagavad Gita's in the other. I'd imagined something other than this nondescript gray storefront space where a handful of men sat around a table smoking bidis. I stepped a few paces inside the door, but everyone was speaking Marathi and seemed unsure whether they wanted to talk to me. None of them were faces I recognized from the institute, anyway. And so although I had been trained as a reporter and knew exactly what to do to get them to talk to me, I realized at that moment that it wasn't really these men I should be talking to at all. It was Iyengar's daughter Savita I needed to meet; Savita could explain the connections between family and history, Ramanuja and India's spiritual-brand nationalist politics, yoga and these tangled strands. I stumbled away, resolving that I would get to Bangalore. There I'd find out what I wanted to know about Iyengar and Indian history; Iyengar's family and yoga's Hindu roots; and maybe why I so badly wanted to make sense of it all.

Chapter Ten

The studio was an extension of the Iyengar family home across the courtyard, and Iyengar welcomed us there as a part of that family. In the mornings, I often saw Geeta in the courtyard, dressed in the white sari she'd worn in my dream, combing out her long black hair or quietly reciting prayers as she placed flowers before the many devotional statues — Patañjali, Vishnu, Hanuman, Ganesh. The setting reminded me that I was here not so much to parse this family as to join it, to be bound by its rituals.

In my own family, there were rituals that bound us as well, but because of my parents' divorce, it had always seemed as if there was more to split us apart than bring us together. As much as the idea of clan was important to my grandmother, I always thought of my family as more like two warring strains of cousins. After coming home from weekend visits with my father and stepmother in Boston, my sister and I would sit at the table with my mother and her boyfriend in our small apartment in Manhattan and discuss the exotic ways they did things Up There. My mother's then boyfriend was a Tai Chi enthusiast who had constructed a large mat-board yin and yang that was the centerpiece of our living room. Beneath it, we sat up late into the night discussing art and other bohemian mysteries. In New York, we ate meals at odd hours or not at all; we slept on floor mattresses with comforters tossed on top. In Boston, they kept mattresses on firm box springs and made up beds neatly each morning with hospital corners. Meals were regular and scrupulously balanced. Talk veered to performance in school and career futures. With either family, it took only mention of one side to set off fierce and bitter criticism from the other. This often continued unabated until either my sister or I — if one of us was feeling bold — insisted, "Don't talk about my mother like that"; "Don't talk about my father like that."

When I'd read the Bhagavad Gita here in India, I easily identified with Arjuna. The story followed an epic feud between two rival strains of cousins, the Pandavas and the Kauravas, ending with Prince Arjuna, a Pandava, poised on the battlefield of Kurukshetra to engage in war against his brethren Kauravas. Krishna exorted Arjuna to fight, forcing Arjuna to contemplate the lineaments of duty in deciding whether he could battle his blood.

Partly because of these kinds of rivalries, I'd been living far from my family for over a decade now. The community I found with Gloria and others at the L.A. yoga institute had offered an alternative for those similarly dispossessed, but this too had its share of petty splits. It was not until I got to India that I started to feel the comfort of really belonging for the first time in my life.

This was never more clear to me than on Gurupurnima, India's annual day of the guru. This was the day Indians honored their teachers. The streets in Pune were festive, doorways bedecked with flowers, colorful awnings strung across sidewalks. A ricksha driver told Gloria and me about his guru as he drove us to school. "Very holy man. Today I go see him." Outside a shop by the institute, a colorful tapestry adorned the street front. Inside, the clerk greeted me warmly. "Today is Gurupurnima. Who is your guru?" she asked. "Mine, he teaches meditation." As much as Iyengar yoga was in part a Western craft, the idea of having a guru was as endemic to Indian life as the god statuettes that decorated ricksha dashes and store windows. "Iyengar," I told her, thinking that I would never admit such a thing to a shop owner in the States. I had the unsettling sensation that I was becoming someone else.

That week, I worked with Gloria and other longtime students, Geeta's devotees and Prashant's, to prepare the studio for Gurupurnima. We strung roses from the mural of *Light on Yoga* photos and ran threads through stacks of rupee notes to create banners. We assembled piles of coconuts and pineapples, placed wreaths around a statue of Patañjali at the studio entryway. This was all a natural extension of the tasks we performed daily, punching Iyengar's speeches into computers, rewriting his broken Indian-English, editing the forthcoming commemorative volume. To participate was to join that family. One day around the time of Gurupurnima, Gloria brought me into the house across the courtyard to use a computer to work on the testimonials. We climbed a back stairway to a small upper bedroom, where a grandson reclined in a twin bed. He greeted us, unfazed by the intrusion.

The boundary between family and school was thin — the school itself, after all, was named for Ramamani Iyengar, the wife who'd left Iyengar widowed on the very eve of its opening in 1975. Rama had died two days after blessing the foundation stone for the building, and her presence indeed seemed to pervade the very atmosphere — especially this week. This year, Gurupurnima fell on the day that would have been Iyengar's fifty-fifth wedding anniversary. I'd mentioned the coincidence to the guru one afternoon in the library. "Yes, this is the date," he'd responded wistfully. "Fifty-five years since Rama's wedding."

The barriers continued to fall away. Iyengar yoga offered a total world; it presented a philosophy to follow, a ritual to practice, and people to share it with. Yoga pervaded life. It was all-encompassing, a tradition descended from some supreme lineage whose exact source we didn't talk about but whose pedigree seemed unpolluted nonetheless. Iyengar's warmth made us descendants ourselves, members of an international family of yoga whose common language was a repertoire of physical shapes. Putting our bodies into asanas in classes and practice connected us to one another and to yoga's primordial past. I was one limb in an integral body.

On the night of the Gurupurnima celebration, Iyengar sat on the studio platform surrounded by piles of fruits and gave a talk. It was lacking in his signature fixation on the cells of the body. "Children of yoga," he began, "you and I are so closely related, it's like a father and mother with their child. With affection, you are all close to me, like my family members. Today is a day where the pupils and the master come close together to understand the emotion of the teacher and the emotion of the pupil. It is a communication and communion between you and me. You are free to ask any doubts you have. You are with me; I am with you. I will not say good-bye." His family was large, its world small.

In dreams, Iyengar began to slide into my consciousness as someone I was indeed related to. As he spoke that night, I remembered a dream I'd had the night before that he was my Indian father, arranging a marriage for me. I accepted a husband to please him. "You have made me very happy," he told me. *Who was I?* I thought with alarm now. *An Indianized shell of my former self, carrying on lineage at the order of a patriarch?*

This was the sort of thing students at the school actually did.

Not only had many of his longtime followers adopted Indian dress and social mores, but some had made the conversion official. Biria, the Frenchman who had instructed me about Ramanuja, had told me how his own hard-won intimacy with Iyengar culminated nearly a decade before with his conversion from his natal Islam to Hinduism. This was commemorated in an unorthodox ceremony presided over by Iyengar himself, meaning that Biria didn't convert to Hinduism exactly — doctrinally, the religion did not accept converts — so much as to Srivaisnavite Brahminism, the particular strain of worship followed by Iyengar and the descendants of Ramanuja. Biria's "conversion" was, rather, an induction into Iyengar's clan, an adoption. Biria was a native of Azerbaijan. Today, he was an odd figure, with his Central Asian features, his French–Middle Eastern accent, his iconic sacred thread looping across his chest like a celestial tether. Biria had learned the family's rituals, he'd explained to me, by studying the *Laws of Manu,* the two-thousand-year-old Vedic text that encoded the customs of daily life followed by Ramanuja himself. Just as I did in my dream, Biria had also allowed Iyengar to arrange a marriage for him. In a traditional Brahmin ceremony, he married a French yoga student of Iyengar's choosing under the gaze of the matchmaker guru. I wondered now if I too was slipping from my roots, casting off my culture like so much Western dress.

After Iyengar's talk, we all lined up and bent, one by one, in front of him. Gloria and I had outfitted each other in luminous silk saris for the occasion. Iyengar placed his hands on my head when I passed. When I looked up after, I caught his gaze; it was a quick and penetrating blessing. I felt a physical charge. I'd once cringed at the idea of paying obeisance by touching his feet, as I'd seen students do my first day. Now the gesture struck me as no less natural than a handshake, only hierarchical — and I knew it was un-American not to be bothered by it. Outside we ate prasad — dinner, but coated in that patina of sanctity. It was sweet rice, sticky with raisins. Because of Srivaisnavite food restrictions, Geeta cooked all Iyengar's meals. The food we ate now also had been prepared according to a strict Hindu kashruth. I knew from my Jewish grandmother and I knew from my experience with anorexia how the ritual of restrictive eating could bind you to, and separate you from, others. This was "clean" food, Gloria was saying as she stood next to me.

Within this clan, I imagined myself a favored daughter, my status partially conferred through my friendship with Gloria. Gloria and the guru were close, in part because Gloria had devised a project much like Iyengar's to institute yoga syllabi in schools in California. Iyengar also warmed to me because I'd suggested he sit for several interviews. When he agreed, I detected no suspicion that to be a journalist was to observe the culture of the school from a detached distance, that reporting and devotion were in any sense at odds. In fact, Nivedita Joshi had already envisioned Iyengar as the subject of a journalistic biography — in her case, a hagiography meant to win acolytes through Indian TV.

But as much as I was a student engaged in the mission of the school, at times I was aware of the ambiguities implicit in my role. When I came to visit Iyengar in his library, he welcomed me with a generous expression of the eyebrows. One day, I sat across from him at his desk, arranged my tape recorder, pulled out my laptop computer, and prepared to take notes. I felt my role as a journalist pushing me out of the fold at the same time that my study and camaraderie with Iyengar were bringing me in. Iyengar eyed my accoutrements, impressed. He shifted the tape recorder to ensure that his words flowed directly into it.

The grandson whom I'd seen in the upstairs of the house floated through, in gym shorts and a sports T.

"Hey, what has happened in the park? Was he out or he was not out?" The guru interrupted our conversation.

"Harbhajan's out." Cricket.

"Out? He does not touch the ball, he says, the ball hits my chest, and he was out? He was looking at the sky, and they pull him out? That man is really a force man."

After Iyengar began speaking to me again, I realized I'd forgotten to unpause my recorder. I reached out to touch it. A minute earlier, Iyengar had been so engrossed in his subject that he'd seemed almost oblivious to my presence. Now he fell silent. He watched my hand, full of anticipation. The recorder wasn't running. I picked it up, fingered the button, and placed it, now operational, back on the table. The guru's face was stricken. He was still staring at the tape recorder, his expression a mixture of panic and rage. "Did it stop?" he asked, his eyes flashing. "So we have got none of that?"

I felt a scare of my own. I had to remind myself that it was not merely my charm and ability to come up with an endless stream of questions about the history of yoga that had won me Iyengar's affection. Iyengar had not become the world's best-known yogi without an intense will to present his craft to the public. He was at heart a performer.

As if sensing my trepidation, he turned to the subject of his death. He did this often, enough to inspire a lingering anticipation in Geeta and the many students. "Now I am retiring," he began. "It took me ten to twenty retirings and still I haven't retired." And then, non sequitur though it was, he mentioned a camera crew. "Trying to keep the body warm," he said mysteriously, "for the cameras." He winked.

The next morning when I arrived for my class with Geeta, a crew had indeed rigged the studio: floodlights beamed down on the podium; wires snaked across the floor. Students prepared for class in the usual array of asanas, seemingly unaware of the commotion except when Pandu or Geeta called out for someone to acquire some piece of yoga furniture to assist the filmmakers. Nivedita Joshi was shooting her television series about the Iyengars — India's first family of yoga.

Iyengar was not in his usual elaborately strapped reclining posture between pillar and wall, but on the stage in a type of backbend I'd never seen anyone perform with so electric a presence. The lights were on him. One leg stretched to the ceiling; his chest arced so that his head and torso reached all the way beneath his body. Gloria came running up from the library. "You have to come get me if he performs!" she scolded me, and then her face transformed, absorbed in euphoric concentration.

Geeta and Pandu were watchful as well, like birds, moving students when they blocked Nivedita or the cameras. "Please stand and watch," Geeta ordered. "Not there! So the camera can go!" The cameras were hallowed visitors from the magical West. "Camera is here!" Geeta shouted again, pushing students from the sight lines.

Finally, Geeta began class: "You people," she said. It was a stock phrase, a shorthand sentence, its second half rarely spoken. "You people" meant "You Westerners are too materialistic, too driven by goals, too disrespectful of the Indian masters."

"You people," she said again, shaking her jowls. We nodded. We knew we were those people, knew that to fit in we needed to become somehow otherwise.

"Your Western marriages," she went on. She marched over to a Frenchwoman who was sitting in a cross-legged, twisting asana and had a cowed expression, perhaps owing more to Geeta's badgering than to any innate predisposition toward shyness. Geeta stood behind her and, gripping one hand over each of her shoulders, dug her knee between the student's shoulder blades. Geeta pulled, causing the woman's sternum to move forward from her shoulders several inches. The woman looked instantly more confident, though the illusion faded as Geeta moved again across the floor. "Your marriages are always falling apart," Geeta went on. "Your poses are like your Western marriages. You think, *I want to do this nice pose, this pretty pose.* You think, *I want, I want.* That is why your marriages are always falling apart. They would not fall apart if you would look at the inside, not the external. Always the external. For you, even the falling in love is external. You people.

"Ladies," Geeta continued. Women, Western and Indian, accounted for about three-quarters of the eighty or so students in class. "Tuck in the T-shirts. Who has said you can do yoga with the T-shirt out? Please tuck in." She glanced toward a Western woman with an untucked shirt and then quickly looked away, as if embarrassed by her immodesty.

Now Geeta was behind me. She slapped the top of my head. *Slap.* I adjusted myself in reflex, not sure exactly how I'd erred.

Before I left for India, people said yoga at the institute in Pune would be tough in a way I had never known yoga could be. But the toughest thing I came upon was not the yoga but the teacher.

Geeta Iyengar appeared in public in only two different outfits. Outside the studio it was the white sari she'd worn in my dream — the costume, in India, of a celibate. But in my dream, I'd miscalculated. Accentuating her dark features and piercing eyes, the sari gave her the pinched look of a severe nun. Geeta had inherited from her father his hawk nose and the deep brown skin of a South Indian. She had his sharp jaw too, set in a gesture of disapproval that was perhaps a less forgiving feature on her than on her father. Her other outfit, the uniform of yoga, consisted of

Kelly-green balloon shorts and a dull-looking white Izod, tucked in and fastened at the second buttonhole with a large safety pin. This was her less assuming aspect, revealing a chunky middle and thick thighs, the safety pin on her shirt suggesting not merely her humility of character but a charming, even girlish, lack of vanity. This was what she wore today.

"Stand up!" she called. "Uttanasana." We all stood and bent forward at the hips, held our ankles, pulled. Then I heard a confusing thing — Iyengar's voice: "Sirsasana," headstand, he called. He sauntered across the stage. The cameras were on him. Geeta loped out of view. "Sirsasana!" Iyengar barked again.

"Move from camera please." Geeta pushed students from the sight line.

We lifted up into the pose as Iyengar shouted in his signature style: "Do not throw legs back! Abdomen tightens if you throw legs back! Keep inner leg tall! Horizontal pelvis! Vertical stretch of chest! Sockets of hips in! Latissimus straight up! Front legs narrow! Back legs broaden! Tailbone in!"

I felt something sharp, like metal, jab into my tailbone from behind. My pelvis arced forward, and Iyengar walked out from behind me. It had been him. Before I could think about it, my body had complied. The movement caused something to relax in the spot in my shoulder that had torqued fourteen years before when I'd first dangled from the live oak in Santa Cruz. Once again, I was reminded of something; it hurt me in a way that suggested it had hurt there for a long time, only I'd stopped feeling it. I'd avoided that pain by standing and moving in such a way that it was never aggravated. When I came down from the pose now, I felt a surge of sadness, the same emotion I'd touched mysteriously in Santa Cruz.

I listened vaguely to Geeta's instructions for the next pose, wondering at the same time if Iyengar had unlocked something just then, simply and quickly. "You never see a person who is depressed walking with an open chest," Geeta was saying, having reclaimed the class. She instructed us to lie on our backs with wooden blocks pushing our sternums forward. "Life's sadness collects behind the sternum. Your sternum is like an introverted child. Make it the extroverted child. When the mind is lifted it is pure. When the mind is dropped it is impure. Have the lifted mind in the chest."

I lifted, and listened to the sadness, and waited for it to dissipate.

When Geeta wasn't teaching or cooking or editing or directing the camera crew, she was taking charge of preparations for her father's eightieth birthday. She was ever shorter of patience. There was something foreboding about the rounded number of Iyengar's advancing age, an awesomeness heightened by Iyengar's many asides about his pending death.

Her father's mortality was weighing on everyone, but it was Geeta who bore it in her mood and in her body. She'd been missing a lot of classes because, Gloria told me, she was suffering from exhaustion and a flare-up of bad kidneys. "How much can I tolerate; how much can I have my patience now?" she pleaded one evening in her weekly class on pranayama breathing after a student from Europe lifted the wrong hand after an instruction to block a single nostril. She'd misunderstood: Iyengar-English was a tongue of its own.

"Did I say take your left hand up on the nose?" Geeta hollered. "Here is person doing with the left hand on the nose. Can you understand? This continues. You also understand my patience? These days I have really started getting irritated. After all, what can I do? What can I do, tell me? If you were in my place, what would you have done? All this yelling, it is unyogic." She

125

shrugged her shoulders as if galled by the sudden appearance of an image of herself. "You are making me unyogic."

I tried to shut out Geeta's tirade by concentrating on the sounds of cuckoos and traffic outside, on the children screaming, the dogs barking, the pulsing sound of Pune. Frog chirps. Cicadas. Yoga was teaching me to ignore the irrelevant stresses. And still, after Geeta finally paused and then shifted back to give directions on how to breathe, it was hard to stay focused, hard to perform the "slow soft quiet inhalation" that she instructed — "the inhalation which should not be aggressive, should not irritate any portion of the body."

A week later, the nostril woman was still aghast. "I've been having a hard time," she confessed to me. "All this getting yelled at, feeling like I'm Geeta's problem child. I think I'm getting disillusioned, with India, with the yoga. It's not fair. You come here, your heart is opening up. You're breaking down defenses, breaking through to new places. And then it turns out it's a place where you can't afford to be vulnerable."

I imagined that the yogic equanimity I was cultivating in Pune enabled me to rise above these nominal stresses. I felt I was becoming more emotionally receptive, yet I experienced none of this woman's vulnerability.

Then, one day, I was the woman with her finger on the wrong nostril, so to speak. There were certain inalienable rules of Iyengar yoga, and among the most unforgivable was that you did not turn upside down when you were menstruating. Teachers ticked off any number of pseudoscientific justifications for the injunction, but the most commonsense explanation worked just fine: the flow goes downward, why thwart it by forcing it upward? Geeta took the proscription to a further extreme, teaching that during menstruation women should avoid all strenuous yoga as well.

Today, we did strenuous poses for an hour. Then Geeta called out sirsasana, headstand, the first upside-down pose of the day. I hadn't had much of a period for the last few years — a lingering amenorrhea that my gynecologist attributed to my previous anorexia. Birth control pills gave me scant bleeding one or two days a month, and today was one of those days. Did this count? I didn't know. I did know that headstand was, on the contrary, considered beneficial in cases of menstrual irregularity and amenorrhea. Two years earlier, Manouso had advised me to stand on my head ten minutes every day until my periods came back — I'd been doing so ever since.

I stood in the center of the studio, unsure what to do. The students assembled their props. I was lost, standing dumbly. A hundred and sixty legs shot upward toward the ceiling, and soon everyone was in either headstand or an alternative pose that Geeta had prescribed for them. Finally, an assistant noticed me. I began my long story.

"What?" Geeta walked up.

"Menstruation?" the assistant prompted me.

I nodded, beginning to explain.

"Menstruation?" Geeta cut me off, incredulous. "Menstruation?" Her voice rose. "And you have been doing these poses for an hour, strenuous yoga? Why do you come all the way here? Why? Eh? Why? You come to do. You do not come to learn. I know you. You people. You are all business. Who is your teacher?"

I stuttered, pointing lamely to Gloria.

Geeta stalked over to Gloria. "She is your student, eh? And she does not know? They tell you, you do the strenuous yoga when you have the period?" Geeta turned back to me. I met her eyes. I couldn't remember ever seeing a pair of human eyes so focused. They were clear, dark, and still. It was only my surprise at witnessing such wrath that kept me from crying. My tears hung just at the breaking point. "Haven't you read my book?" Her tirade continued. "What do I say when there is bleeding? Eh? Eh?"

"Okay," I whispered.

"Okay? No, it is not okay. Why you say *okay?* Eh? Why? Why? You don't answer, you leave. Leave!" Geeta pointed to the stairwell. "This is her punishment," Geeta added calmly, nodding to the assistant.

"Point the eyes straight ahead," the assistant whispered to me as Geeta turned to her next problem child. "It'll staunch the tears. Look straight ahead. This is how yoga works." I heeded her advice as I collected my belongings from the changing balcony and hobbled out of the studio. My tears never came. Such was mind-body yoga. Such was the wisdom of a science that gave you tools to cope with its tyrants.

That night at home with Gloria, though, I cried. The accomplishment of yoga that day had not been its technique to harness emotion, but to pull up from the depths tears like I hadn't cried since I was a kid.

As I cried, memories from my childhood began passing before me — banal slights and hurts: fighting with my father over a glass of orange juice I didn't want to drink, bawling in the backseat of a Volvo. They were random memories, but all pegged, I realized, to the time of my parents' divorce. I'd never actually felt regret about their split — my parents had always seemed as poorly suited to each other as, it occurred to me now, the very sun and moon. So it was hard to understand why troubling images from the last days of their marriage were now flooding in: me, three years old, refusing to wear a pair of shoes that would correct my duck feet; my parents disagreeing about how to assuage a screaming stubborn child; my father pacing away from our old

Volvo, huffing, *You can stay in the car.* The family walking out, my father stalking, my mother grimacing, my sister gloating.

The next morning, I woke up with a sore throat and a sour stomach and a plenty good excuse to stay home from school. In fact, I was not sure I was welcome back at school at all. Had I been expelled? Gloria promised me I had not.

I sat still for a minute, concentrated, tried to quiet my frenetic thoughts just as I had learned to close out the sound of Geeta and her followers in the noisy studio. I was angry, I noticed. A rage at Geeta grew inside me; I felt not sad but potent, as potent as Geeta herself. No one had presumed to yell at me like that since I'd been a child. How dare Geeta keep me away from the yoga school. I thought of the awesome power of her boring eyes. The Yoga Sutras ascribed to the cobra Patañjali, thought to be the oldest extant treatise on yoga, began with the explanation that yoga was the "cessation of the fluctuations of consciousness . . . the stilling of the bodily perturbations." I'd never locked gazes with a person for so long whose eyes did not waver a bit, not a quiver. It had been the truest manifestation of Patañjali's aphorism I'd seen. Geeta had something to teach me. I would not be denied her wisdom.

Gloria poured me into a ricksha, and under her arm I arrived to class. Geeta, striding in with her Kelly-green balloon shorts and Izod, did not acknowledge me one way or the other. It struck me that her rage had been pure, spent in its moment and gone. For her, I became just another Western woman with her shirt untucked.

I might have shifted from Geeta's frame of vision, but in my own unconscious, she was writ large. At night, I began to have dreams of rage. My anger recalled the rage I felt for Geeta, but Geeta, I knew, was only a symbol. In dreams, I was also scream-

129

ing at my mother, my sister, my father. In sleep, I was empowered as I'd never been awake. In Geeta I had found my fury.

In one dream, my mother yelled at me, and I yelled back as I had never done as a child. When I woke up, I understood even better the power of Geeta's rage: in Geeta's face I'd seen my mother's anger. Olive skin, aquiline cheekbones, black French-Canadian eyes. When my mother was angry, she raised her eyebrows, great arching film-star eyebrows. Her pupils filled her corneas. She lifted her hands, curling long manicured fingers into claws. She made herself big, arms bowed outward like eagle wings. My mother growled, towering and inarticulate.

What was my mother so angry about? In roundabout ways and direct ones, my father. I was their go-between.

I remembered asking my mother for money to go to the store.

"For what?" she challenged me.

"Food?"

"No!"

"Why not?"

"Because we don't have any money. Look in the cupboards. There's food."

I scavenged, found a small plastic bag of dry rice, some loose tea. In the refrigerator: half-and-half for coffee. I went back to her bedroom. It was painted a rich gray. She called it her cave. "Pizza money?" I pleaded. "For school?"

The eyebrows arched, the eyes turned to pits. The claws. The growl. "I! Have! No! Money! Ask! Your! Father!" Implication: You are as materialistic and bourgeois as he is and probably belong in the suburbs of Boston.

My father harbored equal if opposite anger at my mother. When he picked me up from the train in Boston, he looked me over. My jeans were too short — I knew it; it made me self-conscious. I grew too quickly, and my mother replaced things too slowly, for my jeans to reach past my shins. I was a long pole of a girl, like my mother. Everyone commented on our likeness. Perhaps it provoked my father.

"Your jeans are too short," my father helpfully pointed out in the car. Implication: You are as incapable of functioning respectably in this world as your mother is.

I shrugged.

"Why don't you get new clothes?" he pressed on.

I remembered my mother's words: *Ask your father!* "Why don't you buy me some?" I responded.

I watched my father in the driver's seat of his Fiat. He was silent. Through the skin on his cheeks I could see teeth gnawing. "Ask your mother."

In Pune I had another dream, in which my sister and I were screaming at each other about, mundanely enough, vegetarian food. My sister offered me meat, and I became incensed that she couldn't remember I didn't eat it. She accused me of being sanctimonious. We started punching, pulling hair, shoving. I swung to pummel her, but then I heard a voice, too clear for a dream. "Elizabeth!" It was sharp and pointed, and it woke me up. It brought me back to the day Manouso called my name to me in my yoga class, willing me to be solid. I didn't understand the voice now. Was it a call for courage, or a reflex to get out?

Over the next few weeks, the nightmares developed the clarity of visions. Each object was brighter than its real-life counterpart; time was slowed, the universe hyperreal. I was an observer endowed with extrasensitive faculties, calm and focused as a yogi in an ecstatic trance.

One night, a gun was pointing at me, luminous and still. I watched a bullet shoot from the gun and move toward me in slow motion. The bullet went through my neck; it was painless. I could see a rupture in my skin, as if I were watching from outside my body. I stopped breathing, as if dead, and everything and everyone became silent, motionless, and bled of color. I breathed again, and everything moved and gained color, and then I stilled the universe once more by halting my breath. I wondered, with an almost pleasant detachment, whether I was dead or just dying. I was amused to see that the choice was as simple as drinking in a gulp of air.

Around this time, Manouso showed up to visit Iyengar. Manouso had met Iyengar on a trip to India in 1977 and grew to become one of the guru's closest American disciples. He was intimate with the family and passed in and out of the home on the other side of the courtyard as if its walls were porous. In America, I'd only seen him wearing T-shirts and elastic shorts or hiking pants. Here, like Biria, he dressed in an Indian kurta and sandals. I told Manouso about the nightmares. Was yoga giving them to me?

"It's because you're dying," he told me with a reassuring nod. "Spiritually. It's a process of death and rebirth. The first time I came to India, I woke up in cold sweats, gripping the edges of the mattress, five nights out of seven. I was losing myself. I had no idea where I was. I didn't know who I was. I woke up in terror. It was a spiritual death. I was being completely remade."

How did this work? Were we remaking our bodies? I thought of the spot in my shoulder blade, rendered invisible after so many self-protective years. Now, the pain was a new piece of me. Pain, I'd read in a book by the literary critic Elaine Scarry, "brought about an immediate reversion to a state anterior to language, to the sounds and cries a human being makes before language is learned." Through pain we could experience distant parts of ourselves.

I was struggling to feel my pains more precisely, so as to someday erase them. Eventually my body would become clear, empty of these places where ache gathered. I'd recently read another book describing the method of physical yoga from the point of view of Western psychology. Writing in 1934, the author, Geraldine Coster, described "fixities of habit"— patterns of thinking in our minds and habits of posture in our bodies that congealed like cement. By using concentration techniques, we could build new patterns, physical as well as psychological. We could unclench muscles that had grabbed for years, change the ways we sat or stood that once protected emotions that lived inside us. And at the same time, we could come up with new ways of conceiving of ourselves, we could intercept those looplike patterns of thinking that forever reminded us of the ways we disappointed ourselves. In our bodies, we made new frames in which to sit and live, and we re-created our psyches as well.

Where did the old self go? I wondered now as I listened to Manouso. Where did the old beliefs about ourselves disappear to? The "fixities" once added up to everything we were. Who did we become when the fixities had crumbled, like so much string dried to dust?

In the institute lobby one day around this time, Pandu raced through with a hand on his cordless. He slammed the phone on his desk and shook out his head as if to say he'd worked enough today. Sitting, he rubbed his eyes with his palms. Instants later, he stood up, the stress of a minute earlier absent. He looked at me with moon eyes. "What is your name?" he asked. "I see you here, you come in and out, but I do not know your name."

I told him.

"You worry. Why do you worry?" he said.

"Yes," I conceded, unsurprised he'd detected it. "I worry a lot."

"You have anxiety, but why? You must learn, in the past you

worry and everything it came out fine. So why you think to worry for the future if in the past everything it is fine? Westerners, they live in the future. The Indian, he lives for today."

"Well"— I considered, trying to locate the exact source of that familiar and vague, yet ever-present, sense in my body and in my brain that things were not right — "there's financial debt," I offered. "Student loans. You mortgage the future, and then you live in the future."

"Let me tell you something. The Westerner, he wakes up in the morning and he says, 'I have this problem today.' The Indian, he wakes up and he says, 'I have this hope.' The Indian who has nothing, and the Westerner who has so much. The Indian has no worry."

"Yes," I agreed. "I have too much anxiety."

"By the time you leave, I watch, you will be better. No worry. No anxiety. You leave here free from your problem."

I wondered what my problem was, and if Pandu knew. My emotions seemed pasted onto my body, lines of text etched in my skin from my head to the hard bone covering my heart, passages from a physical narrative legible from every view but my own.

Chapter Eleven

Iyengar often referred to yoga as a "Science." I had always considered this quirky and less than rigorous, the certificates in his stairwell referring to him as "doctor" quaint and rather kitsch. But now I found myself considering yoga more seriously than ever before. It was certainly more than exercise, without a doubt related to that part of the consciousness that experienced pain as preverbal awareness. It worked in profound ways that circumvented the rational. Its method could not, need not, be explained. It held an intuitive logic that only the body could grasp — not the mind. "You are working from the Western calculative mind," Iyengar had once admonished me.

Whether or not this justified a designation as science, it was Iyengar's version of yoga's more numinous methodology that I found most suspect. I had always relegated the idea of yoga as supernatural craft to that part of me that appreciated the ways yoga was exotic and enchanting, scenic and humble. But for Iyengar and his family, the notion that yoga worked in magical ways owing to its mystical roots was tangible. Prashant once asserted to me that the asanas originated in the heavens. They were, he insisted, "primordial." Speaking of the legends explaining yoga's origin, "The myths are not a myth. They are history," he insisted. Never mind that brass-tacks points such as whether Ramanuja existed, whether Nathamuni existed, and certainly whether the snake-man Patañjali existed despite having left behind the famous Yoga Sutras were, historically speaking, open to debate.

Just as Iyengar learned early on not to question the meaning of rituals, the Pune institute was not the place to examine too closely certain assumptions about how the mystical resonance of yoga was embedded in the Iyengar family's traditions. The family was organized around their customs and so, by extension, was the school.

These customs seemed to affect Geeta the most. Since her mother's death a quarter century before, Iyengar's first daughter had become both codirector of the school and resident housekeeper across the courtyard. Her duties were especially arduous since Srivaisnavites could eat only food cooked by other Srivaisnavites. For this reason, Iyengar's other daughters — Savita, Suchita, Vanita, and Sunita — made frequent trips away from their own families to take some of the load off Geeta. Unlike her sisters, Geeta had wed herself to yoga, but this did not mean she'd escaped her domestic duties.

One daughter I occasionally noticed around the courtyard was Savita. I knew about her in advance of her arrival because Nandu had mentioned her and because I'd read a family tree she'd composed for an institute publication. This tree asserted that Iyengar's link to Ramanuja, through an unbroken line of Brahmin births, was at the heart of Iyengar's mystical and genealogical legitimacy as a yoga teacher. It pointed back fourteen generations, from Iyengar to Ramanuja and then a few steps further to Lord Vishnu. Savita spelled out the significance of Iyengar's ancestral connection to Ramanuja by suggesting that genetic as well as psychical pathways had been at work in the form of samskara, or past-life memories, shaping her father as a yogi.

Iyengar's connection to yoga, therefore, reached back much further than his tutelage with Krishnamacharya. And although Krishnamacharya had his own family tree linking him to yoga's roots, it was only Iyengar's line, Savita's literature made clear, that was unsullied.

This was not the reading forwarded by another yoga school, in Madras, headed by the son of Krishnamacharya, a nephew of Iyengar's named T. K. V. Desikachar. Desikachar had also learned yoga from Krishnamacharya, and his rival genealogy showed him as the inheritor of an unbroken line bridging Krishnamacharya, through ancestral and mystical links as well, not to Ramanuja but to the medieval yogi Nathamuni. This tree traced "a family of yoga teachers" through twelve generations and, in spite of gaps of several hundred years, asserted that Krishnamacharya's, and by extension his son's, inheritance included a claim on the *Yoga Rahasya,* that lost yoga text composed by Nathamuni. This text, recovered by Krishnamacharya in his vision with the tamarind tree, had been lost during the ninth century when Nathamuni bequeathed it to his grandson, who would later become the wise man Yamunacharya, Ramanuja's teacher. Unforeseen circumstances kept the future Yamunacharya from arriving at the appointed time and place to retrieve the book from Nathamuni, however, and so the *Yoga Rahasya* was lost.

Yoga flew off into oblivion alongside the text, until the serendipitous manifestation a thousand years later for Nathamuni's modern heir Krishnamacharya. Desikachar's telling put a fine point on the significance of Krishnamacharya's vision: "A lost text was brought to current knowledge in this mysterious manner, perhaps preventing the dying of this tradition."

In excavating yoga's roots, I was curious about how the idea of a primordial source informed modern yoga. Where, really, did yoga come from? And would the answer to this question clear up any confusions about the true identify of its legitimate shepherd for the modern age? Was its forebear Patañjali, who may or may not have been a cobra? the ancient saint Nathamuni, who may or may not have been a man? a two-hundred-and-thirty-year-old hermit in a cave in Tibet, who may or may not have really lived? Did physical yoga begin with the *Rahasya,* a lost text that may or may not have been reconstructed? Did it descend from a maharaja's palace? Had it originated in Krishnamacharya's, or even Iyengar's, own imagination?

Iyengar had made clear to me when I'd asked for a definition of yoga that he believed the place to start such a quest was with his ancestor Ramanuja. Iyengar's daughter Savita, the guru also instructed me, was his family's expert on things genealogical. With Iyengar's encouragement, I began planning a trip to see Savita in Bangalore, where I could further plumb the topic of modern yoga's roots by visiting the village where Iyengar was born. Here I might gain insight into not just the yogi's ancestral past but where he actually came from.

The extent to which Iyengar conceived of his own lineage as connecting him to a past more godly than factual, however, started to become clear when I got involved in arranging my travel. Iyengar had been born in a village called Bellur, his first name. "How do I get to Bellur?" I asked the guru before I left.

"This town is really beautiful," Iyengar said mistily. "You see the temples."

I wrote the word *temples* in my notebook. I asked if there were carvings that looked like yoga postures that had impressed him when he was young.

"Later. Yes. Not as child. Manda!" he yelled to the librarian. "This book! This, this. The temples. Get!"

I heard the sweep of the librarian's sari as she got up from her computer and began searching through stacks of heavy art books. "Yes, temples," she mumbled. "Bellur you will find."

Soon the librarian had placed a thick volume at my place at the table. I began leafing through pages of spectacular Hindu artworks of scenes from the Mahabharata and the Ramayana, many of them depicting figures that suggested yoga postures. In one relief dated to the seventh century, Vishnu stood on one leg while the other extended parallel to the ground from his hip. This was a posture we knew as padangusthasana. I imagined a preconscious Iyengar internalizing such wondrous shapes as his mother strolled past them, her belly swelling with the future adept. But as I scrutinized the chapter on a South Indian temple town named Belur, I realized it was not where Iyengar was born. It was the wrong Bellur. As it happened, there were at least three Bellurs in India. Temple Belur was the most famous and well traveled because of its memorable art.

I brought the book to Iyengar. "Guruji, where you were born. How do I get *there?*"

Iyengar brushed off the confusion casually. He promised me Savita would bring me to his natal village and went on to have the librarian copy names and phone numbers of old friends and relatives from a well-paged address book.

But it was very odd, I kept thinking later, that the name of his hometown recalled for Iyengar not his childhood so much as a distant place, a destination where art aficionados imagined a mysterious Hindu past. Just as Iyengar spoke Tamil despite never having lived in a place where Tamil was spoken, where he came from was not where he was born but whence the gods hailed. I was on my way to find yoga's roots. But if they resided in a mythical, ancestral beyond, how, exactly, would I locate them?

An official sign in English greeted travelers to the Bangalore train station: EVERYONE'S RELIGION IS PERSONNEL MATTER WITH HIMSELF.

This attempt at wisdom stayed with me while I searched for Savita Raghu's house in a quiet enclave behind a busy Bangalore throughway. There were two or three temples to the block, each one crowded with crouched old women in saris waving incense, or processions of chanting men dressed in orange.

When Savita greeted me at the house, I saw that she was unmistakably a relative of Iyengar, with the same strong features of Prashant and Geeta. On her face, the Iyengar family's rounded eyes and hooked nose took on a particular sadness. "Please, you sit," she said warmly, directing me to wait for her on a couch while she finished her prayers. She moved to a small candle- and incense-laden altar in full view of me and her eight-year-old son, Sharan, where she began chanting in a low singsong. Sharan skipped through the living room in traditional Brahmin dress singing folk songs.

Savita had offered to arrange a taxi to take us to the village of Bellur, and outside the house there was indeed a taxi waiting. It was a large one, more like a van. I wasn't sure why Savita had rented a van. It concerned me — I'd offered to pay.

I didn't mention this as I climbed into the first row of backseats alongside Sharan and Savita, who was dressed in a fancy pressed silk sari. They conversed quietly in Tamil while Savita's husband gave instructions to the driver from the front seat in Kannada. "You don't mind?" Savita added nonchalantly in English, gesturing to the empty seats. "We'll pick up some people."

As we set off, Savita handed me a large bound manuscript, her thesis, "A Study of Sri Vaisnavites — Modernizing Aspects of a Hindu Religious Sect." She'd gotten her doctorate at Pune University, she explained, with research based on a collection of surveys taken from a small population of Srivaisnavite Brahmins living in Pune. As I scanned the research, I got a sense of why Nandu, the khaki-wearing might-be Hindu militant from the institute, had directed me to Savita. She'd chosen as her sample the membership of a social organization of descendants of the saint Ramanuja. That organization was the Sri Ramanuja Siddhanta Sabha (RSS), the same that had inscribed the Hindu nationalist manuscript in Iyengar's library. Savita was not a member of either that RSS or the national one, she told me, but she certainly saw some connection between her own roots and the fundamentalist cause. Brahmins had had a hard time of it since independence, she explained. Tamil nationalists had identified Brahmins as the scourge of India, she lamented, and the nationalism of the RSS was often dismissed these days as "Brahminist." But contrary to its reputation for exclusivity, the RSS was more often on the scene helping flood victims than promulgating violence against Muslims or insisting on Hindu ethnic purity as the most important marker of Indianness.

Savita went on to discuss the countless pressures on Brahmins like herself to modernize. Brahmins were the target of constant criticism for keeping alive the injustices of India's caste system. Yet most Brahmins had been forced by circumstance to shed many of their exclusive practices. Tap water rendered the Brahmin injunction against sharing water from communal sources irrelevant, and few Srivaisnavites would forego a meal in a nice restaurant these days. Meanwhile, the press was always publishing stories about how the Indian institution of arranged marriage was under threat.

141

Was this important to her, I asked, to maintain her family's pure line? Might her son marry someone outside the fold — a non-Brahmin? a Westerner? one of Iyengar's unorthodox converts?

Intermarriage was the biggest threat to their culture, Savita affirmed in a resolute voice. "Are you a Jew?" she asked, out of nowhere.

"Yes," I answered in reflex. The question caught me off guard.

"I had a feeling," she said. "It is very nice to speak with you, you know. Many of Guruji's students are Jews. These are the students I think we get along with the best. You have a certain quality; I don't know what. We can understand each other right away I think. This is how it was with this, this, Miryam. Do you know her?"

I shrugged. "Maybe." I was thinking that whoever Miryam was, she probably was a Jew, but I was also wondering if in her ignorance Savita had conflated the qualities of Americanness with what she thought Jews might be like. I wasn't aware of Iyengar having a particularly large number of Jewish followers, and even in America, people rarely assumed I was Jewish.

"As a Jew," she went on, "you feel you are proud to be born a Jew as you have a code of conduct. We can guide the other people and be a preacher. For Sharan, see, we teach him the mantras; they have such power. It reminds him that we are a part of a tradition. He recites this, and he tells to which clan he belongs. He recites the names of the rishis. You can do, no?" She nodded to her son.

Sharan instantly turned his attention from the finger puzzle in his lap and began reciting. I recognized the names of several saints I'd heard Iyengar mention at one time or another. Sharan had learned these chants before the coming-of-age ceremony at which he donned his sacred thread, Savita explained. The ceremony was conducted by Iyengar himself and attended by some of the guru's Western disciples.

"So you see," Savita said, holding her son by the shoulder, "he knows the lineage of our Vaisnavite tradition. What happens if a Jew marries a Jew is you don't have any problems." She gave me a penetrating look. "If a Jew marries a Christian, then you have a problem, whatever problem. It's a different culture, the rites and the rituals, and the customs; everything changes, and then you are becoming another American society."

Just as I had when my grandmother raised questions about my split identity, I felt like something of a fraud just then. I should never have admitted I was Jewish when it meant so much less to me than Savita imagined. And I certainly should have offered her the caveat that I was in fact "mixed."

"If you are all having these intercaste marriages, and all the children don't know to which caste actually they belong to, to which religious group they belong, they will be all confused. No?" she went on. "They will say, I am not a Jew; I am half a Jew; I am half a Christian, or half an Iyengar, or half a Vaishya, or something like that. And then what? Tell me."

I nodded noncommittally.

"We are very similar to Orthodox Jewish families, you know. When you meet a Jew, you are so happy. You know you both go back to Israel, you know this and that about each other, and it's great. So you understand."

I shook my head no. I knew, however, that in India a nod of the head from side to side in the American "no" actually meant "yes."

Savita paused, considering. "I am proud to be born a Brahmin," she said. "Brahmin is good thinking, helping others and not expecting any fruit from it. You are the ideal of the society. People know, he or she is a Brahmin. So you cannot cheat or use bad words or think ill of others. This is what it means to be orthodox. Orthodoxy is a cleanliness. It's a cleanliness in our bodies without having from the outside. You wash your feet, you might have stepped in something. It's hygenic."

It was true that practices at the yoga institute went a long way in counteracting the pervasive filthiness of the Indian outdoors. One day early on, Gloria had instructed me how to wash my feet beside the squat toilet in the institute ladies' room before coming into the studio, and I'd noticed it was customary in several Brahmin homes I'd visited to not only take off one's shoes upon entering but wash one's feet as well.

But as much as I appreciated these small acts of resistance against the Indian dirt, it also occurred to me that Savita was speaking of the contamination of one's body and the contamination of one's bloodline as if they were the same thing. As a mixed breed myself, I didn't share her associations. Yet I knew that much in the way my teachers at the institute in Pune taught us that yoga purified your body, they also put great stock in its status as a pure form, inherited through unsullied lines. The chart Savita authored was unambiguous in its assertion that Ramanuja was the legitimate progenitor to yoga — and Iyengar its legitimate heir. That the Madras school held Nathamuni was the source — making Savita's uncle Krishnamacharya and his direct descendants the better inheritors — was an important disagreement. The Iyengar family's preoccupation with its genealogical tracings really did put it in the same camp as those militants who had a stake in the idea that Indian identity — and yoga — was intrinsically connected to its ethnic homogeneity. In this light, the Iyengar family's tolerance of the RSS, if not enthusiastic collaboration, made sense.

So I brought up Savita's research. Were the distinctions between Krishnamacharya's family tree and Iyengar's really all that significant, especially given yoga's gesture toward universality?

Savita assumed a pensive expression. "We can go back to the eleventh century, you know," she responded, shaking her head

FIRST THERE IS A MOUNTAIN

emphatically. "Guruji's family is traced from Ramanuja. That is significant. My father belongs to a very scholarly family. He came from a family where in the fourteenth century, our ancestor Prathivadi Bhayankaram went up against the biggest thinker of his time. Our family started here with the winning of the debate. He became the great philosopher Prathivadi, 'the one who wins the debate.' From the six sons of Prathivadi, my father is the fourteenth generation. It is my father who has taken the wisdom. This has come into my father, definitely. It's genetic. Krishnamacharya showed him the way, but my father developed his own nature. It was all written in the history of our forefathers."

She looked at me long now, pursing her lips and cocking her head. "The funny thing about Krishnamacharya's family, I will tell you," she added, speaking now in a conspiratorial whisper. "Krishnamacharya's family is not family from Tamil Nadu. They are originally from Andhra. They are Telugu. Telugu-speaking." She paused for a moment to let the significance of her claim settle. I knew that Nathamuni, like Ramanuja, was believed to have been Tamil. Her reasoning indeed cast doubt on Krishnamacharya's claim of a relation to the medieval yogi Nathamuni. The Iyengars, on the other hand, were Tamil, her look said. Read: legitimate heirs to the medieval Tamil craft. The Krishnamacharya family, she continued portentously, "follow all the Telugu customs. Even their calendar is the Telugu calendar. Lunar calendar. We are the followers of the solar calendar. Tamil calendar." Nathamuni, she repeated, was Tamil. Krishnamacharya was not. "That is that. You know." She gave me a knowing look.

We'd been driving around Bangalore for over an hour now, through ticky-tacky streets with sharp turns, past acres and acres of street-front markets, vegetable wallahs, sweets shops. We picked up a handful of relatives, made another stop back at the house, and, then, finally, six of us packed in and set off through the same backstreets, already several hours behind schedule. I thinking the entire time, *Did the taxi need to be so big, the route so long?* By the time we got outside the bounds of the busy metropolis, the meter read more money than I had budgeted for hotels on my entire trip to the south. I kept glancing at the meter, unsure of how to bring up the subject of money in what was fast becoming a family outing. All this talk about Judaism had made one thing very clear. If my tribe had so much in common with the Brahmin one, I was as good as a member. As in my own family, this was as much a matter of responsibility as of privilege. The price of inclusion was the price of a taxicab.

Upon arrival, whatever roots I'd expected to find in Bellur were no more palpable than in the photos from the other Belur. As in most of India's now impoverished rural villages, the Brahmins had long since fled — the Iyengar family in 1924. They had left no trace; probably all their peers had gone as well. *You can't go home again,* I thought of the obvious truism, learned firsthand by generations of East Coast Jews who'd moved on from places like Brownsville and Roxbury. But in this case, it was perhaps less poignant, since "home" had been a mystical place from the beginning.

The village was pleasant and pastoral, framed by a lagoon and mountain in the background and hard granite formations and green pools along its outskirts. A crowd of close to fifty barefoot peasants greeted our taxi. As we stepped into the dirt street, the villagers led us from majestic rock formations at one end of the village to a temple made of granite blocks at the other, speaking in a dialect of Kannada with the family. This temple, according to Savita, figured in Hindu mythology. "This village can be traced to the Mahabharata period," she noted, as if tossing me a small consolation prize. A man that the family introduced as the former caretaker of their old property brought us to a nondescript house, a hut really, with blue paint splashed onto a wooden door. This, the man said, shrugging, had been the Iyengar family's home. As Iyengar had intimated before I left, it was truly unspectacular. We so often invested the homes of our heroes with undeserved significance, yet they always carried so much less of the past than what we'd already imagined.

The man then brought us inside a stone-floored hut with mud walls, where his wife served us gummy glucose biscuits and Nescafé. And then, because the trip had taken several hours longer than expected and the sun was lowering toward the hillside, we turned around and left, passing on the road outside the village a hand-scrawled slogan on a chicken shack: LEPROSY IS CURABLE.

On the drive back, we were all tired and quiet. I resigned myself to covering the taxi — the fare would eventually tally nearly half a month's rent. I was famished; we all were. As the sun set, our taxi stalled in a long line of cars backed up for a railway crossing. The sky darkened to twilight, and hawkers from the nearby station swept in to sell platform food to the autos. The chants of the vendors reminded me of my first train journey in India. They were sinuous and soothing. *"Moong phali! Moong phali!"* Peanuts. I reached in my purse for a loose rupee — I knew that a cone of peanuts cost one cent. A peanut wallah looked in the window and caught my eye. As I looked back, I noticed that the faces of the family members were all pointed resolutely forward. The peanut wallah seemed to notice the same thing at the same moment, and I detected him make a small calculation before he edged away slowly. Just at that instant, Mr. Raghu's hand went to the automatic window control and sealed the auto.

Chapter Twelve

When I got back to my flat in Pune, I leafed through a coffee-table book about asana that I'd recently uncovered in a dusty esoteric bookstore. It featured a collection of mid-nineteenth-century paintings of yoga poses. Rounded forms drawn in a loose calligraphic stroke sat with legs spiraled into lotuses and Matsyendrasanas; chubby figures wearing loincloths twisted their arms above their heads and pointed their eyes to the extreme right or left. Their corkscrew ponytails pointed to the floor as they dangled with bemused expressions in head-, shoulder, and handstands.

The introduction to the book described the art as illustrations from a newly recovered Telugu text authored in the 1830s by the Maharaja of Mysore — the grandfather of the maharaja who later patronized Krishnamacharya. In an introduction, the editor, Norman Sjoman, revealed that Krishnamacharya's teachings had roots in a Mysore Palace tradition that predated the yogi's school by a hundred years. When Krishnamacharya opened his yoga school, he was building on this more-than-century-old precedent, using floor space and even equipment that had served a prior generation of physical culturalists. Already in place were props that Iyengar still used today: wall ropes, those ceiling ropes Prashant liked to hang from, the weights and wooden forms that made up Iyengar's collection of "furniture." The book was one of few to document a direct lineage connecting Krishnamacharya's modern asanas to any specific antecedents.

Sjoman then made a controversial assertion: That forebear was not yoga. Krishnamacharya, like the artist who made these panels, was borrowing material from the Indian martial traditions of wrestling and gymnastics, he claimed. The yoga ropes and even some stretches, Sjoman held, descended not from medieval sages but from wrestlers. As for the relation of asanas to any longer-standing Indian tradition, there was no backup to support the "modern students of yoga who claim ancient authority." He went on: "The history of yoga lacks virtually any kind of historical continuity apart from that of the sparse texts on yoga which are far apart in time, lacking in substantial idea content between them, and without the context of a surviving practice or surviving tradition." It was damning to anyone who wanted to believe that yoga was a primordial Indian spiritual craft. Iyengar was such a person.

I mentioned the book to Iyengar. He wanted to borrow it.

When I walked out into the courtyard after class a few evenings later, Iyengar was stretched out in the open doorway to his house. He was dressed in his usual white dhoti and cotton kurta, and was watching soccer on TV. It was the World Cup final, France versus Brazil. Iyengar had been glued to the games every night. "Hey," he called out when he saw me. I walked over.

He had the book on his lap. "This book. Full of lies," he said. He waved the book in front of me. I wasn't surprised. Yoga was supposed to come from ancient sages, not from the Indian equivalent of sumo wrestlers.

"About wrestling?" I asked.

"No! That man." I had no idea who he was talking about. "Why he is saying that he taught me? You think I didn't know who was teaching me, my Guruji and no one else? Here, here," he said, waving the book more emphatically. He was ranting. "Why would he lie? He says I am his student when I am not his student at all. Now what can I do? Tell me."

I blinked. "I don't know, Guruji. What man? Teaching what?"

"Pattabhi, that man!"

Pattabhi. Of course. Iyengar was referring to a brief reference in the book to Pattabhi Jois. Jois was a contemporary of Iyengar's who, like Iyengar, had studied with Krishnamacharya in the Mysore Palace. He now taught what he called "Astanga Yoga" to a fashionable and primarily American clientele at a school not far from the one-time yoga headquarters in Mysore. Along with Desikachar in Madras and Iyengar in Pune, Jois had been responsible for bringing Krishnamacharya's teachings to America. The embrace of Jois by such celebrities as Madonna and Gwyneth Paltrow had recently thrust Jois into an international spotlight that Iyengar was once accustomed to occupying alone. Jois was quoted in the book as saying that he and Iyengar studied with Krishnamacharya at the same time. Jois, being Iyengar's senior by three years, had been Iyengar's guru, the interloper held.

I believed Iyengar's protest that Jois's statement was false — I eventually spoke with several people who hung around Krishnamacharya's studio in those same years who all remembered Jois studying with the master only briefly and primarily for Sanskrit, not yoga. And Jois's memory was famously unreliable. He once claimed that he and Krishnamacharya traveled to Calcutta together in 1934 and retrieved a lost yoga text written on palm fronds called the *Yoga Korunta*. In that document, he said, they discovered a lost ancient form — the sun salutation. The *Korunta*, however, was still lost, and many cast doubt on this story. In any case, sun salutations appeared in the Aundh maharaja's treatise, *Surya Namaskars*, which predated this supposed excavation by six years.

But Iyengar's disgruntlement seemed out of proportion to the misrepresentation, and I wondered if it didn't have something to do with other, deeper-seated rivalries with Jois. For instance, I knew that aside from their passing acquaintance at the yoga school, Iyengar and Jois had family conflicts that were similar to Iyengar's with Krishnamacharya. Like Iyengar and his teacher, Jois was a Tamil Brahmin. But whereas Krishnamacharya and Iyengar sprang from different growths on the Ramanuja tree, Jois descended from a different branch of Tamil Brahmanism altogether. I now understand that he was, like the man on the train, an Iyer and not an Iyengar — the Iyers were the inheritors of the philosophical tradition headed by Sankara. Jois and Iyengar, it occurred to me, might in some atavistic way be carrying out a centuries-old disagreement — between Ramanuja's embodied teachings and Sankara's abstract ones.

Even that explanation failed to satisfy me, however. Both teachings espoused "embodied" yoga, after all. And in the following weeks, Iyengar's concern for the matter of Pattabhi's falsehoods reached a pitch of obsession. Iyengar stopped me regularly after class to complain about the book. In practice one day, he was demonstrating on a student in sirsasana but drifted to the topic of Pattabhi. "He says he went to Calcutta for this, this *Yoga Korunta*," Iyengar said, his hand sweeping the air emphatically so he nearly toppled the student. The others seemed mystified by his non sequitur. "Krishnamacharya and Pattabhi never went to Calcutta. First of all, that you should know." I was standing at the back of his small audience, but he was addressing his comments to me. "You mean I did not know where my Guruji went? I am a student of my Guruji since 1934. Guruji went somewhere in 1934 and I did not know? I don't want to say the name of Pattabhi even. He is copying my book. Even. Let him at least be honest."

Pattabhi, Pattabhi, Pattabhi. The word became a mantra, uttered in practice, snorted from the back of the room, groused about with Geeta and Pandu and Gloria.

And then, finally, one evening after class, Iyengar answered the question I'd actually asked. He lay in his customary position watching soccer. "Hey," he shouted, calling across the courtyard. "Also. That book. What that man says about wrestling. All lies."

This was the caveat I'd expected. But why had the guru conflated his jealous feelings about the ancestry of yoga with his siblinglike resentment toward Pattabhi Jois? It occurred to me that perhaps it was because the book exposed weak limbs in two family trees that were of enormous significance to Iyengar. The one I'd already known about was the family tree of yoga, which connected Iyengar to his ancestor Ramanuja and, through him, to yoga's primordial past. But the book had exposed a bitter feud between two of Krishnamacharya's disciples.

I couldn't help thinking that somehow at the root of Iyengar's irritation lay the history of his painful rupture with that patriarch. In this world where loyalty was as central a marker of spiritual character as one's daily performance of ritual, Krishnamacharya had gone to his death in 1989 believing that Iyengar had been a *guru drohi* — a guru betrayer. Although pictures of Krishnamacharya, garlanded in orange flowers, still hung in the stairway to Iyengar's asana hall; although, year after year, Iyengar's books honored the guru as Iyengar's "Guiding Light"; although Krishnamacharya eventually submitted to appear at the dedication of the institute in Pune and wrote a prologue to Iyengar's *Light on Pranayama,* what was memorable about their relationship today was that Krishnamacharya nursed a lifelong grudge against Iyengar for what he did.

What Iyengar did was grow increasingly estranged from his guru while simultaneously winning fame, connections, and intimacy with others — new patrons, a wider foundation of clients, and, ultimately, the West.

Iyengar's success did not come easily. In the wake of his funding emergencies following the close of the Mysore school in 1950, Iyengar, now married, became unflagging in his ambition. Today he claimed, if hyperbolically, to have done as many as fifteen thousand demonstrations in his lifetime, sometimes five in a day.

As Iyengar struggled to piece together his livelihood in the 1950s, his yoga began to transform. Perhaps because he understood implicitly the preferences of modernization-minded Indian power brokers, or perhaps because he was swept up in the technophilic mood of the moment, Iyengar began to embrace Western science. This flew in the face of the asana-as-devotion model he'd learned from Krishnamacharya. "The question 'why?' we were not supposed to ask," was how a student from Krishnamacharya's school in Mysore explained this to me. "If we were to ask, 'Why study yoga?' we could have got the beating." Iyengar, on the other hand, began inventing precise permutations of Krishnamacharya's postures in the service of an end. Iyengar's postures could treat illness, and this he discussed in increasingly complex Western terms. He began referring to yoga as a science. He became interested in things Krishnamacharya had never heard of: hydrocele, nasal catarrh, lumbago, inguinal hernia, coronary thrombosis.

Around this time, one of Iyengar's connections in the nationalist movement suggested they make a photo album. Iyengar agreed, only to discover that the friend had just two days to do it. Iyengar meditated, rested, fasted. Then, in the allotted time, he performed 150 postures for the camera — several of them in just a single take. This was nearly five times the number of asanas mentioned in any available yoga source to date, and several of the poses had been invented by Iyengar himself.

As a result of the exertion, Iyengar got a high fever that put him in the hospital. "After my discharge from the hospital, I ran all over Pune to tell my students that I was processing to Bangalore for rest, as I was not well," he writes. "This brought about a relapse, and when I reached Bangalore, the doctor diagnosed my fever as malaria. I was confined to bed for about twenty days."

The outcome justified the toll. When the photos arrived in Bangalore, they were spectacular. He presented the album to Krishnamacharya, but his guru "gave a sweeping statement at once, 'All the poses are wrong.'

"I said, 'Please, tell me where I am wrong so that I can correct them.'

"He said, 'Everything is wrong.'" Krishnamacharya would repeat these same words a decade and a half later when Iyengar published *Light on Yoga*. The poses were wrong, Krishnamacharya insisted. "Where did you get these?"

"By the grace of God," Iyengar retorted firmly. "By the grace of yoga."

Iyengar's transgression was that by publishing his book — in English, for a Western audience — he had revealed an exclusive Indian code: "It should be kept secret very carefully, like a box of jewelry," the medieval sages admonished in the *Hatha Yoga Pradipika,* after all. Iyengar had let the West into the family home, in a very literal sense. For writing, Iyengar bought a table and chair. These forever altered the family's custom of eating on the floor. Seeing the chair also gave Iyengar the idea for one of the first props in his "furniture yoga"— a backbend support. It would become a powerful symbol of his willingness to be supported by Western patronage.

After showing his guru the photos in Bangalore, Iyengar bowed his head and went back to his traveling show. Soon, he shared his album with a wealthy socialite from Bombay named Mehra Vakil. Vakil later contacted Iyengar with exciting news. Vakil was friends with the Indian violinist Mehli Mehta — father of the future conductor Zubin. Mehta was handling the schedule of a man named Yehudi Menuhin, who was seeking out meetings with yogis in Bombay. Iyengar had never heard of the man, but Vakil explained that he was a world-class violinist on a concert tour in Delhi and Bombay. In a doctor's waiting room, he'd once seen a book on asanas. Now that he was in India, he wanted to meet with yogis who would consider taking him as a student.

Vakil proposed that Iyengar travel to Bombay, at his own expense, to meet with the musician. The musician would give him five minutes, she said enthusiastically. A proud man, Iyengar initially balked. Changing his mind proved to be the pivotal decision of his life. He took the train to Bombay. Walking into the Government House, where Menuhin was a guest of the new government, the yogi discovered a sort of wealth and ostentation he hadn't seen since the spectacular palace in Mysore. In Menuhin's room, Iyengar stripped to his shorts and sacred thread. The musician wore loose pants and a polo shirt. The musician was fatigued, it was obvious. So instead of insisting that Menuhin explore his threshold of pain by performing a strenuous asana, Iyengar simply instructed the musician to take off his shoes and socks and lie on the ground. The yogi gave him slow instructions for relaxing each limb of his body and shortly lulled him to sleep.

The musician later described the encounter in his memoirs: "[I] awoke an hour later feeling more refreshed than I had felt for ages." Iyengar had won the competition. His prize was the West.

Iyengar took his first trip to the West as Menuhin's private yoga trainer. The Menuhin family financed it, hiring him as a paid employee at their summer residence in the ski resort of Gstaad, Switzerland, in 1954. If the hotel in Bombay recalled the enchanting Mysore Palace, aglow with a thousand lights in the optimistic haze of a child's dreams, the Menuhins' "cottage" was unlike anything Iyengar had imagined. The lifestyle was different too. In India, you did not wear shoes inside. Here, he didn't even know where to deposit them. The bed was lumpy — not even a distant cousin of his pallet back home. And how cavernous and lonely was his private room. How different were his interactions with Menuhin and his family from those with his students in India. There, no matter how much he had to beg for his work, his Indian students deferred to him as master. Here, he was something else entirely: a man who worked for hire.

Perhaps most unsettling was that the vegetarian offerings were spare — potatoes, he remembers, every day, only potatoes. At home, he still adhered to the codes inscribed in the *Laws of Manu* that required a female member of his clan to prepare all his food. This, like so many other customs, quickly fell away.

One time in Pune, I asked Iyengar if there was someone who could explain to me exactly how the *Laws of Manu* functioned in the day-to-day life of a traditional Srivaisnavite Brahmin. I wanted to understand how breaching those old rules of food, as Iyengar had at the Menuhins', exposed his clan to the outside in a threatening, or perhaps exhilarating, way. It was those trips to the West, after all, that most offended Krishnamacharya.

Iyengar first suggested Biria, who, though he hadn't been born into the clan, had learned its rituals and devotions with the particular enthusiasm of a convert. But then Iyengar alighted on a better source, an eighty-year-old distant cousin who was his daughter Suchita's father-in-law, a man named Rajendram Vijay-araghava Seshadri.

When I went to visit Seshadri, a barefoot middle-aged woman let me into a spacious and airy flat. His daughter, she was busy preparing a meal for her father. When Seshadri came out, I was taken aback. Many people in India still wore traditional clothes of one sort or another — kurtas, balloon pants, bindis, saris. But Seshadri looked as if he could have stepped out of an Indian village circa 1920. His most modern accoutrement was a pair of Coke-bottle glasses in thick black frames that probably dated to before independence. He wore a white outfit that looked something like a linen sheet tied in the shape of a sari. It looped over one shoulder, exposing a bare chest on one side so that I could make out his sacred thread, a necklace containing an amulet with a scroll of the Srivaisnavite's gayatri hymn, and the Srivaisnavite underarm tattoo representing Vishnu's conch shell. His face was painted in elaborate red-and-white markings in the shape of a U, Vishnu's one foot.

His daughter set a cup of coffee in front of me. It was black, the way I drank it, in a country of milky and sweet coffee. I looked at her gratefully. "We heard you don't take milk," she said, smiling.

I was immediately reminded of having once let slip to my grandma, Bea, that I was going on a date with someone who was a native of her own hometown, Brookline. She casually asked his name, which was a Jewish one, and I forgot all about it until I got back to my father's house a few hours later and heard that Grandma had called. She soon informed me that my date was the grandson of her old friends the so-and-sos, who were friends with our cousin so-and-so, whom she'd just been on the phone with and happened to mention his name to.

You can't keep any secrets in Boston, I'd thought ironically at the time. Far from being annoyed, I had a feeling of belonging that instantly erased any bitterness I'd harbored after she insisted I wasn't a Jew. Today, I thought back to what my grandmother used to say about the Boston Brahmins. Each clan was strung together by elaborate wiring. Like electrical charges, those networks kept us alive.

As Seshadri sipped his milky coffee, I asked him why Krishnamacharya so begrudged Iyengar the publication of his book and his visits to the West. Was it because the trips required him to flaunt Srivaisnavite eating restrictions? The Brahmin paused for a long time, shaking his head. "He handed over the yoga, that was all," he said finally. For Krishnamacharya this was next to defiling it. "There are certain customs that with a Westerner, the teacher does not know whether the student is following," he added. In the old palace yoga school, students followed a strict program that crept into every aspect of their lives. "For Krishnamacharya, performing asana was a form of puja, it was a prayer. You, you are what religion?" he asked abruptly.

The question, as it did when Savita asked it, startled me. I shrugged. "Nominally, Jewish. Sort of."

"If someone is not a Jew, he does not go inside the synagogue, correct?" he asked. "It was the same for Krishnamacharya. The teacher wants to know, are they good Hindus? Are they pious? Are they eating right? Do they know the rituals? Does the foreigner take the bath every day?" Krishnamacharya, he went on, did not want to share yoga with the man who didn't understand the integral way it embedded itself in one's life. "On this he was wrong, by the way," Seshadri then stated.

I was surprised by his sudden and strong judgment against

Krishnamacharya. In spite of Iyengar's negative portrayal of him in his autobiography, the late guru was still something of a sacred cow around the institute.

Seshadri continued: "Ramanuja believed in taking all people into Srivaisnavism. He called out his secret mantra from that temple. Do you remember this? So everyone could hear. This was for all castes." Referring to Iyengar as "Guruji," Seshadri added that this was the reason Iyengar, and not Krishnamacharya, was Ramanuja's legitimate heir. He brought yoga to a wider audience. His explanation reminded me of the atavistic split among followers of Ramanuja that had left Iyengar's strain — the Y-Srivaisnavites — more populist than the rival U's.

This confused me, however. As a follower of Ramanuja, wouldn't Krishnamacharya also seek a broad audience? Though he never sought Western readers, Krishnamacharya had in fact published his own primer on asana, a slim how-to replete with photographic illustrations that came out in two Indian languages in 1934. Wasn't there something more specific that could be pointed to, some violation of the *Laws of Manu,* that could more precisely explain the guru's outrage?

Seshadri considered again for a long time. "Yes," he said thoughtfully. "You should not touch the sea, nor should you bathe in it on an ordinary day — only on the new moon or the eclipse. In the old days, you went to a foreign land only by ship. So crossing the ocean would pollute you. Now you go in a few hours in an aeroplane. You don't have contact with the sea. Whether that will apply crossing the ocean today, it is a matter of your views." Krishnamacharya chose the ancient interpretation, he added. Iyengar's modern choice rankled him.

But still, I pressed, this was a question of interpretation. Was there some more incontrovertible betrayal?

Seshadri looked at me long again. Sitting under his gaze, I

once more had that uncomfortable conflicted feeling I'd had so many times during my interviews in India. Here I was, presented on invitation from the guru, asking people to discuss intimate matters of family significance. I told people I was a journalist, but journalists in India were men and wore suits and used big microphones while interviewing people such as the president, and they then put their subjects on TV. In my baggy cotton pants and embroidered Indian blouse, I looked like a yoga student. I was a yoga student. And I was Iyengar's student. This wasn't the first time I'd felt that a person's hard stare was extracting a promise from me. Just as Krishnamacharya wanted to keep his wisdom within the fold, Seshadri's look told me that this revelation he was about to share with me was meant just for us.

"The poor man, he was jealous of Guruji," Seshadri said finally. "Guruji was Krishnamacharya's disciple. Krishnamacharya was proud. On the other hand, he was jealous." Seshadri now recited a verse in Sanskrit. "You remember this?" he asked. I didn't. It was from the Bhagavad Gita, he said, translating: "'A man should defeat all persons except his own sons. If his own son succeeds him, he should be proud.' Unfortunately, in these days, the guru is jealous of his pupil."

I now realized that without my noticing it, Seshadri's daughter had slid up to the table. She was sitting at the far end, resting her head in her palm and watching me with a stare that struck me as friendly and curious, not the least bit mistrustful. She shook her head now as if this was a conversation she had visited many times with her father. "He should overcome that jealousy. He was a yogi," she said.

"Yoga should make people humble," her father agreed, once again giving the impression they'd had the conversation before.

"This is human nature," his daughter said, shrugging. "What to do?"

"You know the Pandavas?" the Brahmin asked, addressing me now. I nodded yes. He was referring to the family in the Bhagavad Gita that tried to avenge its defeat by declaring war on Arjuna's cousins, the Kauravas. "They had fear. They had jealousy. That was their downfall." He rested his head in his palm now in a gesture much like his daughter's. "It's a cruel fate," he added, nodding grimly.

Chapter Thirteen

As I traveled back to the institute, I thought about how often the idea of family came up when people talked about yoga in India. There was lineage, there were rivalries, there was dirty laundry, and there were family secrets. There was joining the fold, converting. In my own family there had been similar alliances, splits. These were often accentuated by talk of who looked like whom, whose qualities each of us had carried across generations — I looked like my grandfather, my sister like our grandmother.

Many families worked like this, but it always seemed to me that the structure of my own family, built as it was around my parents' divorce, heightened issues of loyalty. I'd been negotiating hundreds of permutations of grudge between my mother, my father, and my sister for as long as I could remember. It was exhausting. I'd once read that the hallmark of a dysfunctional family was that you couldn't step away from it without upsetting comfortable patterns. The family member who dared step away invited the hostility of those she left behind. I had certainly been that person.

In my family, loyalties were even further complicated by the fact that my parents' marriage had been, in the social terms of the city where it took place, Boston, a mixed one — Catholic and Jewish. While the couple that stays married reconciles this kind of difference, the divorce only gave my parents, and their families, the opportunity to exaggerate it. This probably explained why twenty-five years after the divorce my grandma, Bea, still liked to tell the story of how my French grandpapa — a real Catholic gentleman, a cigar-smoker and a cardplayer, broad-shouldered and handsome — took her aside after my parents announced their engagement. It was 1961, at an in-law dinner, where, as happened often, a vast cultural chasm revealed itself over the food. They were in my French grandparents' neighborhood — an Irish suburb of Boston — my grandmaman cooking a roast until, as my cook-a-brisket-to-perfection Brookline grandma put it, "it was dead."

"Bea, I'd love to have the wedding here, but if a rabbi came into my house, my neighbors would never speak to me again," my grandpapa reportedly, if apocryphally, told Bea. She graciously offered their Brookline home for the Jewish wedding.

When Bea told this story, it reminded me of what the marriage spawned: the idea that *they* were over there, and *we* here. My French grandmaman once put this to me in very succinct terms herself. I was about twelve, and someone had raised the possibility that I live in Brookline with my father and his new Jewish family. "They'll treat you like their maid," my grandmaman warned me. "If you go over to them, your grandmaman will never talk to you again." Her eyes, black and hawklike, bore into mine. "We won't see you anymore."

The degree to which this intense charting out of territory had left me feeling stateless, so to speak, became clear much later when, on a visit with my father, I borrowed his car to go see my grandmaman on the other side of Boston. The car was a red Jeep Cherokee — the vehicle of choice in Brookline, I slowly realized. As I wound north out of Boston, I found myself in suburbs where there were no Starbucks, no SUVs, no Metro, and no Jewish girls in bright-red cars. No *other* Jewish girls.

My grandmaman was by now too foggy to feel what I did when I showed up in that car, but when I stopped in a convenience store near her house to get directions, I understood how lost I really was. An old man in checks grumbled something in a Boston accent ten shades off from Bea's. I recognized in his cadence the lawn-mower rhythm and long vowels of my Catholic cousins. The man's directions were vague; the North Boston equivalent of "You can't get there from here." I so wanted to shake him and say, "I *am* from here. I'm from *here*. Too."

At the institute in Pune, the Iyengars often made similar demands on our loyalties by discouraging students from attending other yoga schools. Like the injunction against standing on your head while you had your period, another inalienable rule of Iyengar yoga was that you did not dabble in other systems. Even American forms of exercise such as running or weight lifting were discouraged when I was in the teacher training program in L.A., while in India the competition was the garden's yield of yoga strains: Bikram, Bihar, Integral, Sivananda, Astanga, Vini, Anusara. There was any number of objects for the Iyengar family's feelings of rivalry — most notably his nephew Desikachar's school in Madras, Jois's in Mysore. In fact, when I later visited Jois's school in Mysore to interview that guru, I saw a woman I recognized from the Iyengar institute in his class. She approached furtively and begged me not to tell anyone in Pune I'd seen her.

The attitude of my teachers had always confounded me. Iyengar believed yoga helped everyone. What did he or Geeta or Prashant care if another school won students or standing? Wasn't more yoga better than less yoga?

One yoga institution lesser known in the States but no less a source of consternation for Iyengar was nearby Kaivalyadhama. In a hill town outside Pune called Lonavla, Swami Kuvalayananda, a contemporary of Krishnamacharya, had run this ashram from its founding in 1924 until his death in 1966. It was now the oldest continually functioning yoga ashram in India.

I knew Iyengar disparaged the school, but Kaivalyadhama had an important place in India's history. When Menuhin came to India, it was likely Kuvalayananda's work he'd seen abroad, and this swami was among those other yogis beat out by Iyengar for Menuhin's contract. Kaivalyadhama's place in yoga's lore being what it was, I decided to make the trip there.

After the founding of Kaivalyadhama in 1924, the town of Lonavla, nestled into a mountainside that sparkled with natural springs and mineral-rich mud, became known as a center of natural healing. When I arrived, brochures at the train station called attention to the mountain air — at 635 meters, it was indeed exhilarating — as well as the "salubrious climate" and the existence of no fewer than twenty-one health resorts. The brochures referred to Kaivalyadhama itself not as an ashram but as a "sanatorium," and when I arrived at its gates, I was amused to see that its own signage dubbed it a "yoga hospital." Another sign advertised Kaivalyadhama's ties to the state political party most closely affiliated with the ruling BJP, the Shiv Sena.

Kaivalyadhama's alliance to the government was not surprising given what Iyengar had already told me about the center. According to Iyengar, over Kuvalayananda's lifetime he had enjoyed longtime government favoritism at the expense of Iyengar and others, benefiting from a level of cronyism among India's post-independence rulers that Iyengar had always been denied. Documents from the ashram indeed showed that Kaivalyadhama now received several thousand dollars a year from the state and federal governments. While Iyengar had taken commissions from the government here and there, he'd never received outright support.

How this disparity developed was a touchy subject for Iyengar. In his autobiography, he wrote that after the new government cut off funds to the Mysore yoga school, Iyengar and Krishnamacharya learned that government money had been earmarked for yoga after all. They discovered that in the Bombay area, Kuvalayananda was getting most of those funds. Meanwhile, Kuvalayananda had become Bombay's director of the Board of Physical Education, meaning he also controlled the board's monies. Iyengar had his own friend in the Bombay government, Chief Minister B. G. Kher. Kher had once written to Iyengar that his yoga demonstrations were "the best I have seen so far." Iyengar filed several applications with Kher for a share of the monies. All of his appeals went unanswered or came back from the post office as dead letters. Iyengar later discovered why when he learned that Kher was Kuvalayananda's nephew. Iyengar never got over it. Still bristling over the more than twenty-five-year-old conflagration, in 1976 Iyengar wrote a letter to Kuvalayananda's successor at Kaivalyadhama accusing the ashram of "narrowness" and a "lack of cooperation."

Today, it was hard to imagine the two schools competing for the same clientele. As I passed through the gates onto the campus, I saw several officious-looking men in blue jogging uniforms with Kaivalyadhama logos stitched onto their lapels. They were speed-walking through picturesque curving pathways that connected several Raj-era tile-and-stone structures. Much like those at a real hospital complex, each building was labeled according to function: LABORATORY, ASANA HALLS, NATUROPATHY CENTER, FAMILY WARD — though in this case, signs were in Sanskrit as well as English. Inside a main reception area, antiquated and modern scientific and pseudoscientific gadgets were arranged inside glass cases: blood-pressure bracelets; biofeedback machines; gauges to measure pulse, respiration, and galvanic skin response. Dusty bookshelves contained magazines and reports produced by the school; the original edition of one famous book by Kuvalayananda had indeed been published by the government.

Photos and news clippings traced the rise of the late swami's career. What immediately struck me about the images was how different Kuvalayananda appeared from Iyengar. While Iyengar and his mentor spent the 1930s wearing caste paint, lungis, and sacred threads, the white-cloaked, bespectacled Kuvalayananda looked more like a doctor than a yogi. It also couldn't have escaped the notice of his supporters that unlike the more traditional yogis from Mysore, Kuvalayananda had also been a freedom fighter.

Kuvalayananda, according to these write-ups, considered yoga a medical enterprise and undertook hundreds of scientific and pseudoscientific tests to prove its validity. The title of one ashram publication seemed to most aptly sum up his persona as a yogi: *Swami Kuvalayananda: A Pioneer of Scientific Yoga and Physical Education.*

The texts in the ashram's collection revealed that, although few people in America knew Kuvalayananda's name today, his work had in some important way created the foundation for what we now practiced in the West. Iyengar's own transformation from palace yogi to yoga-therapy maverick seemed strongly influenced by Kuvalayananda's own leanings.

In 1933, Kuvalayananda published a guidebook in English describing thirty-two Hatha yoga poses called *Asanas.* He borrowed the poses from two currently circulating medieval texts —

the *Hatha Yoga Pradipika* and the *Gheranda Samhita* — which had been recently rediscovered and distributed through India by those mystical Western Theosophists. But unlike these medieval texts that counseled secrecy, Kuvalayananda's promiscuous writing was meant to reach as many people as possible, Indian or Western. Kuvalayananda also reconceived the postures mentioned in those texts, adding point-by-point instructions and assertions about their salubrious effects — a Westernized technique for the numinous craft. The book recast asana as a mind-body therapy in keeping with the physical-culture vogue of the time. With his pseudoscience, Kuvalayananda laid a Western lexicon over yoga, just as the French doctors Brosse and Laubry did. Names of poses changed; limb placement shifted; health benefits were heightened and specified. Kuvalayananda's take on the *Hatha Yoga Pradipika*'s instructions for headstand, for instance, bolstered the original's claims about bodily well-being by adding a pseudoscientific level of detail.

> *Hatha Yoga Pradipika:* Place the head on the ground and the feet up into the sky, for a second only the first day, and increase this time daily. After six months, the wrinkles and grey hair are not seen. He who practises it daily, even for two hours, conquers death.

> Kuvalayananda: The best way is to start with 15 seconds and to increase the time very cautiously. . . . Some of the most important endocrine glands are situated above the heart. When a man stands upside-down these glands are richly supplied with fresh blood and their health is promoted.

On the shelves beside Kuvalayananda's books, there was also a whole generation of knockoff manuals that repackaged his message. These primers made it even clearer that Kuvalayananda had an undeniable role in creating what yoga later became — something Westernized, goal-oriented, and populist. Reading them brought home the fact that even if B. K. S. Iyengar fulminated against competitors who he believed had stolen his licks — at one time or another Iyengar told me he'd been plagiarized by everyone from Swami Sivananda to Pattabhi Jois to countless former disciples who'd gone off on their own — his mind-body therapeutics, his Western scientific jargon, his commitment to the worldwide spread of yoga, all of it bore the stamp of this rival.

Working through the shelves, I found myself most drawn in by several books published by a follower of Kuvalayananda's named Indra Devi. While reading her books, I got the feeling that even Devi had laid important groundwork for Iyengar in the West. A Russian, Devi helped bring yoga across the Atlantic with her 1959 guidebook *Yoga for Americans* — a forerunner to *Light on Yoga* by six years — which featured photos of the starlet Gloria Swanson twisted into the range of postures. In her own day, Devi's work apparently did for yoga in Hollywood what Madonna and Gwyneth were doing for it today.

I was admiring a photo of Gloria Swanson in eagle pose, suited in full makeup and a fashionable black stretch outfit with shoulder pads, when a man named O. P. Tiwari, the ashram's current director, interrupted me. A gray-haired, bespectacled Indian of about sixty, he was powerfully built, if somewhat soft around the edges, and dressed in a formal kurta. As he led me into his office, I noticed that he spoke flawless English with a slight American accent. Inside, he began chatting with me about sites in New York, and I soon discovered that both of his children were scientists with degrees from American universities and now lived there. He had made upward of thirty visits there to see his children or to speak at American yoga schools. Most recently, he'd visited Jivamukti in Manhattan, a yoga school I remembered for its bright-green and fuchsia walls lined with devotional photos of John Lennon, Mother Teresa, and JFK.

"It's not yoga," he said, referring to the school in New York and shaking his head firmly. "Mostly people in the West have left the tradition and are doing something more physically oriented. One of the aims of doing the postures is to make the channels, the nadis, free, so the pranic movement can flow everywhere. But it doesn't happen if you do athletically. As exercise, the postures act on a muscular level; they don't go deeper." It amused me to hear the director of the institute that had sewn the seeds of yoga's Western manifestation now disparage the results. To listen to Tiwari, modern yoga in the West — faddish, goal-oriented, and physical though it was — was not some Frankenstein monster created in these very labs but a foreign being altogether. In his thinking, as I soon learned, the cause of these unfortunate tendencies could be attributed to certain rival yogis.

Tiwari was describing how Kuvalayananda had revolutionized the practice of yoga in his day by deigning to teach it in classes. On Gurupurnima one year, Tiwari told me, Kuvalayananda went to his guru and asked him to endorse a revolutionary proposal: he, like so many of his contemporaries, wanted to go to Tibet. "Do something for society," his guru admonished him instead. And so, starting in 1916, the future swami began to teach groups, first on his own and then in schools. "Yoga would have died practically if he had gone to Tibet and hadn't done what he did," Tiwari said. "All over there were isolated yogis and monks who kept it alive, but Swami Kuvalayananda brought it to institutions. Gandhi and Nehru all learned from my teacher. Now twelve hundred people a day come to our center. We have forty yoga teachers and six doctors. This is all because Kuvalayananda was the first man to propagate."

I mentioned that Krishnamacharya, through his disciples

Iyengar, Jois, and Desikachar, had also made an important contri-
bution to yoga's longevity.

Tiwari considered. "To me that is not a Patañjali tradition," he
said in response. "Krishnamacharya was very physical. I know
Iyengar got it from him. He must be teaching what he learned.
B. K. S. Iyengar," he added, sniffing slightly. "He is very physical."
It was a searing dismissal, and it would be unwise, to say the
least, to tell my guru.

Chapter Fourteen

Back in Pune, I spent my spare hours outside of class walking or bicycling around the streets, sometimes passing out cookies to the child beggars who clung to the pant legs of travelers. "No mami, no papi, no rupee," they chanted, like a conscience.

One day at the train station, as children tailed me and as flies swarmed in front of my eyes, a girl in a tattered dress suddenly ran up to me. She thrust a bandaged limb in my face. It was leprous. LEPROSY CAN BE CURED: the message appeared on ubiquitous highway signs. Many beggars had it. Pus oozed from the edges of her bandage. Around one side it was black. I saw movement beneath it: maggots. The girl looked at me with a theatrical expression of misery. I would have liked to have given her rupees as I did to the girl my first day, but instead I turned and walked away.

Since I'd made the journey from Bombay, I'd become skilled in rushing through public places, keeping a bearable distance from the suffering all around. But after so many weeks of yoga, I had lost my defenses. Yoga was supposed to make you sensitive. India was a terrible place to do yoga. How could you block out the horrifying inequities at every turn? Yoga was also supposed to make you strong, but I felt too weak for the rigors of the Indian street. How I wished for that practicality I'd had when I got here. No matter how hard I tried, I couldn't reconcile the differences between the streets and the school. I could not make this world coherent.

In the intense environment of the yoga studio, and with the strenuous physical and mental work of developing asanas, I understood more than ever my need to make myself, unlike that world, whole. It had been three years now since I'd experienced that odd feeling in L.A. that had been my mind losing touch with my body. But I was still drawn to hunger as a drug, still missing periods, still enchanted by the thrill of weightlessness as I flipped from backbend to standing. Was I further from the goal than ever? In daily classes and practice and in listening to the ravings of my teacher Geeta, I could see that I was now becoming emotionally vulnerable. In an environment where we were all undergoing profound psychic and physical changes, it was easy to be trusting. At a certain point, though, I wondered if I had left myself too exposed.

Previously, I'd found Geeta amusing, an anomalous character with a bit part in the curiosity that was Iyengar yoga. I realized now that the spectacle was not funny at all. I was learning, as everyone did, that it was impossible to forever avoid breaching rules when your upbringing did not prepare you for a culture as ritual laden as India's.

Away from the school, students groused. A friend who'd gone home sent me his account from the newsletter of an Iyengar yoga association in Europe: "People may think of or go to Pune expecting an immaculate jewel — certainly it is a jewel in the Yogic crown, but it is not immaculate." He went on to describe a class with Geeta identical to what I now witnessed almost daily. He recounted one incident I had been present for in a class on breathing, when Geeta instructed students to practice a particular form of pranayama, "one of those ones where you twiddle your nose with your fingers," my friend wrote. "Geeta found that not everyone had the prescribed length of fingernail and then proceeded to rant on about how people come to pranayama classes with long fingernails." He lamented that she didn't offer the people with long fingernails a different breathing exercise, something perhaps compatible with their manicures. "It would not take too much imagination to suggest this sort of solution to the problem," he concluded. "After all shouting at people does not make their fingernails shorter."

I, like those manicured ones, was erring daily. One day, Geeta instructed us to lie so the soles of our feet pushed into the wall. I searched for a spot, but finding none, I pressed my feet into the marble base of a statue — of, as it happened, Patañjali. The marble was cool. Something felt wrong, but I was tired and light-headed from an hour and a half of contortions. Annie, an assistant from France, came rushing over. "Elizabet'!" she said. She pronounced my name like my French grandmother. "You know the feet are unholy! On Patañjali! You soil the founder of yoga?"

Despite my schooling before I came, my feet were destined for missteps. One day, I placed a plastic bag on the changing balcony before I entered the studio to practice. The bag contained several objects I planned to unload, among them a pair of sandals that I'd bought but never worn. As I did a headstand, I heard a whisper from the balcony. "Chappals?"

The word circulated the studio as in a game of telephone, whispered.

"Chappals?"

"There are chappals?"

The whisper grew to a conglomeration of increasingly frantic sounds, until finally an assistant shouted from the balcony, "Who has brought chappals into the studio? There are chappals on the balcony!"

"Chappals?" I heard the word uttered more, and then, finally, the translation that had eluded me: "Sandals."

My sandals, unworn, had violated our ritual of leaving contaminated shoes outdoors. I immediately whisked the contraband to the courtyard.

When I came back, a petite woman from France rolled her eyes at me conspiratorially. She was a slip of a woman — her boy's body and pale skin gave her a virginal look, accentuated by her attire. Like Geeta in her daytime outfit, she wore all white. She appeared about twenty years younger than she really was, like a child. Her name was Susanne, and I had gotten to know her at a party where she'd talked at length about the tray of food she'd brought: raw vegetables decontaminated in Clorox water for five hours. She'd spent the day preparing them. Susanne, I suspected, was anorexic. Watching her in practice was like seeing a ghost. Frail and white, she looked like someone I'd been once. Knowing her reminded me that I had changed.

In practice, Susanne did not count herself among the women who lay around Geeta in supine poses discussing institute business. Like me, she preferred active poses. I had often watched her arch her back into upside-down circles from which she then lifted a leg or flipped to standing. One day right before she left Pune, Susanne hung from a ceiling rope, Prashant-style. No one was paying attention, really, when she came down. I looked up when I heard howling. Susanne was standing on the ground, grabbing the ropes with her arms as her body went slack and dangled. She kept shouting, big sounds belting from small lungs. Then she crumpled to the floor. Several yoga students rushed toward her to arrange her body in a resting position.

Afterward, Susanne was shaky. She gave me a wiggly smile and said she was glad she was leaving Pune. Her smile crumpled in the same way her body had, her paper-thin skin shrinking like a page in fire.

Later, Annie told me Geeta was angry with Susanne. Susanne had been practicing asanas too strenuous for her constitution. She'd brought this collapse upon herself.

Susanne's specter stayed with me. Gloria was en route for the States and leaving our flat in Pune, so Susanne had arranged for me to take the flat she'd been staying in, a pleasant Raj-era monk's cell with foot-thick walls and painted shutters that looked out on a mango tree. She'd left small jars of health-food products and a container of bleach with which to sterilize raw vegetables. When I moved in, I threw them all away, trying hard to erase her shadow. What Annie had said also disturbed me. If Geeta suspected a problem in Susanne's practice, why hadn't she intervened? Was Geeta secretly analyzing her students, not with any intention to help but to discuss them in gossip with her assistants? I wondered if I'd been wrong in assuming Geeta wiped me from her mind after my own transgression. Was she watching me, too, making ticks in a mental notebook?

I decided to take up the issue with Annie. I knew that Annie and Geeta were close, and that Geeta, whom I could never approach in private, accepted messages through her assistants. I asked Annie for Geeta's advice. If she thought my practice unhealthful, could she suggest a better one? Was there something she could recommend for my missed periods?

Annie looked up and down my figure. "You're too thin, is all," she said. "You want a sequence?" she asked, her finger on her chin, her eyes assessing my body from toe to cornea. Her know-ing look made me wonder if the topic hadn't already come up.

My practice consisted mostly of backbends and upside-down poses. I had developed it over my three years of study with Manouso and Gloria in the L.A. teacher training program, where they recommended poses alongside instructions on timing and sequencing. In Pune, I'd added several poses to my repertoire and come closer to achieving the advanced versions of others, but essentially my practice followed my old teachers' advice.

I did not hear back from Annie, though I noticed Geeta watching me sometimes in practice; she grimaced when I did backbends, said things to her assistants that sounded like my name. Was I imagining it? She was certainly willing to discuss oth-ers. She still ranted in the open about what had happened to Su-sanne. "Why she was doing all the backbends? I knew something, I didn't know what exactly. Why she didn't speak?"

Susanne's breakdown was soon forgotten amid the din of cameras clattering into the studio each day. When their lights clicked on, so did Iyengar. In practice one morning, Pandu told us to come out of our poses. The students gathered behind the camera. Iyengar began setting up the stage for a demonstration, barking out orders to staff and students. "Why no one helps? Eh? The bench over there, get!" Several students leaped to retrieve the prop. "No, not that! The metal, the red, yes!"

Finally, Iyengar stood before the camera, electric. The crew got silent as he moved from one backbend to another. He did the pigeon and the king's pigeon, the wheel and the scorpion. Gloria sidled up beside me, gripping my arm like a child at a carnival. The guru was the picture of control. But between poses he seemed winded, shaking out his mane and huffing.

He stood facing forward now and slowly moved a single arm

and a single leg until he was in Natarajasana, like in that photo before the Taj Mahal that had so hypnotized me my first day. As in that photo, his figure rang out with the harmony of the poses' angles. We all watched, awed at the grace of a body so presumably close to death. There was palpable electricity flowing through the passageways in his limbs.

Then that electric current jolted. And it stopped.

What had I witnessed? No one reacted until Iyengar did. His body jerked again. He released the pose awkwardly and quickly walked off stage. He left the studio, and we all stood in silence.

In a few minutes, Iyengar sprinted in again, but he seemed flustered and unfocused. He stood on the stage and called out a few instructions, and then descended into his signature pose, Hanumanasana, of the flying monkey-god Hanuman. The vision of Iyengar in the pose was usually opportunity to believe him truly capable of flying across an ocean like its namesake. But today he sank, like a heavy ship. Abruptly, he pulled his body from position and bolted again from the room.

We didn't see him after. That week, the cameras shut down. There were no interruptions in the classes, no discourses on the straightness of a leg in practice. Nor was there an official explanation. The school got quiet. The library stayed dark, and those of us who worked there did so in silence, without even the whir of the fan from Iyengar's now-empty desk. Geeta wasn't shouting as much, but her mood was no less black. Every afternoon it was hot and sunny, and then as instantly as Iyengar had disappeared from sight, monsoon downpours made deafening noises on the corrugated-metal roofs of the patio. As the drops became heavier, they sounded like plastic bags crinkling in people's hands. I kept looking over to see if Iyengar was among them, but it was only the air getting thick, and the sky dark, and the rains leaking onto our clothes.

Eventually Gloria confided that what had looked to me like a jolt of current in Iyengar's body had in fact been a jolt of the heart. Iyengar had suffered a heart attack. It had been minor, but he was ordered to stay in bed for a month. No practice, no teaching, no fraternizing with the students who were the lifeblood for the incorrigible performer. Iyengar had overdone it. He seemed very human to me in those days. Every morning when I walked into the studio and scanned the empty space of floor between pillar and wall, I felt a pang. I missed him as I missed my own grandfather, someone very dear, and very flawed.

By now, I had switched to Prashant's classes. As Iyengar's only son, Prashant had once been heir apparent to the Iyengar teachings, and he was now codirector of the institute alongside Geeta and their father. But Prashant was "not a yoga teacher," as Iyengar had confided to me. "Prashant, he is an artist," was how Iyengar put it.

A sensitive young violinist, Prashant had been a quiet child. Because of a condition from birth, one eye habitually rolled and pointed to a far wall, making him clumsy in the physical arts. The young Prashant, unsurprisingly, proved a disappointment as a yogi. "I had an antipathy toward yoga," Prashant admitted to me in a conversation one evening in the library. "I was dealing with something very delicate — music. I thought yoga is not my cup of tea. So although people around me were saying that being the son of a legendary father I should be practicing, doing some yoga, I still did not pay any heed. I had that antipathy seeing the powerful personality of Guruji and his influence. That atmosphere of a yoga class did not go well with my musicalized mind, which was going on a delicate path with a greater emotional touch. I felt that this is something very much more harsh than the fineness of music."

On the founding of the institute in 1975, Prashant neverthe-less prepared to teach classes to the burgeoning new clientele. But mostly he wanted to spend his time alone — listening to the classical Indian music that had once been his only love, poring through Sanskrit texts on Vedic philosophy and legend, practicing arcane breathing techniques from the medieval yoga manuals.

Today, Prashant was charismatic enough as a yoga teacher. He still had the wandering eye: it lolled to the far wall as he spoke. Coupled with an ironic glint in his good eye, a mischie-vous twist to his lips, and a habit of rolling his tongue in his cheek, it gave him an almost absurd bearing. To add to these mannerisms and tics, Prashant had been the survivor of a tragic freak accident in the mid-1980s that left him with a mangled right hand and arm. Despite years of therapy with his father, he could now use neither to much effect, which made it impossible for him to demonstrate poses or give adjustments.

Prashant compensated for his physical shortcomings with talk. In class, he led us into poses and then stood at the front of the room delivering philosophy lectures. He quoted from the Bhagavad Gita, occasionally reminding us to watch each breath as "a feather brushes against the interior lining of the body."

One day, he told us to do trikonasana, triangle pose. He stood on the platform, surveying us. "Watch what is the state of mind when you are in that reflective phase of trikonasana," he be-gan. We were not yet tired. It was possible to listen to each word. "It is inward. Study how the mind should be in trikonasana as much as you study the physical alignments. Glimpse the great mind behind the mind. In yoga we get *instacy,* not ecstasy. When you have ecstasy, you dance with the joy. It is external. In yoga we do not dance. We stay inside." I was finding it hard now, after several minutes in the pose, to keep track of his words. But by listening more deliberately, it was easier to ignore my body as it struggled to keep its position.

"Which is the softest, most fluid part of us?" he continued. He grinned, with a little shy smile. "The mind!" he boomed. "It does not take any time for the mind to do something. It is there as soon as it thinks about it, whereas the body takes some time. Do the poses with the mind!" I followed his reasoning, and then couldn't, and then could again.

Prashant continued his speech as he led us through back-bends. "Do not get the craze! Backbends bring the delirium potential! You will become insensible if you allow the arousal of craze; you lose the sense of judgment. You become passionate. For yoga you require an ideal dispassionate knowledge, unbiased." My mind, challenged to keep alert, remained focused. I began to feel light-headed, but in an unscattered way. My thoughts did not wander as they tended to in daily life and even during yoga, but remained locked on each of Prashant's words. I heard each word as a singular ingot of meaning. The space between the words was empty; I heard a bright ringing sound in the silences.

Prashant now instructed us to do headstand in a ceiling rope. I walked to a rope, my body seeming to glide there. My legs carried me, but the rest of my being, inside and out, mind and muscles, was still. I leaned into the rope and flipped upside down. I felt the pull in my upper back that I'd experienced in the same pose on the live oak in Santa Cruz and, more recently, when Iyengar had adjusted me in headstand. It was someplace deep inside my shoulder. I did not feel pain exactly, only sensation. I could see my whole self curled up in the spot where I felt the pull.

Prashant's words continued, like a lullaby. "Let the mind be still, hold it in its single space. Do not wander." He kept us there a long time and then instructed us to come down from the ropes.

As I stood, blood rushed to my head. Little spots of black gathered at the edges of my vision. I was dizzy. Then the black spots lowered from the upper limit of my vision field and crept up from the base of it. Then everything went black. I felt my body convulsing. Something screamed out from my throat. My vision fragmented into splinters of dark and light. I was on the floor, my body shivering and my torso and head shaking with my sobs. When I opened my eyes, a crowd of yoga students had surrounded me and arranged me so I was lying over bolsters. The first thing I thought was, *Susanne was here.*

For several days after, I felt like my body had undergone a kind of dissolution. I walked around slowly, as if I had to give each piece of myself time to keep up with the other pieces. I had come to Pune to make myself whole, but instead I seemed to be coming apart in yet another way. Something inside me had started to unravel with the nightmares. Now it was as if those threads were becoming ever looser and more untangled. I wondered if those strings that once tied me together would now start to trail out of my body. Once they unsnarled themselves, would anything hold me together at all?

Living in Susanne's flat, I also worried that her fracture was repeating itself inside me. Iyengar too had broken down. Broken. We were all breaking.

Later, I asked Prashant what had happened. "You fainted," he said nonchalantly.

"But why?" I asked.

"Perhaps you have debility. Physical debility, mental debility. What I recommend is, you eat some ghee." Ghee was a thick butter substance used in great amounts in Indian cooking that I was not fond of. Ghee could cure me? I looked at him ironically; he returned the expression in kind.

But I did feel weak. I was beginning to get migraines. A

colony of India's fabled amoebas was squatting in my intestinal track. I ventured to the room on the institute's ground floor where assistants used the computer that was the institute's erstwhile publishing engine. This was also a congregating place for the several longtime students I'd joined volunteering editing and other small tasks. I asked if anyone could recommend a doctor. Annie wrote out the name of a homeopath. Another assistant told me she knew an Ayurvedic doctor. Someone wondered how I felt about Western, or allopathic, medicine.

Pandu wandered in, his ever-present cordless phone attached like an appendage at his wrist. He looked at me with his doe eyes. "What kind of path you need?" he asked. "I find for you. But I know what you need. You want allopathy? homeopathy? naturopathy? No. I know. What you need is sympathy. I give you sympathy."

We all burst out laughing at Pandu's quip, but I wondered if Pandu didn't have it right.

Iyengar was still absent when it came time for me to leave Pune. I would return a year later, but I didn't know that then. Iyengar had given me a personal letter on institute letterhead recommending that I receive funding to come back. But today, his letter seemed as divested of meaning as that original invitation on blue parchment. Just now, I'd studied at the institute every day. Iyengar had spoken to me and charmed me, and Geeta had, in her own indirect manner, taught me. It had not been a fruitless time. But I wondered, thinking of the Peggy Lee song, *Is that all there is?* Geeta had never offered a sequence of asanas, and the integrity of my very being seemed more compromised than ever. The man I had come to learn from had pushed himself to breakdown. I had thrust myself into an institution whose very structures and students seemed on the brink of breakdown themselves. And then I too pushed my physical and emotional limits to the point where I, like so much around me, was coming apart. Was this what I had come for?

I saw Annie in practice on my last day. The studio felt barren — with Iyengar's absence, many regular students had stopped coming, and Geeta was off caring for her father. "You're leaving then, Elizabet'?" Annie said in her accent.

"Yes," I said.

"You know Geeta, she never gave you a sequence."

"I know."

"It's because she doesn't want to. She didn't say, but this is what I think." Annie was looking me up and down again.

"Yes?"

"You know it's because your practice; you are doing everything wrong."

Her words stung. I'd learned from dozens of accomplished students of Iyengar who had guided me specifically for years. Iyengar himself knew I was worthy. I knew Annie was wrong.

"It's as if you've never learned Iyengar yoga," she continued. "What I recommend is, you start at the beginning."

I had practiced for fifteen years now. She was ridiculous.

"You take *Light on Yoga,* you know Guruji has sequences at the back for people who are trying to learn on their own. You start there. Start with lesson one."

I didn't have a chance to say good-bye to Iyengar.

Chapter Fifteen

International flights left Bombay at dawn, making the daytime-only trains to Bombay an impractical form of transport. A far cheaper and more convenient route to the airport was via shuttle on the Pune–Bombay Road, a byway whose place in Indian lore was comparable to that of Highway 17 outside Santa Cruz — among the most overused but undermaintained "highways" in the nation. It was said to be a windy two-lane old cow trail paved with speed bumps every hundred meters. Owing to a lack of urban planning and a population explosion in Bombay that had made a suburb out of faraway Pune, this small trail had evolved into a major commuter artery.

By the morning of my departure it had not rained for several days, meaning that the road between Pune and Bombay would be safe — except in the case of an unexpected last-minute downpour. Of course, by afternoon it was pouring. It was too late to get on a train. My shuttle picked me up, inauspiciously enough, an hour late. We wended in the dark through slumlike dirt-pathed villages on the outskirts of Pune, picking up passengers. This took two hours. I prepared myself for the possibility of missing my 5 A.M. flight. As passengers stumbled from hutlike structures addled by luggage, I watched dust turn to mud and slither into gullies on the sides of our wheels. One passenger, a woman wearing a Punjabi dress and with a bright, engaging stare started the immediate drill that was par for the course upon meeting a foreigner. "And you are?" she quizzed me.

I was not interested. "American," I mumbled, looking back to my book.

The next passenger was a portly man wearing an ill-fitting suit; he carried a briefcase with the stitching coming apart. "Which country?" he demanded.

"America," I said, looking down.

I was thinking about how I was bored of yoga, sick of Geeta, fed up with people saying "yes, yes" when they meant "no, no" or weren't listening to begin with. I was tired of reeking toilets and hundred-year-old roaches and talking to Italians and Russians and Maharashtrians with whom I could not communicate with any nuance or specificity. I'd lost patience for the way Maharashtrians said "ayy" at the end of every phrase in a way that meant "Sure, even though I have no idea what you're talking about." I felt the pain in my sacrum and the first dizzying hints of a migraine. I'd had it with India, with dirt in the air, amoebas in the water, contaminated chappals that caused blisters, and I'd had enough of blisters that drew foot fungus that prevented them from ever healing; hard mattresses and mosquitoes and ricksha horns and pigs on the street and filthy sacred cows with crooked painted horns and limbless beggars and lepers with damp bandages thrust in your face and mean little boys demanding spare rupees and the fake smiles of merchants. I was done with the isolation of my foreign language, the impenetrable wall of noncomprehension, the lonely symbol I embodied as a foreigner in India. I was aching to leave India and thinking that if this shuttle never traversed this makeshift pass, I might never get to.

Outside Pune, the highway stretching ahead was indeed little more than a street, pockmarked by potholes, broken up by sharp ninety-degree turns, and made barely navigable by speeding tin-can Marutis careering from the other direction carting neatly dressed businessmen with Nintendo eyes.

This vista lasted only a short while, however, for we were only minutes beyond the slums of Pune when we got a flat. The driver cursed and swung open his door, and a torrent of rain and mosquitoes flooded in. The buoyant woman in the Punjabi asked me what time my flight was leaving. She settled back comfortably into her double bench and said that hers wasn't until 10 A.M. She began to crochet. The man with the briefcase nodded cheerfully. His flight was at noon.

I watched out my window as the driver kicked at the tire a few times before prying it loose. He walked to the side of the road and stuck out his hand, hitching. Soon he got on the back of a scooter, holding the tire so it made a large O on the seat behind him. I watched the O slowly disappear into the mist of rain and dark on the long road reaching out to Bombay. The O was like the shape of someone's mouth, saying, "O look at the mess you're in."

The road was now deserted. Without the driver's flashlight, it was as dark as it was quiet. "Is he coming back?" I asked my shuttle mates.

The woman in the Punjabi shrugged, crocheting.

"Oh, sure," said the man with the briefcase. "No problem. Just ten minutes." Soon everyone else in the bus was nodding at me, echoing in false voices, "Just ten minutes, madam. No worry. No problem."

Two hours later, the driver had not returned. It was now 11:00 P.M., and the trip to the airport was four hours in good weather. Or so it was said. There were six hours left until my flight.

The driver did return, tire perched behind him on the back of another scooter. "Come down," he said to me. "Your flight is at what time?"

I told him.

"Come."

Outside, the driver directed me and another passenger from the shuttle into a Jeep packed with young Indian men. "Who are they?" I asked.

"Please, madam," the driver said.

"Where are they going?"

"Yes, yes. Safe journey!"

A chorus erupted from inside the shuttle bus, the passengers all urging me inside the Jeep. They sounded like paid promoters assuring me of the efficiency and goodwill of this nation called India.

"Yes, madam. Inside!"

"Yes, madam. Ten minutes only."

"Your plane, you will get!"

I got in. I was the only woman. I was wedged in the middle of the backseat between two young men, one of whom shoved his thigh practically into my lap. The other leaned over me with a seedy grin. "Excuse me, madam. Which country?"

"America," I offered, staring fixedly at the dark road.

We were silent for a long time, but the second man, a boy, really, was still watching me eagerly. "Because, madam, I am going to Chicago." He pronounced the *ch* hard, as in *chortle*.

"Good," I said.

Hindi film music blared loud from the front seat. The Chicago-bound kid beside me began singing along, bobbing his head from side to side with the music. I slid my carry-on bag from my lap onto the seat between me and the boy on my other side, shoving his thigh away from mine. He snorted.

We passed through a town. A ragged sadhu clung close to the walls as he hobbled down the street. There was first a woman, barefoot, and then a dog, limping, blocking our path. The driver bleated his horn at them. I thought once again of how India looked to me the day I got here, and how it had not changed much, and how the world inside the yoga institute was very far from the world that was India.

Chicago Boy leaned over me. "Are you hungry?" he asked, his head still bobbing so that he seemed to be looking at me from upside down. "We could stop for dinner."

"No time!" I cried. But I had no cards. I suspected that the boy had rented this Jeep to get to the airport himself. The other men were his drinking buddies and a hired driver. The other shuttle rider and I had no more rights than hitchhikers would. "If you're hungry, I have food," I offered, sliding a tofu sandwich from my carry-on. Chicago Boy frowned at it.

"Ten minutes only," he assured me.

Shortly, we pulled into an outdoor garden restaurant. The air was cool. We were in Lonavla, home of Kaivalyadhama — "land of freedom." Chicago Boy had never heard of Kaivalyadhama or the seminal mind-body experiments conducted by Swami Kuvala-yananda. He knew Lonavla as a posh retreat for stylish Bombay-ites — "a place to come picnic." At 2 A.M. it was bustling with well-dressed and giggly Yuppies. I remembered the man I'd met on my first journey across this pass: *India doesn't give a damn about yoga.*

"You take food?" The other boy leered.

"No," I insisted.

"We buy you pop," Chicago Boy pressed.

I followed them to a table. The other men from the car scattered at other tables, and quickly all were shoveling down large portions of chicken biryani and roti. I tried not to feel disgusted at the food. I hadn't seen an Indian eat meat since I got here — in our world, meat was as impure as shoe soles. No one at my table talked until the food was done. Then Chicago Boy, wiping biryani grease from his mouth with the back of his palm, looked at me balefully. "Do you know Chicago?" he asked. Suddenly his eyes looked very big, and his face and body very small. He had light-brown eyes with dark ridges at the edges of his corneas and deep black shadow lines around his eyelids. His skin was very dark. He told me he was going to Chicago to take a job as a computer engineer. He'd lived in London for a year doing the same thing, and he didn't like London. One time, he'd been walking down a street in London and was surrounded by a group of adolescent boys. They started throwing pieces of garbage at him and calling him names — "beast" and other things — until he ran away.

"Tell me something," he asked, leaning forward to hold eye contact. "In U.S., how are people? Friendly?"

At that instant, I saw him in America, a young man with dark skin and a foreign accent who had every right to be welcomed. I felt, strangely, a surge of national defensiveness not unlike what my shuttle mates must have felt when I hesitated outside the Jeep by the side of the Pune–Bombay Road. I didn't want Americans to make a bad impression; I didn't want him to meet one Chicago racist, and if he did, I wanted him to know there were people he could call.

"Some of us, yes." I gulped. He still held my gaze. I saw nothing challenging, nothing mistrustful, only the open face of a person at the outset of a daunting journey. I'd been there myself.

Chicago Boy got me to my plane on time. When we got out of the Jeep my shuttle mate and I offered to give him money to help cover the cost of the car, but he refused. "I was just trying to help out." He shrugged. I gave him my number and e-mail in the States and told him to get in touch if he had any problems. He was my goofy angel.

Something changed in me on that traverse to Bombay, through that tunnel that was the Pune–Bombay Road. I had come to India to do yoga, but in the process I was being drawn to the place, to its irreconcilable contradictions, to the way that what repelled me one minute called me the next. I knew that to understand yoga, I needed to engage the country it came from, needed to understand how it, like me, could come to make *sense,* how it could look like something whole.

I also knew that Iyengar called, not Iyengar the head of the yoga school or even Iyengar the yogi, not Iyengar the healer or Iyengar the magician or Iyengar, as he was once known, the Man of Rubber. But Iyengar the Indian, Iyengar the patriarch, Iyengar the man who had made me feel welcome despite the flaws at his school. Iyengar the friend, whose presence in my life I cherished, Iyengar who had welcomed me to his family.

Chapter Sixteen

Back home, I followed Annie's unsolicited advice. I practiced the sequences in *Light on Yoga,* starting from lesson one. I quickly progressed toward Iyengar's advanced curriculum. I'd never examined the lists in his book carefully before, and as I came to feel their logic in my body, I doubted that Annie had either. They represented Iyengar's philosophy of physical yoga from forty years before. The sequences consisted of strenuous postures I'd never been exposed to in an Iyengar class. To get through a series took over two hours. Their effect was not unlike what I'd felt when I'd been starving and sick: I was euphoric, hyperalert, calmed, meditative. Had my earlier, however unhealthful, experiences of reverie been somehow essential to my development in yoga? Had they been a prelude to what I was discovering now, to something more sanctified and mysterious? There were saints, ascetics, and so-called holy anorexics who experienced God after extreme acts of physical sacrifice. Were my previous otherworldly feelings related to the flights of these figures: Jesus fasting at Tiberias; Ramakrishna in ecstasy after days in lotus; Saint Catherine of Siena starving before she communed with God? Was it the grueling rigor of these new sequences that connected yoga to the divine? A holy experience seemed encoded here, in the very way that pain helped you encounter a different world. I wondered if it was the practice in the book, and not necessarily the therapeutics of Pune, that made this world accessible.

I also felt as if I'd stumbled into another realm of yoga. I'd heard the term *subtle body* applied to yoga, and now it rang very true. Slipping between states, feeling the very *slip*periness of the physical world, was something I had perceived many times: in dreams; as a girl, when I believed I was levitating; once or twice in savasana after a yoga class; in the druglike haze of starvation; in the park during the monsoon in Pune; and even when I'd fainted in Prashant's class. The edges of the world sometimes became indistinct, and I slipped across them in a liquid state, without boundaries myself. By practicing these sequences alone now, that slipperiness was becoming a state I could access at will.

One time, in Pune, in response to that challenge that so irritated the family, Prashant said, "We have the question which really puts our back to the wall. 'Your yoga is really physical yoga,' they say. The best way to counter a question is with a question. What is *physical?*" Understanding a new definition of *physical* suddenly seemed at the very heart of yoga's ability to heal me. Doing so was showing me a large and awesome universe. My capacity to feel was unbounded by the constraints of my physical outline. Kaivalya, or freedom, was sometimes defined as breaking the bonds that tied you to the material realm. But that was Sankara's vision, in which reality was actually maya, freedom the act of transcending it. Just now, the material world

193

seemed to be seeping into a larger and boundless entity. As in Ramanuja's breakthrough philosophy, the goal seemed to be a state in which the material and the metaphysical were integral and interconnected. Why it felt like bliss I did not yet know.

I did know that I would go back to India, to understand yoga at its most essential, to understand where it came from and how it changed when Iyengar channeled it to our modern West. What *was* yoga, really?

"I have never been in a country," the novelist Paul Scott wrote about India, "where the past impinges so little." I already knew the many ways yoga lacked a deep history. Now I wanted to know the ways it had one.

When I was in India, Biria had recommended one book for its sketch of yoga's philosophical and anthropological roots. *Yoga: Immortality and Freedom* was written in 1954 by Mircea Eliade, a Romanian who had been a protégé of the great Indian philosopher Surendranath Dasgupta. I read it when I got home. The book stressed how little was known about yoga's history. The sources on ancient yoga disagreed over even the dates of key texts. Patañjali's Yoga Sutras were authored anytime between 2000 B.C. and 500 A.D., and there was no consensus whatsoever as to whether their author was human and not a thousand-headed cobra. Even the works of Ramanuja had no grounding — great spans separated them, suggesting multiple authorship or even ghostwriting. The dates of medieval Hatha yoga and its three best-circulated extant texts — the *Hatha Yoga Pradipika,* the *Siva Samhita,* and the *Gheranda Samhita* — stretched between the tenth and seventeenth century. Where and what period the asanas came from was an open question. Some pointed to the Indus Valley seals at Mohenjo Daro, dated 2000 B.C., in which figures could be construed to be sitting in the lotus position; others convincingly pointed out that they just happened to be seated cross-legged.

One thing the sources agreed on was that in the absence of a clear lineage, yoga movements *did* borrow from that early philosophy laid out in the Patañjali sutras. These, while adhering to the rough outlines of Vedic thought, encoded an eight-step system to attain union with God. With lengthy tangents about how to simultaneously exist within the physical and metaphysical realms, the sutras offered a "sadhaka" practical training to gradually become more sensitive to the metaphysical — to the point of ultimately performing supernatural feats. The steps began with instruction on following ethical principles and then led the student through the practice of breathing and asana before finally embarking on four levels of meditation. The discussion of breathing and asana was more concerned with extolling their virtues than with actually describing them, mentioning only three particular asanas — or seats — to facilitate meditation. Meditation, too, was a means to an end: samadhi, the description of whose bounteous glory took up the bulk of the text.

Some thousand years after the Sutras were written, medieval ascetics began developing ritualized practices that, like Patañjali, aimed to realize unification with God. There was no evidence as to how the term *yoga* reached them, but because these ascetics believed it took a great act of will to achieve this union, they called their system *hatha* yoga, or the yoga of force. Texts from this period discuss a total of thirty-two painful physical postures. The detailed descriptions of these postures formed the basis for twentieth-century yoga.

Eliade's book described medieval yoga as the result of a nearly accidental synergy, an encounter between several coexisting cults that employed mystical, physical, and often metaphorical programs to accomplish spiritual oneness. The alchemists, for instance, believed that making alloys of different kinds of gems and metals not only promoted immortality but also figuratively stood in for the fusing of self and God. Also influential were Sufis, Tantrists, and many small cults, including the followers of the twelfth-century saint Gorakhnath, known for his magical abilities to tame wild animals, heal the sick, and control his breath by swallowing the tongue.

For Eliade it was especially significant that the yogis of this time did not, strictly speaking, descend from Patañjali. They were part of a "new magico-religious synthesis," he wrote, which explained why the term *yogi* soon came to describe almost anyone dabbling in mystical arts: "from the sorcerer and fakir who perform cures and miracles to the noblest ascetics and loftiest mystics, taking in cannibal magicians and extremist Vamacaris (celibates) along the way."

Unlike Patañjali's yoga, medieval Hatha yoga was as concerned with the physical as with the metaphysical. Where Patañjali's metaphysics survived was in the idea that all must be merged into the universal spirit as, in the words of the *Hatha Yoga Pradipika,* "camphor disappears in fire, and rock salt in water." The yogi, wrote Eliade, "sees the element of earth become 'subtle' and dissolve in water, water dissolve in fire, fire in air, air in ether, etc. until everything is reabsorbed into the Great Brahman."

If yoga meant *union,* as in the English cognate *to yoke,* then the Hatha yogis would "yoke" themselves to the divine. But for them, self joined firmament by way of the body. This required fusing the body's various channels, or nadis, which represented the masculine and the feminine; the moon and the sun; and the great rivers of India, the Yumuna and the Ganges. The term *hatha* also cryptically referred to the joining of sun and moon, an idea symbolically embedded in the two syllabic Sanskrit characters *ha* and *tha.*

If the body could contain things that were not actually physically contained inside it, it was because there was this "subtle body" overlaid onto the material body. It was in this body that the yogi accomplished, in Eliade's words, the "abolishment of all experience of duality." The subtle body, like the tether around the torso of Vishnu that so impressed Ramanuja, resided in that ether between earth and the divine.

Just as the Brahmins of Ramanuja's time believed that their spiritual endeavors depended on their purity, these medieval yogis also believed that to abolish duality in the body required, above all, becoming pure and clear. The *Hatha Yoga Pradipika,* probably written in the fourteenth century, guided the practitioner in ablutions including asanas and breathing patterns to cleanse the channels, or nadis, running through the body. Kriyas, or cleansing rituals, involved physically clearing the openings of the body with water, air, and strips of cloth.

Like their twentieth-century successors, these yogis saw a connection between cleanliness and godliness. "When the body becomes clean, the face glows with delight," the *Hatha Yoga Pradipika* promised. When the "eyes are clear, body is healthy, *bindu* [semen] under control, and appetite increases, then one should know that the Nadis are purified and success in Hatha Yoga is approaching."

Unfortunately, the only documented link between these medieval yogis and those popularizers from the twentieth century is the resurrected texts. The travel literature of curious onlookers hints at a loose continuity. But through the eyes of these outsiders, it's hard to pick out the esoteric from the freakish — *yogi,* after all, referred to all mystics.

Modern yoga can only be traced back to the time when the medieval texts were recovered — barely more than a century ago. The two oldest visual depictions of actual asanas are roughly contemporaneous and possibly unconnected. One appears in a

German survey from 1907 of the Hatha yoga literature by an aficionado named Richard Schmidt, *Fakire und Fakirtum*. He included thirty-two loopy, matter-of-fact watercolors titled in Sanskrit that closely correspond to the written descriptions of the thirty-two postures in the *Gheranda Samhita,* which itself might date only as far back as the seventeenth century. Schmidt writes that his mentor, the German Indologist Richard Karl von Garbe, commissioned the illustrations in 1886 from a yogi in Benares, who re-created the postures working from Garbe's copy of the *Gheranda Samhita,* newly translated from Sanskrit to German. The outcome prefigures the postures taught by Krishnamacharya a half century later.

The Mysore Palace panels from the book that so disturbed Iyengar were created at roughly the same time as the German attempt. The panels include poses with names that appear in the *Gheranda Samhita,* though these postures don't much recall the written descriptions. The collection also shows several extra postures that the book's new editor traced to Indian gymnastics exercises from the nineteenth century. To find a continuous lineage between these postures and the asanas of the medieval yogis would be, as those yogis would have appreciated, an act of will.

Something resembling what we now consider yoga nevertheless caught the interest of travelers to India across the centuries, from the rationalists and Spiritualists of the nineteenth century to the Orientalists of the eighteenth, from rogue traders to colonists, from explorers to conquerers. Whether it was through a lens of science, mysticism, voyeurism, or opportunism, everyone had their own way of looking at these mystics. Today, with so many overlapping lenses, what remains of the history of yoga is like an image through polarized glass — shiny but murky.

The travel literature tells a story of grotesque characters and bizarre ritual. In one of the earliest recorded yoga "sightings," probably dating to even before the *Hatha Yoga Pradipika,* Marco Polo, on his Eastern tour from 1275 to 1298, came upon adepts at the chili ports on the southwestern tip of India in Malabar. Here, wrote Polo, were "Bramin" enchanters who performed the mystical art of stupefying fish. Some of them were austere religious types devoted to "temperance and chastity." They called themselves "chugis" and lived to a hundred and fifty years in "health and vigour."

After the fifteenth century, evangelical-minded wanderers came to portray yogis as magicians and fortune-tellers, bearers of elixirs of immortality and alchemically transmuted metals. The seventeenth-century French Jesuit François Bernier, writing in his memoirs, attempted to construe the yogis' cosmology as they plied him with mystical tonics and pastes made of crushed gems:

> Frequently these pious jauguis are absorbed in profound meditation. It is pretended, and one of the favoured saints himself assured me, that their souls are often rapt in an extasy of several hours duration; that their external senses lose their functions; the jauguis are blessed with a sight of God, who appears as a light ineffable white and vivid, and that they experience transports of holy joy . . . which defy every power of description.

Dara Shikuh, a Mughal prince who was a contemporary of Bernier's, reportedly sought the spiritual counsel of one such "Hindu ascetic" in 1653. "Dara Shikuh attempted to have Baba Lal Das analyze, in Hindu terms, his own religious experience as a Muslim," interprets a French account of their meeting written in 1926 by the Orientalists Louis Massignon and Clément Huart. "Upon pronouncing the holy syllable *Om,* does man enter paradise?" the Muslim reportedly asked the ascetic.

"In truth, there are good results from reciting the supreme

word," the wiry saint began ambiguously. "But it really brings you the same understanding as the fact that consciousness is never counterfeit. It knows the real coin from the forgery, even if both are stamped from the same mint."

Philosophical conundrums had no place in the accounts of the Westerners who traveled East. For the gem traders, it was alchemists who captured their interest. A French diamond merchant named Jean-Baptiste Tavernier, who came to India with a wave of seventeenth-century Dutch spice merchants on a chase for legendary stones — he is believed to have spied the Koh-i-noor diamond long before it was known to the West — discovered an "infinite multitude of *faquirs* that swarm all over." He included in his travelogue a detailed engraving illustrating eight loinclothed and longhaired sadhus who performed several categories of ritual for the trader. One suspended himself from a tree, Prashant-style. This ascetic, wrote the witness, "never slept day nor night. When he finds himself sleepy, he hangs the weight of the upper part of his body upon a double rope that is fastened to one of the boughs of the tree; and by the continuance of this posture, which is very strange and painful, there falls a humour into their legs that swells them very much."

Magical yogis continued to hold the attention of traders, a generation of economic voyeurs mystified by exotic, magicianlike faithful performing believe-it-or-not acts. The British industrialist James Forbes described encounters with "gymnosophists" during his stint as a senior merchant with the East India Company. John Fryer's *A New Account of East India and Persia,* dated 1698, described how one adept held "his Body with his Feet bolt upright, and so continued standing on his Head the space of three hours very steddily, that is, from Nine till Twelve; after which he seats himself on his Breech cross-legg'd after their way of sitting, and remains so without either eating or drinking all the rest of the Day."

In 1829, a report from Calcutta testified that a Brahmin levitated in a seated position four feet in the air for forty minutes with his hand lightly resting on a crutch. By this time, the accounts had turned toward the preoccupations of an industrializing world. Could mystical acts be explained through rational techniques? Was there such a thing as magic? Yogis seemed to defy the dichotomies. Their "tricks," as the rationalists saw them, or "feats," as the Spiritualists saw them, required extensive testing, probing, questioning, and systematized trial. The rope trick, the basket trick, the cobra trick: a whole genre of literature alternately praised and debunked the handiwork of yogis. The most controversial illustration was the burying-alive trick.

There was one practitioner of this craft who received a large share of the scrutiny. He performed his miracle in the princely state of Lahore, now part of Pakistan, at the behest of the maharaja, a legendary palace figure named Ranjeet Singh. Miniature paintings from Singh's court, in lurid reds and oranges and blues, illustrated the beginnings of future relations between maharajas and yogis. They showed a rotund Singh on his dais, in capacious white robes and colorful turbans, surrounded by sweetmeats and hookahs and consorts. In an atrium of white marble flooring, entered through archways astride patterned stained glass windows, Singh held court with an endless stream of exotics. There were court jesters and astrologers, miracle workers and eunuchs, harem guards and yogis.

When I saw those miniatures in an exhibit on Sikh art, I imagined that among those yogis was Haridas, who claimed he could lie buried underground with neither air nor food to sustain him, corpselike, for forty days. I was particularly enchanted by Haridas's story because his technique harked to those skills that Krishnamacharya carried from his Tibetan tutor a century later. And, unlike the rope trick and the basket trick and the cobra trick, the burying-alive trick seemed related to a practice recommended in the *Hatha Yoga Pradipika:* "He whose mind is neither sleeping, waking, remembering, destitute of memory, disappearing nor appearing is liberated." Perhaps this man was the link — to both future and past.

Maharaja Singh too was beguiled by the man's claims. The maharaja was skeptical, wrote John Martin Honigberger, a chronicler from the princely court, in his memoirs, *Thirty-Five Years in the East,* published in 1852.

> To convince himself of the truth of the assertion, [Singh] ordered the faqueer to be brought to court, and caused him to undergo the experiment, assuring him that no precaution should be omitted to discover whether it was a deception. In consequence, the faqueer, in the presence of the court, placed himself in a complete state of *asphyxia,* having all appearance of death.

Claude Wade, the British Resident in the Lahore Court, wrote in a report about the 1837 "exhumation": "Runjeet Singh, who was attended on the occasion by the whole of his court, dismounting from his elephant, asked me to join him in examining the building." An illustration accompanied the text: with a weak chin and an idiot's grin, Haridas is portrayed as a quaint magician freak. "As my object was to see if any fraudulent practices could have been detected," Wade wrote,

> I proposed to Runjeet Singh to tear open the bag, and have a perfect view of the body before any means of resuscitation were employed. . . . The legs and arms of the body were shriveled and stiff, the face full, the head reclining on the shoulder like that of a corpse. [The medical gentleman] could discover no pulsation in the heart, the temples, or the arm. . . . A few minutes afterwards the eyeballs became dilated, and recovered

their natural color, when the fakir, recognizing Runjeet Singh sitting close to him, articulated in a low sepulchral tone, scarcely audible, "Do you believe me now?"

One of the things that most intrigued me about these travel stories was the extent to which Westerners seemed to have had most stake in keeping alive the legend of India's exotic and magical past. It was British chroniclers who immortalized Haridas, Theosophists who recovered the medieval texts, the German Garbe who commissioned the first illustrations of the *Gheranda Samhita*. This led me to the natural next question: If the actual practitioners never told the story of their practice, had there been some element of fraud, mixed with willful fantasy, at work in keeping Hatha yoga alive? Even Kuvalayananda owed a debt to the Russian Indra Devi, not to mention to the author of one popular guidebook to yoga asana that predated his own: *Hatha Yoga, or, The Yogi Philosophy of Physical Well-Being, With Numerous Exercises,* published in 1904 by a self-styled mystic with Spiritualist leanings named Yogi Ramacharaka. But Ramacharaka, it turned out, was an American — his real name was William Walker Atkinson. The name Ramacharaka was but a "borrowing" from a yogi who reportedly came to the World's Fair in Chicago with Vivekananda in 1893, but even that yogi may never have existed.

For those invested in the very Indianness of yoga's roots, the preponderance of figures like Ramacharaka — "that English trickster," as Eliade described him — had long been a sore spot. As Eliade put it, yoga risked being overtaken by "all the popular superstitions about a mystical, magical India, all the nonsense of Ramacharaka's books, all the foolishness of the Indian pseudo-culture, so fashionable in Anglo-Saxon countries." And yet as much as Eliade fulminated against a "false" yoga, he well knew that most of yoga's history was equally flimsy.

It seemed to me now that a lot of people were invested in defining yoga as one particular thing. But for me, to experience yoga was to encounter its very slipperiness. This was the beauty of it. With so many overlaps and falsehoods, yoga's most defining characteristic was not its legitimacy but the very uncertainty of its paternity. Yoga was something we assimilated into our contradictory, multilayered world, something that was never wholly Indian, never one particular authentic anything.

Even the maverick Iyengar seemed caught up in the problem of the corruption of yoga, especially at the hands of those Westerners who so romanticized it. Yoga's various monikers had always been a minefield for me. Iyengar claimed to teach the eight-limbed "astanga" system of yoga derived from Patañjali. So when I referred to "Iyengar yoga," he exploded. "My friend," he shouted, "I don't know why they came up with that term. Maybe in America this is what you say, but I don't understand how you can put the name of a mortal to the word *yoga*. This is Patañjali yoga."

Another time, I let slip the term *hatha*. "Don't say *hatha yoga*," he rebutted, as if it was at all conceivable that his teachings had leapfrogged straight past the medieval texts to bridge Patañjali with the present. "It is not the kriyas. We follow only astanga yoga, not the kriyas."

On the other hand, Iyengar found the terms were too limiting. The word *Hindu* raised a different kind of red flag. "Don't use the word *Hindu*," he protested when I asked about his orthodox upbringing. "I said I was born in India, but yoga is universal. Probably if I was born in America and if God had graced me to do yoga, I would have done yoga, too, with the same mentality."

In those conversations with Iyengar, yoga splintered into so many contradictory shards. The system I was learning was indefinable: an amalgam of Kuvalayananda's borrowings from Western science; the nationalist reinvention of yoga; the sinister authoritarian bent of its Fascist past; vestigial medieval traces; the innovations of Krishnamacharya; the orthodoxy of Srivaisnavism; and what spilled over into Iyengar's own modern sensibility from sources as far-ranging as Zen Buddhism, Freudian psychology, the Vegetarian Society of Britain, Gandhi, Theosophy, Indian dance, Western medicine, gymnastics, and even soccer — not to mention an Americanization encompassing such practices as chanting, breathing, meditation, gymnastic feats, step class, and burning incense before a photo of John Lennon.

Iyengar resisted being defined precisely because he wanted to define himself. The fuzziness of the facts about yoga created a void in which yoga could become exactly what its disparate promoters wanted it to be: for Iyengar, a past-life dream whispered by ghostly ancestors; in India, proof of an illustrious tradition of discipline and learning on a subcontinent where centuries of colonization had undermined morale and national pride; in America, a feel-good alternative to a competitive sports culture; and for all of us, a way to imagine a time and place where occult and secret ritual could open up a universe of awe and the unknown, a world less mundane than the here and now, a practice, a philosophy, and a way of life into which anyone could pour everything one wished to believe about one's self.

Mutable and lacking in definition, yoga, like the idea of a universal spirit, was becoming for me not a site on which to reconcile differences, but a receptacle into which many contradictions could simply intermingle — *like camphor in fire, like rock salt in water.*

Chapter Seventeen

A year after I left India, I stepped off a plane back into that same wet heat to study again at the institute with Iyengar. This time I landed in Delhi, and from there a friend and I decided to visit Agra, site of the Taj Mahal and its echoing geometries. The train would have gotten us to Agra in three hours had we caught it, but we didn't. We went to the bus stand. There, we found none of the signs, lines, gates, or information agents of those orderly airports back in the States. With buses scattered about randomly, it looked like a graveyard for abandoned transit vehicles. Hawkers and passengers thronged around the dilapidated buses. I'd been studying Hindi, but it was too soon to discern key words. Outside of several buses, men chanted a word that sounded like "Agra," our destination, but they couldn't all be going where we were, and as it turned out, the word was *agla*, or next, as in *next bus*.

Signs on bus fronts were in Devanagari — the script of Sanskrit, modern Hindi, and Marathi. Each word looked like a shantytown in the overcrowded megalopolis that was the script. Each letter was a building, with additions built on — up top, on the sides, down below, a clutter of curls and dashes and corners, cupolas, porches, basements, minuscule markers whose meanings I could glean no more intuitively than I could the logic of Delhi.

We stood on the pavement working our jaws as we sounded out words. The words on storefronts and street signs had been impenetrable to me when I'd been in India before, ever present but invisible against the busy Indian streetscape. Reading them today felt like watching a mist come into focus. Slowly, order emerged out of a chaos that I hadn't even been aware existed. I remembered my first introduction to the yoga asanas — so foreign, so impossible to replicate — and the feeling of epiphany when I could finally fit my body into a prescribed shape. If I could read the script, maybe someday I could understand India — read it like a text, a tangible object with a finite number of pages.

The feeling was elusive, though, for when we did read out place names, none said *Agra*. On buses with names of cities that might be close to Agra, it turned out the signs were from old trips and hadn't been updated. How did anyone get around here?

"Agra?" a man asked us.

"Ji haan," my friend replied. *Yes.*

The man answered in a stream of incomprehensible chatter and directed us to a bus whose red metal panels had been pried loose at the edges. "Agra?" we confirmed skeptically.

"Ji, ji. Ji, ji. Haan haan. Milega, milega. Sirf das minut." This, I quickly learned, was the Hindi equivalent of "Yes, yes! Madam! Yes, yes. You will find! Ten minutes only!" We tiptoed on board, the vessel rocking exaggeratedly with our weight. "Agra? Agra?" we called down the aisle. Several passengers nodded blankly,

with anything close to comprehension it wasn't clear, and when one said, "*Ji, ji. Agla. Agla,*" we considered the possibility that our whole communication had been misguided.

We stayed on the bus nonetheless. A third man shared our bench, which was the size of a schoolbus two-seater. A baby lolled in his lap; it was red-faced and limp, possibly feverish. Its head rolled onto my thigh and became heavy there. I caught myself worrying that I'd catch something. I wondered how long the ride was, if the bus was really going to Agra. I watched out the window as the crunched-up pavement of Delhi gave way to "highway" (in the Indian sense) and the landscape turned dry and desertlike, and, quickly, darkened.

The road stretched on. It was dark for a long while; dinnertime came and went. We'd packed nothing for the presumably three-hour ride. We'd been traveling now for five hours. I was faint with hunger, aching from the hard seat and the bumpy, shock-absorberless ride. Having learned by now that when things Indian are beyond control, it's best to give in, I rested my head against the metal handrail over the back of the seat in front of me and drifted off, not to sleep exactly but to a dream in which it seemed I was awake. I was passing through a tunnel with vacuum pressure inside, swimming through the air to get to the other end. When the bus bumped my forehead on the metal rail, in my dream I was knocking against the sides of the tunnel trying to get out.

After six hours, the bus made a rest stop. We found ourselves in a dirt field with plastic tables and a shantylike building at the back. The men filed out and peed, in full view, everywhere. People drifted to the building and emerged with plates of food. We sat in plastic chairs and set about figuring out where we were, where we were going, when we would get there. When we asked people if we were going to Agra, they all nodded yes. We'd get there in "ten minutes."

Later, after months of traveling in India away from the company of Iyengar yogis, I would learn how to eat in these roadside "hotels." I eventually figured out that if everyone else was eating it, the food was in fact "edible," and whether you got sick from food in India had more to do with how thoroughly it had been cooked than with who was cooking it or where it was being cooked. Living according to the idea that food in India was essentially contaminated reinforced the vestigial caste dynamic asserting that eating certain food, dining in the presence of certain company, or touching certain people was polluting. These deep-rooted beliefs still separated Indians from one another and separated Indians from Westerners like us. Whether you were the equivalent of a Brahmin traveling among the poor or the equivalent of an untouchable in the company of Brahmins, this was the trap that was laid for you. And yoga, I would come to realize, was not hostile to this thinking.

That day, however, it didn't even occur to me to eat. It was as if there was no food. The food, like the once-ubiquitous-but-unreadable Devanagari script, was invisible to me.

The bus passengers were mostly young men dressed in loose-fitting canvas shirts and slacks that looked like farm gear. The few women wore brightly colored saris and had silver dangling from noses, ears, ankles, and hems. They wore their sari throws pulled low over their foreheads so that their eyes were almost hidden. The passengers' faces were very dark, and many had similar features. I knew this meant they were from rural villages, where the poorest and lowest-caste Indians lived in economic servitude. I tried to make out words in conversations, but soon understood that it was unlikely they were speaking even a relative of Hindi.

The women huddled together far from the men, and the men gravitated toward us. I noticed one man staring at me. I turned away. When I looked back, he was still staring. I wanted to brush his look off of me, like dirt. But I stared back, smiled. He didn't flinch. My friend said something to him in simple Hindi. Another man turned, and now there were two men staring at me, neither appearing to understand nor caring to respond. After a while, a few more men stared. One finally ventured a question to my friend, a man. Inductive reasoning suggested it might translate to "Which country?" though when he repeated it slowly, we knew it wasn't in Hindi.

"America?" we offered.

He said something at length, to which we replied in Hindi, "Do you speak Hindi?" He and all his friends gestured no and giggled. A relay went on for a while, they shooting questions in their language, we trying our pidgin Hindi, until finally everyone accepted the absurdity of it. By now, more had gathered. A crowd of several dozen young men surrounded us. No one tried to speak. We all just stared. I looked at each of the men's faces, thinking that they looked so much alike they could all be cousins. They looked us over too, perhaps thinking the same. It was very quiet now, and for the first time, I heard the sounds of the Indian wilderness — frogs, crickets, hoots, empty sky. We sat like that for a long while, contemplating the uselessness of language, comprehending exactly how close, and how far away from one another, we all really were.

The bus let us off in Agra at two in the morning. Like the trip with Chicago Boy to Bombay, this short traverse from one place to another seemed to change me. I was that much farther from where I'd come from, and that much closer to something else. What I understood now was the vastness of what I didn't know, and would never completely know, about India. But I also had a feeling that India had let me come a little closer, and that if I kept walking toward it, something would become clear.

I'd already learned the language of asana. I'd come to understand poses as they resonated with national and religious meaning. There was something implicit in the shapes of the poses, something I could fathom by fitting my body inside them. Indian music, Forster once wrote, was "like Western music reflected in trembling water." Yoga was our bodies reflected in a different language.

I had returned to India to immerse myself in another, less tangible language, the nuanced culture of symbols and repartee that I would find when I got back to Pune. The Iyengar institute was its own island, a nation of gestures and idioms in an idiosyncratic dialect. I believed I could learn this language, believed it would lead me someplace I'd never been.

These goals, and this institute, were very far from the homes of the people on the bus to Agra. I was reminded of this when I finally arrived in Pune. That day, I read in the *Times of India* about a cyclone on the other side of the subcontinent. It caused a flood that wiped out miles of agricultural land and took ten thousand lives. The paper described bodies floating in canals, train tracks submerged — the land "a vast sheet of water dotted with devastated villages." Photos showed scenes of horror — the greatest toll on villagers like those on the bus.

It was big news in India, yet at the institute, I heard no mention of it. I found out later that Iyengar had donated money to the relief effort, as he often did in times of national crisis. But this was done quietly. We students were kept insulated in the tiny fiefdom. Here there was yoga, there was practice, there was philosophy. When India spilled in, it was a mythologized India of sages and enigmatic history. Our isolation from the world outside our courtyard seemed calculated to speed our spiritual progress, but I began to wonder if it somehow hindered it.

*   *   *

This India of sages nevertheless welcomed me, or so Iyengar made me believe. He stopped me in the institute foyer my first day back. "My friend. So you have come back. Your research, how is it coming?" Before I could answer, his gaze left me flustered. He looked at me intently, for a time longer than a second and less than a minute, a moment when all I was aware of were his eyes, dark and large.

Over the next few weeks, I had several similar interactions with him. In daily practice, he often trailed off after lecturing to a crowd of students, raising his eyebrows with that question-mark face used for rhetorical effect. When he finished speaking, I would sometimes discover his eyes seeking out mine in the back of the crowd, and then boring into them. When he did this, time seemed to stop, and I felt something inexplicable rushing over me. For hours after, I experienced a sense of well-being. It was a feeling of profound contentment, an ease that reminded me of the "boundless bliss" described in the Bhagavad Gita. Was this some version of samadhi, of the "spiritual union" immortalized in the holy text? In *Autobiography of a Yogi,* Yogananda described "receiving" enlightenment from his guru. Was Iyengar consciously "giving" it as well? Was it possible that he was expressing it to everyone in the room, communicating, like Patañjali, with a thousand pairs of eyes?

Iyengar was eager to hear about my research into his role in the history of yoga. "This story, it is very interesting life story you will learn." He spoke with the wistfulness of an aged patriarch passing on life's accumulated jewels. I often felt he was passing something to me. In practice one day, he walked by me slowly and paused, and then simply held his hand to the top of my head, an Indian gesture of blessing, unselfconscious and warm. Whatever doubts I had about the benefits of studying at his school vanished after such moments. If I had come merely to be near him, that was enough. The details — classes, postures — dropped away. Being around Iyengar felt good. His presence enriched the other pieces of my life.

Part of what made him so winning was his way of making me feel that I too enriched his life. "Hey," he'd call from his desk in the library, putting aside stacks of manuscript paper and peeling off owl glasses — he was editing yet another collection of speeches. "So you want to ask one short question?" Thus began our ritual in which I assembled my tape recorder and asked him things. The session would quickly devolve into conversation in which he told me about his health, and I told him about old friends of his I'd interviewed and what I'd read about yoga, and he chuckled over my photos of places and people he used to know. When I came down to the library, his eyes got bright, the way my Grandma Bea's did when I made one of my too-infrequent visits, when all the delinquency in the world was not enough to keep her from loving me. Our chats reminded me of visits with her too, encircled in the kind of warm superficiality of a time whose salient purpose is that it be spent together.

Also like my grandmother, Iyengar talked at length about his health. I, the ever-dutiful granddaughter, listened with keen self-interest for signs that death might be near. Since his heart attack, Iyengar had regained all his previous vitality and several times more. He looked younger; his skin was clearer, his middle trimmer, his mood lighter, and his body sprightlier. He was, however, watchful, with an infectious and scientific curiosity, of the deterioration of his body. Although he was making fewer allusions to imminent death, he had a persistent cough. It was a disconcerting, room-shaking rattle that made it easy to tell when he had come into the studio, in which corner he was practicing, and, at worst, whether he was in the lobby of the building or even in his basement library.

Working in the library, I overheard him dictating letters whose subjects revolved around this cough. "My lungs are tired and infected with cold since four months," he responded to one request to give a lecture. "I cannot [lecture] as I begin to cough as soon as I start speaking. The cough comes and continues, and I feel embarrassed."

"I am fine," he told me later. "Except for this cough. This cough is like my wife. She is faithful to me; she never leaves my side."

Since his collapse before the cameras a year earlier, several institute regulars had filled me in on the details, confiding like cousins whispering across the deathbed of a patriarch. The heart attack had occurred while he'd been demonstrating for the cameras. It was the jolt. Unsure what had happened, he kept performing until, in Hanumanasana, he knew he could push no more. After jumping up from the pose, he went across the courtyard to the house. He lay with his chest open over a block and listened to his heart racing. By breathing slowly, he calmed his heart, and then he lay like a dead man, in corpse pose, for a very long time.

When Geeta discovered him, she begged him to see a doctor, but he refused. So she brought in a specialist. Blood tests showed chemicals in his system that appear when a person has had a heart attack. He was thus sentenced to a month's bed rest: "In bed all the time, using a bedpan," as Geeta put it. She had taken to referring to the incident in an offhand way with students, calling it, simply, "When the Cameras." As in, "You see what Guruji was putting himself through When the Cameras?" or "You think anyone can tell Guruji what he is to do? You think he would use a bedpan for four weeks When the Cameras? With other people emptying for him? No." Geeta was the long-suffering caretaker daughter, eager to commiserate about her difficult patient with us more remote, hand-wringing relations.

We were never too distant to broach the topic of his health. When I asked Iyengar about the incident, he answered as if to an heir apparent invested with the right to know. "That was exhaustion. The entire system gets disturbed. For five, six hours after, I was sweating. It was a very intense case. I did savasana. There was no need for doctor. It was the film I did, and I collapsed. I was going nonstop in order to oblige. The mind, it is the devil's workshop. We are all devils inside." He winked, as if his devilish nature was a congenital trait that all members of the family of yoga must be on guard against manifesting ourselves.

I told him I had heard that the doctors detected heart-attack chemicals in his blood.

"Heart attack," he responded, waving his hand, "that is only maybe."

My grandma had also been cavalier about the deterioration of her body, intimating that she, like the guru, had at age eighty come to an understanding the young could by nature never assimilate. Age was the great liberator, Bea had once told me. You stood outside the set and watched people act out roles that you no longer had to play along with. You could remember how you would have felt about those role-plays back when it mattered to you, but now, with death holding open its luminous doorway, you observed with bemused detachment, your ego disinvested. Iyengar, like her, was watching from afar, amused at his own persistent vanities.

Geeta was nonetheless leading her charges on a mission to dissuade the guru from plans for another ambitious and life-threatening performance, of which there were many. Her father was now preparing to invite relations from all the world over to come pay him yet another tribute. Eight hundred guests, myself included, had paid respects ten months earlier for his eightieth birthday. Now, he was planning an event to commemorate the "silver" anniversary of the institute, which was also the twenty-fifth anniversary of the death of the institute's guiding matriarchal spirit, his wife, Rama.

This inevitable event — the "Silver Jubilee"— quickly became the focus of practice-time chatter. Like all reunions, it served not only to bring the family together, but to expose underlying rents and rivalries.

Chapter Eighteen

When I first returned to the institute, Pandu regarded me with a raised eyebrow, a skeptical cousin. I slid him a bar of Swiss chocolate I'd picked up on my layover in Amsterdam, a small offering, meager compared to what came with the wealthier offspring. "So," I asked him, "can I take morning classes?" I was hoping to circumvent Geeta's classes by studying with Prashant.

His eyebrow crept up his forehead. "You want to take classes with Prashant?" He looked at me as if he suspected a plot in which he might wind up an unwitting sacrifice.

"Can I?"

He shrugged. "So you want morning classes." He looked at me balefully.

I understood only vaguely that the favor I asked hinted at a complex net of loyalties, my place in which was entirely unclear to both of us. I knew that because of the institute's three-year waiting list, many first-time students who arrived in Pune eager to take classes were turned away. Returning students had to get back on the waiting list. The waiting list itself was a fluid entity. How long you spent there had some relation to how much obeisance you offered the guru, how much money you donated to the school, how many bulk orders you put in at the institute store, run by Pandu, for T-shirts and yoga props. My interviews with Iyengar may have counted as a form of obeisance, but this was probably the least significant of the three types of patronage for Pandu.

Pandu nevertheless reached into the desk and pulled out a slip of scrap paper, holding my gaze. He wrote out some times and handed the paper to me. He rested his fingers on mine when I touched it. I pulled my fingers away and looked down at the page. It was a Prashant-only schedule. I thanked him, rushing out of the lobby before he could change it.

The next morning, Prashant showed up for class in his yoga uniform: white zipper shorts and a white wife-beater tank, its ribbed cotton thin enough to reveal the impression of his Brahmin thread underneath. His thick black hair was unruly. One of his eyes pointed ahead; one watched the window.

He instructed us to stand in rows holding our sacrums with our palms while leaning back. "Do not get the craze!" he shouted. We leaned back farther, farther, our heads dangling closer, closer, to the floor. The familiar sequence reminded me that I had come back to an intimate place.

"Do backbend with entire body," Prashant lectured from the stage. "Backbend is not pose only of back. Backbend is pose of entire body. Make each part of body a part of pose, thigh firms it is part of back, open across clavicle it is part of back." We had been arching back now for quite a long time, and slowly people started standing up straight to follow the lecture. "Asana is an integrative art," he was saying. "There are many parts of body, but body works as one, each part doing separate job."

I looked around the studio. Almost everyone was Indian. Unlike in Geeta's class, the room was not packed to the balconies with Western students, mats lined up edge to edge; we stood amiable distances from one another. Most wore sweatpants and baggy T-shirts, while a few of the younger students were dressed in the Pune vogue of white T-shirts and those balloon shorts, like an odious gym uniform I had to wear in junior high school. Most of the students were upper-class and probably Brahmin — I knew this because I had seen them in their daytime clothes, and several had chatted with me in their fine British-inflected English. There were a handful of medical doctors, one a former Fulbright grantee to the United States. Several were "U.S. returnees," people who had gotten educations and even worked in the States — where, ironically enough, some had gotten their first introduction to Iyengar yoga.

That the student body was ruling class reflected how unsuccessful the Iyengars' efforts to reach beyond their own caste and social milieu in India had been. Iyengar had spearheaded charitable projects to fund yoga programs, alongside education and sanitation initiatives, in poor villages. But the school itself catered to an affluent crowd, much as yoga schools in the States did. There was only one student at the school who I knew was from a low caste. She was the Iyengar family's maid. I had seen her scuttling on her knees, sweeping and mopping with a rag and bucket, moving in that crablike way that was the national gesture of the Indian sweeper. I had seen the maid in medical classes too, being treated for, not surprisingly, a bad back. In the courtyard and on the school floor, I'd seen her mopping barefoot with her hands — in India there was an entire caste whose role it was to "sweep," and Indians had been resistant to bettering their lot with the modernizing influence of long-handled mops or brooms. This, V. S. Naipaul wrote, owed to a tendency for Indians to see work as a matter of identity, not labor. The job of the sweeper was not so much to sweep as to be a sweeper. "'Do thy duty,'" Naipaul quoted the Gita, "'even if it be humble, rather than another's, even if it be great. To die in one's duty is life: to live in another's is death.'"

The maid was in class today. Prashant had by now elegantly segued from his thoughts on how body parts must work in harmony to a discourse on the very Gita. "According to Gita, there are different jobs for different people. Society works as whole body. You have teachers, you have soldiers, you have merchants, you have sweepers.

"Society is like body. Like whole society, you have whole body," Prashant continued. "Hand has job, arm has job, leg has job, foot has job. Not equal jobs, but equivalent value. Every job is needed for functioning of whole. Different job, equal value. We have our jobs, each different; parts of body have their jobs, each different. So this is how you have difference, with equality. You must discriminate. Use right part for right job. Discriminate so as not to discriminate."

I also knew this passage from the Gita. The Sudra — the feet of the body of Brahma — possessed a "natural duty" to serve, "as is his natural disposition. . . . The illuminated sage regards with equal mind a selfless Brahmin, a cow, an elephant, a dog, and even an outcast who eats the flesh of dogs."

I looked around the room. Faces were rapt, and many heads eagerly nodded. The doctors nodded. The young students nodded. Even the maid nodded. It was a disconcerting image, especially because in India the nod of assent looked like the American "no." It looked like all the people in the room were shaking their heads in disagreement. I started nodding no with them. But I knew that their nods meant yes, and that in this whole sea of nodding heads, only mine meant no, but no one could understand. It was a lonely moment.

At the end of class, we lay in savasana, but I couldn't relax. The Gita's unified social whole was the family that Prashant extolled today, a family that could take in a Sudra maid, but only if she remained in her place. Such a world had little room for a Westerner — an outcaste. I kept worrying the problem. Prashant was a fundamentalist, of course, I knew this: he was a devout yogi and abstainer from alcohol and sex, a literal reader of yoga legends. The idea of a hierarchy of human worth, of a superiority and inferiority encoded in nature, of privilege and hard luck as chits in a divine plan, was deeply embedded in Prashant's Hindu cosmology.

As we lay there, I heard Prashant rush down the stairs and say something to Pandu. A few minutes later, he came back up and ended class, and then walked over to me and held me with his cockeyed stare. He had changed into his civilian uniform of white pajama pants and white kurta top, his Brahmin thread now visible only beneath his collar. White in India was the color of the brahmachari, the celibate. "Pandu wants to speak with you," he said firmly.

Downstairs, Pandu was on the phone. "You just wait. Just you wait. Eh. Wait, you." Pandu-speak. It needed no translation. Finally, he looked down at and up from his desk at me. "Look, uh." He cleared his throat. Grunted. "There is problem," he said, looking down again, fingering something in his desk drawer. "Morning class. Too full."

"But it was empty," I protested.

"You see," he started again, "you were just here since one

year's time. So —" He trailed off, pulling out another slip from his drawer. He wrote some times on it; I didn't have to look to know that Pandu was shifting me to class with Geeta.

"But morning class is empty," I argued.

"Yes, but, well. Beginning of month," he offered. "Next few days more students show up. This month very busy." He paused. "You ask Prashant," he added.

As if on cue, I heard the sound of a classical Hindu raga weaving through the lobby. It was coming from under the door to the room where Prashant slept, listened to music, and did breathing exercises. Prashant emerged from his room. I imagined the music swirling around his head. I told him my appeal — something about schedules, responsibilities for my research, appointments.

"No room," Prashant insisted. The music from his quarters became chantlike and sinewy.

I averred that the classes had not been full, that I'd come here to do research that Iyengar supported, that since Prashant discussed ancient texts in his class, it was especially relevant.

He wove his head, avoiding eye contact. "You see, this is American way. You demand the things. You get schedule. You don't like schedule, not convenient for you, you change. You don't think, Maybe this is inconvenient for us." His eyes darted around both sides of the room. "American way!" he went on. "You all want to choose. You think, *This is what I want*. Not, *This is what was given*. This is American way!" One eye stared at me hard now. Prashant then walked to his room and closed the door. Seconds later, the Indian music got louder.

I decided to duck out of Geeta's asana classes even if I was unwelcome in Prashant's. Instead, I enrolled in classes at the home of a young Maharashtrian named Abey Javakhedkar, to whom the institute often referred its overflow. Abey offered to pick me up for the first class. He showed up on a motorcycle, in tight jeans and a bomber jacket. He reminded me of the middle-class students I saw outside the colleges here. In fact, he had gone to one of those local colleges, where he finished a master's in commerce — as, he told me, did Prashant.

Abey took me to class on the back of the bike, leaving his helmet strapped to the seat. As we rode, I watched whole families brave the heinous exhaust-blackened street on scooters and motorcycles. Father drove; mother sat sidesaddle in her sari; babies and children bent over handlebars, sat in mother's lap, stood on footrest. If anyone wore a helmet, it was the man. I was thinking about how Abey's ability to fit yoga into his modern Indian life was utterly different from Prashant's. The fact that Abey neither took the helmet himself nor offered it to me seemed a kind of compromise with Western ways. As the street tableau made clear, the Indian rule of the road was not the chivalrous one — a female passenger or a child was never coddled with a helmet. In the Bhagavad Gita, women were lower than even Sudras — it called them "womb sin." It was the strong who were valued.

I watched the usual street hierarchy from the back of Abey's bike. Buses sideswiped scooters, rickshas ran down bicycles, pedestrians ceded to everyone. I imagined each vehicle occupying a rung on a social ladder, its crude physical power determining its place. A schoolgirl, wearing the requisite uniform of braids and plaid skirt, was stranded in the middle of the busy throughway on a bicycle. Abey and I wove past her, and I knew no one else would stop for her either.

Abey braved the traffic at top speed, easily carrying on rapid conversation. He was saying that his friends still teased him about his decision to quit commerce and "go into" yoga. "Indian driving doesn't bother you?" he interjected.

"Indians, they think they know yoga," he went on. "You say, 'So you'll study yoga?' And they say, 'Yoga I am already knowing. I saw my grandfather when I was growing up; he did the exercises. I know the exercises.' You say, 'Yes, but have you ever done?' They say, 'No, but I am knowing. I am knowing since a very young age.'"

Another Indian yoga teacher I knew made the same point one time with a Hindi adage: *Ghar ki murgi daal baraabar* — When you're eating at home, even chicken tastes like dal. Indians did not appreciate the native art at their doorstep. It occurred to me that we had the opposite problem in the States. Yoga seemed so exotic to us that we invested it with all kinds of meaning that it didn't necessarily hold, wishing to immerse ourselves in a culture of yoga that we imagined somehow more resonant than anything mundanely native. Maybe Jane Fonda was our chicken. Maybe the so-called spirituality I had come so far to find was indeed no more distant than my gym, provided I entered it carrying a shield of light.

Abey was saying that he liked having Western students. He was excited to work with a longtime practitioner like me.

As we pulled up to the house, I mentioned what I'd discovered practicing the advanced sequences in *Light on Yoga*. Abey turned to face me, and I could see his eyes get bright. I wondered if he too had worked on his own to master the challenging poses. I'd seen him twist himself into impressive shapes for an exhibition at the institute once. Had I found that teacher to guide me in this wisdom? I was glad to quit the big classes at the institute, I added, where they covered only a narrow range of asanas.

He jumped off the bike excitedly. "The balancings you want? The backbends? Ah! Great! Really first-rate!"

Abey's parents, Anagha and Vijay, were waiting for us outside. They were early "sprouts" on Iyengar's Pune tree, they explained as they invited me inside their simple living room. Abey started taking classes for children when his parents got involved in 1974. By now, the family had built a small studio on the roof of their house, where all three taught yoga.

As Abey's mother went to prepare tea, I read the title, written in Marathi, from a book on the coffee table. Abey explained that the book was by a pop nationalist who had taken the names of landmarks and heroes throughout history and traced them to Hindu names and concepts. The book maintained that Indians had provided the seminal genius behind most developments of note. Christ was named after Krishna; Israel, the Yamuna River; China, the Ganges. The Egyptians built the pyramids using proto-Hindu techniques. Two thousand years ago, Indians had discovered the secrets for building the nuclear bomb. Nationalist historic revisionism was big here in Maharashtra state, of course. I laughed uncomfortably. Abey rolled his eyes coyly.

"You can read it. Good. Here, read this, it's better," his father interjected. He pulled a slim volume from a plastic bag. It was covered in brown paper, so I turned to the title page. It was, like the Marathi, also in the Devanagari script, but in Sanskrit. *The Yoga Sastras*. This was a collection of Sanskrit yoga manuals from medieval times.

I put the books down, and the event passed unnoticed after Abey's mother returned with tea. But for some reason, it stuck in my mind. The two books embodied two versions of nationalist pride, the crude model of the newer text and Abey's father's embrace of a more classical one: two books, two generations. The contrast caught my attention, and I wasn't sure why, but after we moved upstairs to the studio and class began, I kept thinking about it.

The three teachers worked together in class, trading off instruction fluidly. The students were largely middle-aged women.

Most were covered from head to toe in clothes that looked like they'd get in the way if the students tried anything vaguely contortionist: big sweatshirts and sweatpants; capacious Punjabi tops with cotton balloon pants underneath. Class was in Marathi, though the Sanskrit nomenclature and English loan words made it easy enough to follow. *"Change kara! Trikonasana!"* meant "Change into trikonasana." *"Hath press kara!"* meant "Press the hand." Each time Abey taught a pose, he came over to me to justify himself in English. "Don't think I always teach like this, just today we are doing this pose because the weather, you know, it is cold," he promised, and I found myself assuring him that I'd really never questioned his methods.

"Paschimottanasana," his mother called out. The students were chatting in Marathi.

"Psssshhh!" his father yelled.

I listened to more conversation I couldn't follow in rapid Marathi, and then heard Abey's mother teasing a female student in English. "Tell her what you told me, tell her!"

I looked up; all eyes were on me. I'd been sitting with my legs straight out in front of me with my head resting on my shins. Had I done it wrong? One woman was grinning and looking especially shy. She giggled and buried her head in her sweatshirt.

"She says she can't believe how beautiful the poses are when you do them," Anagha told me.

I was embarrassed, but now Abey was explaining more to me, in a hush. "For them, yoga is something they do, maybe for one hour, once a week. You see how after so many years they still don't do it well. It's not part of life for them. They are so amused to see someone come all the way to India to do this and to do it so seriously, to do it so well. They are a little shocked."

The women were all looking at me and smiling; I smiled back.

"Pshhhht! Paschimottanasana!" his father called out.

I put my head back down on my shins. Soon, I felt something hard against either side of my rib cage. It was Vijay's shins. He was straddling me. "Forward!" he shouted, pulling my torso with a strong shove of his legs. The gesture was stern. It was a good enough adjustment, but it also struck me that Vijay was issuing a challenge. In this room, with so much Indian admiration heaped upon so foreign a practitioner, I wondered if I wasn't being put in my place.

I remembered the two volumes downstairs, and I understood that I had stepped into a kind of playing court. The soul of Hinduism was at stake. It was the same fight I perceived in Prashant's classroom. Yoga had become an object of jealous competition, hovering over a net between East and West. As much as Iyengar had tried to make his institute a summer home for a large extended club with players from every continent, there were misgivings about some of the members.

Indians perceived yoga to be a precious prize, tugged at from two sides, I thought now as I buried my head in the crevice between my shins. On one end was a phantom Westerner, with my face painted on. I had no particular claim on yoga myself, yet I had become an unwitting contestant in this match. For Abey's father, a kind and gentle man, I was a towering figure of domination. To Prashant, I was an image representing the might of Western arrogance and materialism.

But somehow this didn't seem so important to me right now. Around me were all kinds of splits and tears, people ripping their worlds in two as they tried to wrest away what they thought was theirs. I didn't have to be torn in two while I watched them. I would go home soon, and when I got there it might not seem so grave that I still had parents who warred on a playing field of conflicting cultures. They would continue to make claims in my own family, continue to pull me from either side. This bitterness had caused me pain once, and I'd felt that pain in my body. I still didn't understand exactly why it had hurt me in my shoulder, or in my sacrum, or why it had once run through my whole being and made it difficult to eat or let myself feel. But I could also see that over the past several years, while I was focused on the undoing of small aches in my muscles and bones and in my insides, I had undone a wrenching in my heart.

Chapter Nineteen

Soon, celebrations for the Silver Jubilee began. The distant relations arrived — two hundred and fifty senior Iyengar yoga teachers from abroad. They were white, they were aging, they were the West. All my old teachers were there. It was a strange sight, my American mentors on foreign soil — tourists to this land of yoga. At the opening ceremony, Mary Dunn, a teacher I had studied with in New York, talked about Iyengar's "family of yoga." She described how she had first come to India for an intensive teaching along with her mother, Mary Palmer, who had arranged the guru's first American workshop in Ann Arbor, Michigan, in 1973. "We were doing janu sirsasana," Dunn said. "My mother was looking over at me to give me a hint, but I thought I shouldn't listen to anyone but Guruji or I'd be in big trouble. Guruji saw that look too. He came over to her and said, 'Mary, out of class she's your daughter, but in class she's my daughter.'"

Iyengar turned to the audience with a beaming smile, and even from the back of the room I could see his white locks shaking with laughter. Later he addressed the new arrivals: "You are my family," he said, "my many children. We are the family of yoga."

I too was among these offspring. It was impossible to deny, especially when Geeta got on stage and announced the release of the commemorative volume we'd all been laboring over for so many months. She thanked each of us by name. When she read my name, one of my American teachers looked over and nodded, grinning. Finally, her look seemed to say, you and I are united by our bond to a common patriarch.

Then, a strange thing happened. An Indian student got onstage and began flipping through slides of Iyengar's life. They included photographs of his birthplace, Bellur. I recognized it. And then I recognized the photos. They were my photos. I'd given the snapshots to Iyengar as mementos. Apparently he'd passed them to Geeta. She'd barely acknowledged me since she'd ranted at me about headstands. I'd asked her to participate in my research several times, but she'd waved me away each time until finally she looked at me with a wiggly smile and said in a quiet voice, "This I can't do." I squirmed in my seat now, not sure why her appropriation of my photos seemed like a violation, and knowing I had no right to think so.

Over the next ten days, the Western students gathered at the studio and at outside venues for chats, teachings, and lectures headed by the Iyengar clan. Only a handful of Indian students showed up, wearing badges that identified them as "observers." This distinguished them from participants. This event, according to program notes, was designed to keep Iyengar in touch with his global spiderweb of "certified" instructors.

For me, it was disconcerting to see the kinds of disagreements and discussions I remembered from back in the States play out here in India. While the network in India was tightly organized around the paternalistic Iyengars, in America teachers ascribed to a hierarchical system of certification. This created countless disputes and rivalries that often lent the community an air of pettiness. During the festivities, the American teachers used terms like *second-rate* to describe other teachers; open discussions took up rumors about the ways certain teachers taught certain poses in their private classes; it was said that certain teachers used techniques not approved by Iyengar. Rivalrous, tattling siblings, they appeared, for the Iyengars, to be a bit of an embarrassment.

"When one teacher says it could be like this, and another like this, it is just the egos fighting," an exasperated Geeta lectured the offspring one night. "You have to stop the ego fighting. If you just fight with each other, yoga will not go anywhere. Forget all these politics. Otherwise, when you face the outside, you can't become one." Here we all were, one dysfunctional unity, airing dirty laundry, hiding it from strangers.

The participants were dense sometimes as well, asking over and over if Iyengar's method was "only physical yoga"; requesting rules and schematics and sketched specifics instead of a paradigm to help understand the principles behind Iyengar's teachings. "I myself question where the things went wrong," Geeta scolded the charges. "I feel sometimes that something somewhere is not getting conveyed. Guruji's method is not just the asanas. The very philosophical approach, the very clarity in our doing, that your mind must be undergoing some kind of transformation while you are doing, that has not been thought of at all."

Poor, beleaguered Prashant and Geeta.

*   *   *

With all these activities transpiring in halls and auditoriums across Pune, things got very quiet at the institute. I took the opportunity to finish going through the material at the library. As much as I loved his company, I was self-conscious in Iyengar's presence — it made it difficult to negotiate my dual identity as disciple and writer. When the guru was there, I feared that reading certain files might violate his privacy, but when I was alone, I had few qualms about doing my job and reading everything he had authorized me to read.

There was one swath of files that I hadn't yet penetrated, including much of the folder reading "VIPs," which held his correspondence with Menuhin. I knew Iyengar regarded Menuhin among his most cherished friends and benefactors. Iyengar still owned an Omega wristwatch that Menuhin had given him back in Gstaad in 1954. "To my best violin teacher — B. K. S. Iyengar," read an inscription on the back. I'd often noticed that when Menuhin's name came up — at this week's ceremonies it rang practically on the hour, like a distant and hopeful chapel bell — Iyengar got rather teary-eyed for a man who claimed to have mastery over his emotions. One of the events this week had been a screening of another video hagiography about the Iyengar family, *Sculpting Humankind.* It included shots from a meeting that the filmmakers had arranged between the yogi and the musician in Menuhin's London flat. As it happened, the musician died some months later — it was their final encounter.

I pulled out the file and brought it to the table quietly, stealthily even. Inside the file were stacks of newspaper clippings and personal letters. Menuhin too, I imagined, must have found himself negotiating two worlds when he became intimate with Iyengar — dedicated disciple on the one hand, modern on the other. Did Menuhin ever reconcile, as I tried to now, feelings of split loyalty, of ambivalent love, of frustration, of hand-wringing, of exasperation?

In his autobiography, Menuhin credited Iyengar with teaching him something mystical about the relationship of creativity to the body. "All influences pointed toward less tension, more effective application of energy, the breaking down of resistance in every joint, the coordination of all motions into one motion; and illustrated the profound truth that strength comes not from strength but from the subtle comprehension of process, proportion and balance."

But what this file revealed was that Menuhin's impact on Iyengar's life was far greater. After Iyengar's trip to Switzerland to instruct the Menuhin family in 1954, Iyengar made contact with a cultured elite of European musicians, who, on Menuhin's recommendation, took on the yogi as a kind of community mascot. Musician passed word to musician, and soon Iyengar was the guru to the cultural glitterati, making rounds on monthlong visits to musicians' and arts patrons' estates throughout Europe. He set up with a different family one summer after the next, meeting with parents and children for daily lessons, performing his Brahmin rites in the privacy of the servants' quarters. Over the next thirty years, the yogi would make dozens of trips to Europe and the United States, contributing his Indian brand exoticism as a Swiss au pair might infuse an American mansion with airs.

For the provincial Iyengar, the encounter with the West was stunning. "There was the complex. I felt the inferiority," Iyengar once told me simply. "These people were the very cream of the society. I had to overcome that; at first it was not so easy."

Iyengar found himself in this world at the very sunset of Britain's colonial rule. When Iyengar met Menuhin, India had been an independent nation for all of five years. Menuhin was

American by birth, but he lived in England, as did several of Iyengar's first Western employers. Iyengar had grown up in a world of colonizer and colonized. Although his British patrons could ignore the ironies of their prostrations before Iyengar — "We are deeply grateful for your refusal to do less than 'kill' us daily," wrote one of his students, the pianist Clifford Curzon — Iyengar couldn't. The world was upside down. They called headstand "topsy-turvy pose," after all.

Iyengar made his first trip to the United States in 1956, at the invitation of Mary Harkness, the heiress to the Standard Oil fortune and a prominent arts patron. There, the politics of skin color immediately announced themselves. When he got off the plane, Iyengar was asked to exit the airport through a separate doorway for blacks. While an employee at Harkness's home in Rhode Island, Iyengar gave a performance at the eponymous Harkness Auditorium at Yale. *Life* magazine wrote it up, belittling his yoga as "a new twist" and, to Iyengar's chagrin, "contortion." Iyengar was a curiosity, and a black one.

That Iyengar was crossing color lines did not escape the notice of his patrons. The Holocaust had turned Menuhin, who was Jewish, into an ardent civil rights campaigner. He was keenly interested in the taboos Iyengar was breaching. So in 1957 the musician did a bold thing. Menuhin was a member of an organization called the International Arts Youth League, which was planning a congress in South Africa. In South Africa, to be a member of the large population of Indian immigrants was the next thing to being a "kaffir." Menuhin wrote a strongly worded letter to the organizer suggesting that Iyengar be invited. In fact, if Iyengar wasn't welcomed, Menuhin threatened, he would withdraw his membership from the organization. "As a Jew I feel strongly about this matter and cannot accept the privileges for one race while permitting the exemption of the other races," he wrote.

What resulted was a historic visit by Iyengar to racist South Africa. Iyengar's file included several clippings from South African dailies reporting on the controversy, and several from Indian dailies applauding the yogi's courage. But as I read them, I couldn't get over the feeling that Iyengar had been used. There was something cruel about Menuhin's gesture. He made Iyengar an unwitting Rosa Parks, a "test case" as the musician called it in one letter. In doing so, it seemed to me, he was once again repeating that power dynamic implicit in all of their dealings. The yogi became a pawn in a battle that was not entirely his own — for Iyengar, in his own world, was still a Brahmin. Iyengar no doubt suffered unknowable humiliations in South Africa, but it was not an experience he was ever willing to address with me.

The power dynamic persisted in other ways as well. Back in India, Iyengar showered his foreign charges with affection, sending them photos of his family and regular, chatty letters. The mail was never as frequent going the other way. The responses were often only contracts for future employment — stipulating airfare, salary, and room and board — and regrets.

"Dear friend," Menuhin wrote in 1960, "I have had you on my mind for all these weeks and wanted to let you know how I was keeping — but between my *many* concerts and other duties I have failed you."

I have failed you.

As I read the letters, I felt Iyengar's presence in the empty library. I imagined his cough. *Cough. Cough.* I had not spoken to him much since the festivities began. As I thought about the patrons' remorse, I worried that perhaps Iyengar felt that I was slighting him as well. I was distracted as I read. I worried that he thought I'd put in too few hours at the institute since I'd stopped taking classes with Geeta; I worried that he'd expected me in the library more frequently all along; I worried that I had failed him.

I felt the same guilt I felt about not having written my grandmother in two months.

The guilt was familiar, too, from when my parents competed for my loyalty. So many rents and tears. Once, when my mother was staying with me for my college graduation, I gave her a copy of a Gabriel García Márquez novel. The next day, en route to the airport, my father asked for airplane reading. I presented another copy of the same novel. I happened to have many García Márquez novels, in several editions, in Spanish as well as English. I was a Gabriel García Márquez fanatic. My mother saw me pass the book to my father. "That was my book," she'd said, stricken, after he left. *You gave him my book.*

It wasn't your book. I had two books. I have plenty of books. I have plenty of love for all of you.

When I read Menuhin's words, I understood his dilemma. The pangs of guilt I'd felt in Iyengar's library and with my family were for imagined slights and future ones, for insensitivities I might never even know about. This potential to inflict hurt feelings was heightened in India because, unlike with my family, Iyengar and I did not share a common set of cultural values and social expectations, handed down through generations. No matter how much Iyengar saw me as a part of his world, I really held no innate understanding of its workings. Though I felt the unstinting affection of Iyengar personally, I could never join the Indian Iyengar on the terms of his own Indian family. I feared that somewhere down the line, I too would be writing letters apologizing for having failed him. Iyengar had welcomed me into his family. I hadn't even left India yet, and I worried that ultimately I would never be able to reciprocate properly.

It was inevitable that Menuhin felt guilt. Just as I had spent my life negotiating between my mother's demands and my father's demands, the musician was pulled between two worlds with two sets of cultural givens. Trying to cohere those cultural universes was a prescription for misunderstanding. The musician added the yogi onto his payroll much as he might take on a governess or a personal trainer. There was no model of student-teacher relationship that could translate from India to Europe or back again.

To add to the possible misunderstandings, Iyengar was working on the assumption that world was clan — discipleship was indistinguishable from the lifelong devotion of kin. In the traditional guru-parampara, or mentoring, a student moves into the house of his guru, the guru-kul. He is, literally, adopted — as Iyengar's guru, his brother-in-law Krishnamacharya, had adopted him. In this way, the student submits completely. The teachings become as integral as prayer, as regular as toothbrushing.

And then, as I continued to read, I soon discovered something that no one had ever told me. That it had been kept from me felt like a kind of betrayal — like a grandparent going to his deathbed with a family secret beneath his pillow. Despite a lifetime of mutual good intentions, Iyengar and Menuhin had a falling-out. Four years before Menuhin's death, he was still practicing yoga, but the bygone days of one-on-one instruction with Iyengar were now forty years past. In 1995, now close to eighty, the violinist came to Delhi to receive an award. Iyengar learned of the visit from the Indian press just before a note from the musician reached him, sent from Bombay. The guru expressed his hurt feelings in a letter.

"You have no idea what a huge correspondence I have," Menuhin wrote in defense.

Please, dear friend, do not entertain feelings of offence or hurt. Diana's and my days in India were so full and it was

237

our own private holiday that it was absolutely impossible for me to find any time for our wonderful work, which I remember from 40 years back.

I have the warmest feelings of gratitude and affection for you. I felt in your letter a certain resentment; this is not worthy of you.

With my love and loyalty,

Devotedly,

Yehudi Menuhin

How tempting it was to read beyond Menuhin's words. Here, the Westerner put his foot down, finally. He rejected the Indian terms that had defined the relationship for forty years.

The two old men had a short reconciliation for the documentary. The filmmakers raised funds to send Iyengar, some friends, family, and the camera crew to visit Menuhin, now a knight, in his family's magnificent flat in London. Menuhin and Iyengar embraced warmly and drank tea for the camera. This time, though, they were back on Menuhin's turf. It was as it had been in the old days: on foreign soil, Iyengar bedazzled and disoriented, scanning the glittery British space and wondering, perhaps, where he was to lay his shoes.

Chapter Twenty

I had seen Iyengar instruct students many times, but these days he rarely performed the megaclasses in which he presided as legendary patriarch. Today, the second day of the Jubilee, he would teach. Students arranged their mats around a central platform in a large rented hall; two hundred and fifty mats lay edge to edge. Iyengar was dressed in yoga wear marketed by Pandu — a Polo shirt emblazoned with the institute logo and matching balloon shorts. He climbed on the stage and attached himself to a cordless lapel microphone. Geeta and Prashant walked the aisles in their signature yoga outfits — Kelly-green shorts and a muddy-white safety-pinned Izod for her, wife-beater and zipper shorts for him — each carrying a cordless mike and shifting students out of the sight lines of ubiquitous video cameras.

The guru ordered students to lie on their stomachs, toes tucked, palms on the floor at chest level. "Now lift! Lift one inch to chaturanga dandasana!" The bodies rose an imperceptible distance off the floor. It was alligator pose, but the bodies looked to me as mysterious as temple gods — man-lions and winged things. "Has the energy coiled? Have you moved from action in the cells to relaxation in the mind? Feel the strength," Iyengar chanted. The bodies hovered there; they floated in a single plane, shifting in space like meadow grass. Iyengar stood, transfixed, gazing at the gorgeous sight. "See the energy. Feel the energy," he whispered, transported, like me, by the beauty of his creation.

For four hours at a time over the next five days, Iyengar talked about upper inner thighs and outer patellae, about odd toes and consciousness filling the mind as breath filled the lungs. Working hard on empty stomachs, students gasped in appreciation of small sage insights. "Inner top leg is like a journey; why the bottom top leg is not like a journey?" *Gasp.*

His technique was to chide, to hold poses until students buckled, to complain about his quarry in the third person — as if discussing the sorry state of the talent with Geeta or Prashant. His deputies nodded in agreement, heaping on more complaints like smug older siblings. His parenting style was tough love, and he doled it out liberally.

"Take pose again! I am not satisfied with your work that is why. I see some people are so lazy. They haven't stayed."

"Integrated action! Integrated action!" Prashant interjected.

"No! There is no integration," Iyengar picked up. "Don't ask me to repeat. You never make an attempt! I said bend the leg. I never said stretch the leg. Bend the left leg. Can you see they are all twenty years, thirty years teachers, and still they cannot catch?"

"Eh! Stretch out that bottom leg!" Geeta chimed in, slapping the thigh of a teacher from Chicago who was in his fifties. "After so much explanation!" she scolded the man. "He says bend the left leg and see what happens? Not catching." Geeta threw up her arms, shook her cheeks.

"Sorry to tell you, you are like donkeys!" bellowed the master. "Extend the inner leg in downward dog! Now you understand?"

Iyengar looked for his students' weaknesses, and rather than softening to them, he berated. After so many months by his side, this was my first experience with his brutal teaching techniques.

"Who is demo?" Iyengar boomed. He beckoned some long-time students to come to the stage to demonstrate a pose. The usual suspects climbed up: Manouso, Biria, Mary Dunn. Iyengar looked around with a confused expression. He scanned the tableau of white faces. The Indian "observers" were in a back room watching the proceedings on a video feed, or crowded into a one-foot perimeter of floor space between mats and wall. I stood with them, making myself small to keep from blocking the cameras. Iyengar had arranged the teachings so that only those with high-level certificates could attend; Iyengar's Indian students did not have certifications because in India, Iyengar did not feel the need to award them. A conundrum.

"They're all international students; it pains me," Iyengar muttered. The sea of white faces shimmered like froth on ocean waves. "It's not for international students only! Remember, you people have more of my teachings than the Indians." He peered around the room. Indeed, there was only a single Indian student participating, and that student had been born in Africa and had lived in America for years.

A yoga teacher who lived in Bombay, Jawahar Bangera, trotted up from the edge of the room. Iyengar nodded at him. "Now, I am taking him because as an Indian he does not go down and say, 'I'm tired,' like you people wanting freedom in a second," the guru chided. "Don't ask me to repeat because the Western mind is to take this blood, suck others. You come here to get some points and then you say latest Pune points. You are all quick to cash in on your work, but you are not quick to encash on your own selves! Be humble!

"Here you want to be taking but you have not imprinted the new thoughts in your cells. This will be my last class in my life for anyone because you are exploiting!"

Iyengar paused there, looking out on his sad-faced heirs, unwitting descendants of those colonizers who once bled India of gems and spice. "I know, you are all good people," he recanted, his voice retreating. "We are all caught, ordinary people."

After the class, students gathered in a large cafeteria, where they lined up to fill large trays with sticky rice, curries, samosas, and chutneys. The Western visitors appeared suitably dejected. Vestigial colonizers' guilt weighed them down like a bad meal, and they bore it in silence. But as much as the guru had abused his Westerners, the real slight, I felt, had gone to his Indians. The Indians lining up with their thali trays were his longtime faithful. Abey and his parents had come; Nivedita; people who'd traveled from as far as the Himalayas and Delhi. That none of them had been invited to participate in the classes seemed a slap in the face, no matter how much Iyengar fulminated against Western privilege. If he found Westerners so privileged, why did he privilege them further by offering them exclusive classes?

Maybe because Iyengar's anger at those poor Americans seemed so misplaced, I was intent on finding evidence of a Cinderella complex among the Indian left-behinds. Didn't they feel like pale stepsiblings, shunted to the sidelines by the charismatic patriarch? Iyengar hadn't taught a formal class at the institute in a decade — he was "retired." I had no patience for the notion that Indians' proximity to the master justified this lesser status.

Abey's father, Vijay, and Rajiv Chanchani, a yoga teacher from the north who sometimes took classes here, looked at me blankly from across a cafeteria table. The feast today was garnished with horseradish pickle that Rajiv's wife, Swati, who was sitting beside me, was telling me offered little-known Ayurvedic boons. Vijay seemed very different to me from the man who had used his shins to wrench my ribs forward at his rooftop yoga studio. Chanchani, whom I'd once wrestled for a prop during a yoga class, also looked more youthful than usual, teenlike and impish. About forty-five years old, he had sharp cheekbones and an angular beard, and eyes that could be either intense or heavy-lidded and sleepy. Today they were the latter.

I asked Vijay, Rajiv, and Swati why Iyengar didn't resolve the two-tier disparity by awarding Indians the same certificates he gave foreigners.

"It's different for us. This is saddhana," Vijay began, shaking his head emphatically. "In saddhana there is no beginning, no end. Saddhana is a lifelong search. A quest. So when do you know where to give the certificate? This for us is a way of life. It is not something you do like a professional."

"For us you know Iyengar yoga is very small," Rajiv added. "It exists in only three cities. We have large populations in Pune and Bombay and Bangalore. There are only a handful of people making a living this way, so you see for certification there is no need."

I knew it was true that Iyengar's network in India was modest compared to his international one. According to my own crude calculations during the seven-odd months I'd been a student in Pune, ten times more Westerners attended the institute than Indians during a given year. I estimated there were about a hundred regular Indian students at the institute. Counting practitioners outside India skewed the ratio more. The Iyengar Yoga National Association of the United States, which handled U.S. certification, counted fifteen hundred certified Iyengar teachers around the globe, with large concentrations in California and New York. The guru had attracted a thousand students at his last and probably final appearance in the West, in England in 1993, while eight hundred were now signing up to study with Geeta at a workshop planned for Pasadena. *Light on Yoga* had reached more than a million readers since it was first published in England in 1965, but it didn't come out in an Indian language until 1992.

"In India, the name Iyengar is hardly known," Rajiv picked up. "I don't think we have even a hundred teachers in India, maybe thirty. I don't think more than a half-dozen people are doing it full-time. You wouldn't be able to make ends meet. We made a concerted effort to have a workshop in Delhi. Guruji agreed to teach. We couldn't find a hundred students, even fifty students, for an Iyengar workshop in that entire city. Eventually, Guruji didn't come, and all we were left with was a dozen people who were mostly foreign nationals associated with the embassies."

Rajiv and Swati looked at me with their eyebrows raised, as if their eyebrows substituted for hands tossed up in the air. I'd been expecting hurt feelings when I'd asked them about certification earlier, but not once had it occurred to me that those hurt feelings could have been inflicted by their compatriots. "Why is that?" I asked in a quiet voice.

All three were silent for a moment, and then Rajiv began, shaking his head slowly. "After Yehudi Menuhin, Guruji had no students. If Guruji was left in India without Yehudi Menuhin, he would be a regional teacher."

By now a second wave of cafeteria eaters needed our seats. Swati and Rajiv offered to take up the conversation with me at the pleasant wooded ashram where they stayed when they made their frequent journeys here to study with the Iyengars. They lived in the Himalayas, nearly thirty hours from Pune by train.

Rajiv strode with his hands clasped behind his sacrum as we made our way through footpaths to their simple cabin. Despite his homespun knee-length kurta and leather sandals, he reminded me of an Oxford don, an image that stuck when he began pointing out the names of the foliage and instructing me on the Ayurvedic applications for each plant. There was amla, custard apple, acacia, and lychee. "This is prime lychee country," he added, taking a cross-legged seat on their porch as Swati joined us. She was carrying a pitcher of bright-red liquid that she said was amla juice — "good for the digestion."

I sipped my amla. It was sticky sweet. The Chanchanis were telling me that they hoped to undo the injustice inflicted on yoga by the Indian people by working from the root — with children. They had recently begun teaching in the foothills of the Himalayas at the Doon School, "the most elite school in the country, exclusive and elite," as Swati described it.

"It's like Eton and Harrow," Rajiv cut in.

"Rajiv Gandhi went there, and Vikram Seth," Swati added.

"So teaching India's most privileged can bring yoga back to India?" I asked skeptically. From their description, the school's population sounded vulnerable to brain drain.

"The Indian middle classes are looking to the West," Rajiv began, seeming to follow my logic. "Their mind-set is formulated by a colonial system. Even Doon School was founded to create brown Englishmen to fulfill the needs of the Raj. My goal is to get colonial hands off and bring back India to India. So now the kids study yoga as a subject with the same status as chemistry and math. You can stand on your head and get a grade. At least it is now considered as a subject equal to computers."

But wasn't elitism part of the problem? I pressed. Ramanuja broadcast from that temple to reach Sudras. But to this day, Brahmins were still cut off from the masses. Secrecy, exclusivity, and concern for purity, after all, were never alien concepts to yoga.

"Caste is no longer relevant in India," Rajiv cut me off. "In urban areas, you don't know who's what caste."

Swati looked at both of us. "Of course you know, Raju. Of course. Someone leaves the house, the first thing we talk about is what are they. If you know someone's caste, you know fifty percent about the person."

"Caste is dissolving very fast," Rajiv averred.

"Even when we go to America we put Indians into their castes," Swati went on. "In the West, it's a sort of a fun game. There, everyone dresses the same. So we find out, depending on which profession, or we think, *He's a born Brahmin, but he behaves like a so-and-so.*"

"We don't talk about this," Rajiv insisted.

"All the time, Raju, all the time. It determines fifty percent of human behavior. It's all Indians, Raju. We all have this lens."

When I tried to sleep that night, several images kept flipping in my head, like a fan on my eyelids. I kept seeing Rajiv and Swati staring each other down, locked in their ugly banter about caste. And I kept seeing Iyengar, before all those people who loved him, saying they weren't worthy.

We are all caught, Iyengar had said. In that instant, Iyengar, too, looked caught to me. He saw an arrogant old white man snapping fingers at a servant who happened to be Brahmin. He saw the commanding gazes of uniformed guards at an airport in New York City. He saw a dear friend tottering in headstand, veins stark against fleshy cheeks. He saw his children praying to Vishnu. He saw a white head bowing down in obeisance before him. He blessed a black head; he blessed a blond head. Flash. Flash. Iyengar teetered there in the middle, waiting for the world to come in focus.

In the climax of the Bhagavad Gita, Arjuna himself is caught, between God and a row of chariots on Kurukshetra battlefield. Arjuna, the warrior, stands at the midline. On one side of him is this row of chariots, his relations inside, poised to fight Arjuna for the soul of the kingdom. On the other side is God, as the avatar Krishna, telling Arjuna he must decimate his family. Arjuna settles down to discuss the problem with Krishna, for from this dark tunnel he must find light — must choose between family and God.

Iyengar too seemed split between worlds to me, the world of birth and the world of justice, the world of clan and the world of yoga. I once thought he'd brought all these worlds together. Now I saw him, like me, stuck between. On one side stood his family from the West, people who had been loyal to him as long as they'd known him and had helped him rise up. Yet somehow these people were not loyal in the ways he expected, not reliable in the ways he wanted. On the other side was home. But his work in India had not taken. Arjuna chose God. Iyengar was eighty-one years old now, and still he had not chosen.

I was thirty-four now. I had come to a family where I was destined to remain forever separate. But in the meantime, I had learned something about yoga. I needed to make my choice.

Chapter Twenty-One

Did Iyengar abandon India? Was this betrayal the root of Iyengar's rage? Iyengar circumvented a certain path on that fateful day in Bombay, anointed by Menuhin, beating out the favored Swami Kuvalayananda. But had he really pulled out his Indian roots — left them as sacrificial pickings for the bested Kuvalayananda?

Rajiv said that without Menuhin, Iyengar was nothing. I couldn't believe it was true. Vijay had held that Indians did not approach yoga with the professionalism of those in the States. If this was the case, it could explain why there was no Indian equivalent to the unbridled competition and unwieldy bureaucracy of the American yoga establishment. It could also mean that even if it was small, Iyengar's Indian following possessed a devotion that made it strong.

I was still curious about this Indian branch. From the vantage of the Pune studio, Iyengar's Indian contingent had looked small and less than serious. But perhaps there were nuances that had escaped my eye. My ability to overlook things that were obvious to most Indians never ceased to be a source of wonder for me.

It was true that the attendance at the Jubilee represented the legacy of Iyengar's work with Menuhin — those Westerners who, like the musician, nurtured their freighted familial ties to India. What was the legacy in India? I knew whom to ask: those Indians at the Jubilee. No matter how much they'd hung at the sidelines and skulked in the shadowy videoconference room, they were shiny and impressive. Several had shown up for classes and practice in the days before the Jubilee. I had watched them twisting in and out of precariously asymmetrical handstands, chatting together in the corners as they executed thrilling backbends and splits.

One day, I heard someone refer to these students as members of an organization in Bombay called the Light on Yoga Research Trust. The name recalled that era when yoga was best kept secret: *It becomes potent by concealing, and impotent by exposing.* I came to think of the Trust as a kind of syndicate, a Masonic clique of emissaries who humbled everyone with their proficiency in advanced poses and spoke little to anyone who wasn't Pandu or an Iyengar. They reminded me of the syndicate in Hermann Hesse's fantastical search for enlightenment in the *Journey to the East*. "Zoroaster, Lao Tse, Plato, Xenophon, Pythagorus, Albertus, [sic] Magnus, Don Quixote, Tristram Shandy, Novalis and Baudelaire were co-founders of our League," I remembered from Hesse's whimsical tale.

I got to know one of the Trust members, a no-nonsense biologist whose day job was in a fertility clinic, because of the work I'd done editing for Iyengar. Unlike her counterparts in Pune, Rajvi Mehta was a wiry young woman who dressed in jeans and T-shirts and had a rather ironic way about her. "I make test-tube babies," she'd said bluntly. She told me that the Trust had been founded in the sixties to provide a business backbone for Iyengar's growing organization. It was based in Bombay and not Pune simply because Bombay was where Iyengar's more business-minded supporters happened to live. These days, the Trust published an institute journal, did the brass-tacks organizing for celebrations and workshops such as the Jubilee, distributed videotapes and Iyengar-wear yoga shorts, and raised funds for institute projects such as outreach to drug addicts and lepers. Back in the seventies, they'd built the institute in Pune. In Bombay, they also taught classes to a small knot of longtime Iyengar protégés and their now-grown children. Rajvi was, as she explained, "second generation."

Now a yoga teacher herself, Rajvi told me she'd been studying with Iyengar since her father brought her to classes as a child. "I just grew up with it; it was a part of life. On Sunday mornings, there was a ritual, at six-thirty the whole family is out. In an Indian family you don't question. We had to go. My father was very particular. There was no question of bunking classes."

Rajvi became more serious as a teenager after a visit to the institute in Pune when she got personal attention from the guru. The fateful moment occurred, she remembered, when she was stretching out over a folding chair in a backbend. "Guruji was walking by, and he just put his foot on my chin. I had never touched my head to the floor before. It touched that day. I was thrilled."

Rajvi told me that if I wanted to talk to the people who had really made Iyengar yoga possible in India, I should go see a man named Motiwala. I had heard the name at the institute, tossed about with a certain air. She said he lived in Dadar, a wealthy suburb of Bombay, and had been among the original funders of the institute facilitating its opening in 1975.

After the Jubilee, the institute closed for a week, and I took a train to Bombay to follow Rajvi's recommendation. Rajvi met me when I arrived, and gave me directions for the complicated journey out to Dadar. The bus ride took me through Bombay's greatest extremes of urban excess and decay. My bus curved along the shoreline, where one minute, shiny chauffeur-driven Ambassador sedans tumbled like beach balls from manicured estate entrances, and the next, urchins waded in green ocean froth, pulling sustenance from muck.

Sam Motiwala and his wife, Freny, lived in a lushly landscaped out-of-the-way enclave where Art Deco mansions fronted curving streets that spoked out from a central maidan. Kids played cricket on the maidan, but otherwise all was quiet. The Motiwalas' building faced the maidan; a name and date — Italian, 1930s — were inscribed in elegant script in stonework on the front.

I climbed a marble-tiled stairway to the top floor, where a servant led me across a vast patio. Bougainvillea and geraniums sat on an artfully arranged floor mosaic made of small shards of tile. The servant asked me to sit in the den. She returned minutes later carrying a silver tray with a teapot under a cozy and sweets arranged in a half-moon.

Freny Motiwala followed. She was elegant and silver haired, in her sixties. She took a stuffed chair next to me, something Edwardian or Victorian, and explained in an impeccable British-inflected English that she and her husband first consulted with Iyengar in 1961. Freny's dorsal spine had given out. She could barely walk, and the doctors were recommending surgery. She started submitting to Iyengar's fierce therapeutic regimens for her back, and as it began to heal, she found that her life, too, began changing. Soon she brought her husband to Iyengar's upstart classes in Bombay. In a short time, both Motiwalas stopped drink-

251

ing and eating meat; they resolved marital differences; and later, after they got their three daughters involved, they found that yoga had become an activity and a philosophy of life that was the glue that kept their family whole.

As Freny talked, I scanned the flat. It was magnificent, with an upper-class Indian aesthetic I recognized. Hindu devotional objects, Mughal miniatures and archaeological-looking Indic statuary lined the shelves. Seeing my eyes fall on one shelf, Freny added in an intuitive kind of non sequitur, "Yoga is a universal religion."

At that moment, Sam walked in. "Wouldn't you say, Sam?"

Sam was a great white-haired man with a barrel chest and a thick white mustache; he reminded me of an orchestra conductor. He wore sweatpants and a T-shirt and his cheeks were flushed, as if he'd been out speed-walking in the maidan. The couple reminded me of parents I had met in the Park Avenue homes of friends from high school, places I found equally exotic and yet somehow familiar.

Sam assented. Iyengar had always drawn an ecumenical lot of followers, even in India, he said. This, as much as the guru's alliance with Menuhin, proved that yoga not only transcended difference, but was rightfully the domain of outsiders.

Iyengar was an outsider in Central India, after all, he said. "When we met Guruji we could barely talk with him. We knew Gujarati, but he didn't. He knew some Marathi, but we knew none. He hadn't studied English; that's why he demonstrated the poses. We really couldn't understand. It was all Greek to us.

"When Guruji started teaching, he had to deal with parochialism," Sam went on. "He was a South Indian, and in Maharashtra he was seen as different. In Maharashtra they feel that only a Maharashtrian should come forward. He really had to shine to be appreciated."

"In those days, people didn't think Guruji was so great," Freny interjected, daintily pruning the tip off a crescent-shaped cookie with her teeth. "They didn't realize he had these special remarkable qualities." This forced Iyengar to seek out allies in all corners. "We don't have to restrict to our own," Freny added. "We're not cloistered like everyone else. There is no contradiction at all in a Parsi doing yoga —"

"— that's why most of the community was Parsi." Sam finished her sentence.

I looked at them dumbly. They seemed to be speaking in non sequiturs, but I strained to forge a link between their discontinuous thoughts. And then something clicked. It would have been obvious to any Indian: the Motiwalas were not Hindu. They were as foreign to Iyengar as Menuhin. They identified with his plight as an outsider precisely because they too were outsiders. The decor in their house should have been the tip-off. It revealed as exotic a fascination with India as that of any British Indiaphile; the Hindu elements were classical, added on like trim. The Motiwalas were Zoroastrian — Parsis. "You're not Hindu?" I asked meekly.

They nodded together. "Zoroastrian," Sam said in his booming voice.

"Parsi," Freny echoed.

They went on to explain that India's Parsi minority was some hundred thousand strong, based primarily in Bombay. Parsis hailed originally from Iran and had settled in India after the eleventh century, fleeing forced conversions by Iran's Muslim rulers. In the interest of self-preservation, they had since followed a path of assimilation that had led them to discard many of their rightful practices. But the community preserved one ritual, for which they were perhaps most famous. They left their dead on the roof of the great Zoroastrian Towers of Silence here in Bombay for the vultures to eat. But, Freny added quickly, Parsis were also known in India for their commercial prowess. Their wealth and prestige helped them to become India's greatest supporters of the arts. India's wealthiest industrialist, Ratan Tata, was a Parsi, she added proudly, as was the conductor Zubin Mehta.

This rang a bell. I remembered that Mehta's father, Mehli, had facilitated the first crucial contact between Iyengar and Menuhin.

The Parsis, Sam interjected, were often referred to as the "Jews of India."

"And Parsis supported yoga?" I asked in my small voice.

"Of course," Freny said matter-of-factly. "They supported all of the arts."

"This is why Parsis supported yoga," Sam added.

An odd thing happened once I was armed with this piece of information that was otherwise common knowledge. The fact of Parsi participation in the yoga of Bombay was like a password, a key to a whole body of mundane facts that made everything look different. It was as if someone had flipped a switch, and suddenly the entire story of Iyengar yoga in India shifted from the story I thought I knew: the Hindu nationalism story, the yoga-as-the-legacy-of-Ramanuja story. I got the same feeling I'd had once during a class in graduate school in which a teacher presented "readings" of James Joyce stories so that everything the narrator told you was actually false. If you imagined the point of view of a minor character, she instructed us, you could piece together an entirely different version of truth.

In the days that followed, I went about town asking questions about the genesis of Iyengar yoga in Bombay. Mentioning the word *Parsi* was like opening a faucet.

The Motiwalas' claim that Iyengar drew an ecumenical following was in fact modest. Until only very recently, Iyengar's Indian clientele outside Pune had been almost exclusively Parsi.

Those Parsis had been instrumental in creating not just Iyengar's base of support in India, but also his presence in the West.

"When my family started," Rajvi told me, "there were not a lot of Hindus. Guruji's students in Bombay were Parsis. There were more Parsis than any other community."

"When I joined in 1969, 1970, there were only Zoroastrians in the class," added Jawahar Bangera, the student who had volunteered as guinea pig during Iyengar's Jubilee demonstration. "They were so serious. Myself, my father, and one other were the only non-Zoroastrians. This was the monopoly of the Parsis, we used to joke."

This circle of Parsis tried to do for Iyengar in India what Menuhin had done in the West. Their patronage took on a different character, but what intrigued me about the story of Parsis in the life of Iyengar was that it *was* still patronage, with all the same paternalism — *patronizing,* as it were — of Menuhin.

Iyengar's association with the Parsis began when he met a lawyer named Birjoo Taraporewala through Mehra Vakil, a member of Taraporewala's close-knit Parsi circle and a well-connected socialite — the same woman who introduced Iyengar to Menuhin through Mehli Mehta. Taraporewala gathered a handful of families to populate classes in Bombay, and Iyengar began taking an express train from Pune every Saturday to accommodate them. He taught an evening class that night and another in the morning, skipping dinner in between to avoid eating food cooked by an outsider.

After Iyengar's introduction to Menuhin, Taraporewala also arranged for Iyengar to meet another powerful Westerner. This man, like Menuhin, was tapping Indian sources to find a man to do a job. He was a publisher with Allen & Unwin. He had grown tired of the mystical Theos Bernard treatise on yoga and wanted to update it with a more direct treatment by an indigenous voice.

Taraporewala presented Iyengar's album, produced back in 1952, to the publisher. By now Iyengar also had available detailed point-by-point instructions to accompany the 150 photos, as well as a whole cache of letters explaining his philosophy of yoga. The opus numbered some one thousand pages.

The publisher signed on, but as Biria reported to me, "He says to Guruji that you are a great teacher — and a very bad writer." Taraporewala embarked on the revisions and painstaking editing that ultimately cut the thousand pages to a manageable size, and wove the guru's broken English into that poetic synthesis of Hindu philosophy and practical advice that became *Light on Yoga.*

Taraporewala's patronage did not stop there. In 1966, the year after the publication of *Light on Yoga,* he gathered Sam Motiwala and another Parsi investor to help form the Trust. Their first project was to provide seed money to buy the property that would later become the Iyengar family home and yoga institute.

By now Iyengar's students in Bombay had taken it upon themselves to begin teaching classes on their own, especially during Iyengar's frequent absences for his visits West. Taraporewala secured a position teaching yoga at the health club at the five-star, Parsi-owned Taj Mahal Hotel. He soon brought in more of Iyengar's followers as teachers, until the Taj was the "only place in Bombay that had twelve classes a week," as Bangera boasted. By 1990 there were twenty people in a class; teachers were turning away prospective students. And so the ancient Hindu art of yoga found another venue, populated by the "cream of society," as Bangera described it — wealthy foreign itinerants and embassy personnel. Once again, Iyengar's wisdom bypassed the Hindus who were its rightful heirs.

Yoga penetrated other circles in Bombay as well, but none of them were Hindu. The chairman of the Trust, Father Anthony

Lobo, a member of Bombay's large Portuguese population, arranged for Motiwala to lead a class at his Catholic church. Taraporewala and others took on another five classes in Catholic schools throughout the city. "Do you know," Iyengar teased Taraporewala then, "we have a Parsi teaching Christian nuns a Hindu philosophy?"

I had once believed that Iyengar joined the East and the West, like Hanuman flying across the Indian Ocean to rescue Sita, leaping in the shape of a split. His yoga "yoked" opposites. By healing rents and mending dualities, he not only worked his mind-body therapeutic magic but made the world cohere. This was something I could never seem to do. I came from a "broken" family. I'd never reconciled my mother's world and my father's. If I could join those, I'd believed, I could heal myself. But now, it looked to me like the East and the West were not neat domes that Iyengar could join into a perfect, interconnected round. Iyengar sought an impossible synthesis, and I had sought one as well. The world, in all its beautiful complicatedness, was far too dense.

Chapter Twenty-Two

So," Sam Motiwala said, making deliberate eye contact and standing up slowly so that he seemed conscious of balancing his weight evenly between the two sides of his body. He rocked on the balls of his feet. "Are you ready?"

"You can change in this bedroom," Freny offered, leading me down the long wood-floored hallway in their flat.

Sam was teaching a yoga class.

About a dozen Indians dressed in sweat suits like Sam's gathered on the balcony outside, among the bougainvillea and geraniums. Beyond the mosaic railing was an exquisite sunset, blue fading into purple. Class was in English. We began by sitting on woven mats with our eyes closed. "Feeeeel the energy," Sam began. His voice boomed. I imagined him as a great Zoroastrian priest giving rites at a rooftop funeral. "Feeeel the energy moving dooooooowwwwwwn into your fingertips." He lingered on the feeling in the limbs, the flow of sensation through them, the "energy" inside.

This was nothing like the Pune classes, but I did not feel dislocated. In fact, I felt very much at home, someplace warm and familiar. I lay in savasana at the end and tried to remember when I'd last attended a yoga class in which the teacher spoke about feeling the pulse in your temples. And I realized that Sam's teachings reminded me of Santa Cruz in the middle eighties. The Motiwalas were a bit like children of the seventies themselves.

A vast ocean, a continent, and several cultures separated Sam Motiwala of Bombay from Julie Kimball of Santa Cruz. But as I listened to airplanes hovering overhead, and to Sam's baritone uttering soothing formulas, and to kids cracking cricket balls on the maidan below, and to a horse carriage clopping down the cobblestones on the affluent suburban street, and as sunset melted to twilight, and the planet Venus blinked at me in the purple sky, I believed that I could have been anywhere.

That night, another American and I wandered through downtown Bombay. The streets were quiet, and in the moonlight the old buildings took on a silver cast, their crumbling facades becoming ghostly and otherworldly. We passed the Parsis' downtown fire temple. Larger-than-life feline caryatids in pharaoh's garb flanked the entrance, their claws curled under. There was no sign of vultures, but I imagined what the temple might look like if the stealth animals came for bits of corpse, then flew to the vanishing point at darkness — little shreds of human soul, carried off in bite-size flecks of flesh. This was as exotic as India had ever been to me.

We turned onto a quiet alley. Light and noise came from a building farther up the crumbly street, the building freshly whitewashed but as ancient as the Parsi temple. It was a synagogue. It was Friday night. The thought of the Jewish Sabbath hadn't entered my mind since I'd been in India. Upstairs no doubt another arcane ritual was playing out, only this one was a practice I could call my own. How disoriented I felt to discover the familiar in this strange land, on this street where vultures carrying off dead might be as commonplace a ritual as davening. I hadn't gone to temple much in my life, but I certainly knew to think of it as a place where I might, or even should, go, where my absence was felt, where if I paid the High Holiday dues I'd certainly be welcomed — no questions asked, other than "Are you Jewish?" Whatever my ambivalences, I could certainly answer yes.

We heard Hebrew chanting as we climbed the steps. Upstairs, a small cluster of men was gathered up front. With a bar separating them from the entranceway, the men davened — swathed in tallithim, fringes swaying at the edges. A man noticed us and gestured for my friend to come forward; he dangled a yarmulke, beckoning. I counted the men in the group and realized they needed another man in order to make a minyan. My friend would suffice. Another man signaled for me to move backward. It was an Orthodox synagogue, and a woman's presence was not welcomed past the bar.

As instantly as I'd detected the warmth of this familiar culture, I remembered what had pushed me from it. Here was my own family, or at least part of my family. This synagogue might have seemed a warm light on a dark street amid the unknown, but tonight it repelled me. I'd felt more among my kind earlier in the evening listening to familiar relaxation jargon at the Motiwalas'. What a twisted riddle I'd walked into. Hindu and Hebrew were traditions equally arcane, equally arbitrary, as rich with history as that of the Parsis. In between stood the amorphous modern hybrid that was yoga, yoga as executed in English, on an outdoor patio, in the resonant deep-voiced oratory of a Bombay suburbanite. By some circuitous route, I'd come to that patio and found my people.

Asana, it struck me, was a ritual as redolent of mystery as the davening of the old Jews in the Bombay synagogue. *Asana is my prayer,* Iyengar had famously said. I'd never prayed, and my own connection to my ancestors was little more than tenuous. But asana was my rite.

Chapter Twenty-Three

When I got back to Pune, I took the next morning off from practice at the institute and did yoga on my roof. The ambient noise of India was louder there; kites and cuckoos swooped from orange poinciana, making hoot and swish and flute echoes; maids clattered stainless-steel breakfast plates beneath hoses; a woman flung water from laundry on the next rooftop; splattering drops made *whoosh* sounds.

How I missed the quiet of that practice I used to do at home, under no one's stern judgment, with nothing to observe but the way my breath slowed, my muscles loosened, my flesh became sensitive in places I hadn't yet known were there. No phones, no gossip. Nothing.

I was no longer progressing as a yoga student here. Abey and his parents were teaching me more Marathi than asana. We still hadn't gotten to those balancings and advanced backbends. I was still studying pranayama with Geeta, and there, thanks to longevity, I was finally exempt from those errors the new students never ceased making. Wrong fingers continued to fly to wrong nostrils: the same wrong fingers every month, the same wrong nostrils, the same unclipped fingernails, the same tedious rants by Geeta. But I was nonetheless a "backbencher," as Iyengar once called himself. Geeta spent endless minutes explaining the proper seated position for breathing: the angle of the buttocks bones; the orientation of spine to sacrum, throat to ear canal, rib cage to navel. When the actual breathing part of class began, my mind clung to that minutiae, never nearing the focus or emptiness we strived for. I didn't understand pranayama. I didn't grasp what we were doing there. I didn't see how it could point me someplace more sublime than a physical or emotional calm, to something that might be spiritual, to some understanding of spirituality itself.

I began a sun salutation on my roof. As I started, a recent dream came to me: I asked Iyengar what we were doing in our pranayama breathing classes. "What should I be looking for?" I pleaded. Pranayama was an empty hole, holding no particular meaning. In the dream, Iyengar took me to a pond, saying nothing. There was a plank hovering over the pond. The guru, barefoot, walked to the end of it. He picked me up and put me on the plank, and then crossed to the land on the other side without me. I walked out onto the plank clumsily, in big boots, thinking only about how my feet were unconnected to the earth. When I woke up, all I understood was how little I understood. I didn't know how to cross to the other side, where meaning lay, how to make the bridge, how to root myself on either side. Iyengar had nonetheless helped me enter the empty sea. There, I was suspended, footless. Ready.

On the roof, I wrapped my legs into lotus and swung my arms around my back to catch my big toes with my hands. I arched my head back. My right shoulder, under my clavicle and behind my scapula, let out its quiet yelp. I breathed deeply, which heightened the pain. I had an urge to resist the feeling, to protect myself against the tightness in my shoulder by caving forward. After so long, though, I knew not to give in.

I swung forward and brought my belly over my feet, and my chest and forehead to the ground. The stretch in my groin was strong. I didn't flinch from it, as I'd learned to persevere so long ago. I kept stretching, pulling my torso out from my hamstring, pushing my belly deeper down. I felt a pull in my groin. It felt like the grief I'd once held in my chest, the sensation of a knife cutting into me, an ache like a broken heart. Millions of minuscule sobs cried out from singular cells in my groin.

Yoga gives you the strength to face God when he appears, a yoga teacher once told me. I repeated the phrase in my head. The pain did not scare me as it once might have. I stayed. Millions of small sobs gathered into a single sob, a throbbing grief that after a while was only sensation. The feeling didn't go away. It stayed, personified, talking to me. It said, This is the reason to work on advanced poses, to stretch strings of flesh you never felt before. This is how the pain becomes a part of you, with an ache you carry in your body like a well-thumbed stone between your fingers. This is how you learn to feel more, to resist less, to cultivate your senses so you detect so much, smell it and see it and hear it, so much so that the world itself starts to ring, and you realize that as much as you feel every cell in your throbbing hamstring, your senses have become tuned to experience the world in the finest detail, and that world is luminous and alive. This is where you understand that Iyengar's supposition is correct, that the "fluctuations of consciousness" really do reside in the flesh, and when each and every cell quits its constant irritating quivering and joins in with a pulsing inside your body, your consciousness stops quivering too.

After, I did savasana, with a cloth over my eyes to block the light. I thought of one of Iyengar's phrases: *When you still the flickering eyes, you still the consciousness.* I concentrated on relaxing the muscles in my eye sockets, and then on resisting the wandering, circling motion of my eyes behind their lids. When my eyes got very still, the roof sounds got very loud. And the pulsing of each of the cells of my body, in concert, got loud again too, and then the world outside began to reverberate with the same sound, a single thrum that was kites and plates and wind. And I knew that I was asleep and I was not asleep.

And with my eyes closed I saw the blue of the sky sheet out into two dimensions and split into striations of blue and beige. The beige was my flesh, and the strips of blue whirled like banners in wind. My body lost form. Sinuous, it threaded inside the banners, flying to the sound of a rhythmic, musical bass. I merged with the sky and the sky merged with me. And I wondered what exhilarating thing this was. And *whoosh*. It was over. And I was awake again. And I knew that for a second I had collapsed inside of something outside me. I knew that I had been a part of something greater than I was, and whatever it was, it felt like bliss.

Chapter Twenty-Four

There was a story my mother told me once when I was a girl, about how when she was growing up in Maine she got so angry at my grandmaman that she ran away from home. She convinced a cousin to come, and they went to a nearby lake. There, they found a boat, and they rowed out to an island. They wandered around in mist until they found a soft patch of dirt beneath a tree, and they spent the night there, huddling together. When it got too cold, they walked three towns away to an aunt's house. She found them on her doorstep when she got up: two little girls, shivering, cold, and scared.

Whenever I thought about that story later, I imagined the island as enchanted, its mist heavenly. Small shining beacons winked at my mother and her cousin from the sky, telling them, *Yes, make the break.* This story was so dear to me that I never dared ask my mother to repeat it, lest she tell it differently from how I remembered it. In fact, I was never sure I remembered it right. But it didn't matter to me so much whether the story was real. It had become my story, a part of me.

I began planning another trip away from the school. I had the feeling now that I, too, was setting off for a magical island. It was a path that had been trodden before. Wherever it led had already been determined, charted by the footprints of ancestors.

I left Pune. I took a train east and headed for a small community by the ocean near Sri Aurobindo's ashram, where I had heard you could rent cabins cheaply. I was looking for a place to take all the material I'd gathered in Pune and write it down. But without looking for it, I discovered on the grounds a large wooden tepeelike structure where there were yoga classes. I had no expectations. For the first class, there was a teacher named Karen Haberman. From New Jersey. The room was large and round, airy, with sunshine beaming in from a skylight and palm trees towering above. Outside, the air was dry like desert in the afternoon but wet with fog in the morning, an air that made you want to feel your skin, and remember what it was like to feel good inside your body. I had been many places on this journey that recalled my time in Santa Cruz, but this was the first that brought back the attitude of unburdened discovery I found when I got there. Whatever Karen taught, I was here to learn.

Karen was teaching the yoga of Pattabhi Jois. Jumpings. "Astanga yoga." Sun salutations linking postures. An hour of steady breathing while moving. A different practice from Iyengar's, the one Iyengar had learned from Krishnamacharya and disparaged. Karen had been with Jois in India for several years and then left his school in Mysore because she didn't trust him any longer. She had once had, and left, a guru, and in this way she was a little like me. She'd felt betrayed when she understood that her guru was not infallible, not immune from cultural chauvinisms, not a role model or stand-in for father or family — and in this way she was like me too.

Karen still revered the practice if not the messenger, though, and she taught it to me. I studied with her every day for a month. Every day I improved. Sometimes when I couldn't do a pose, I'd assume I still couldn't do it the next day, and then I'd surprise myself when I found I could. One day, Karen was pulling me up from a backbend to standing, and I noticed I was resisting her pull because I thought I wasn't capable. In that month's time my hands reached the floor backward in a difficult standing forward bend; I jumped through my arms; I stood up from a backbend. I learned new poses, ones I'd only read about in sequences that I'd never reached in *Light on Yoga*. I figured out new ways to hold my muscles to get me there.

One day, I swam in the surf. The waves were frantic and kept pummeling me into the shore. Then I figured out how to ride them so they didn't push me down into the sandy ocean bottom. There were palm-shaped fish leaping out of the water by the dozen, and as I watched them, it occurred to me that if I could learn this many things, have this many breakthroughs every day of my life, I could live forever like a child. I could discover my body anew every day, and through it discover the world around me. I could start again, remake my universe.

On my last day, Karen and I played the name game. We were from nearly the same place, after all, and we were the same age. Sure enough, her high school boyfriend had sat next to me in homeroom in high school. She remembered who I was, then. "Didn't you used to go by Liz?" she asked.

For the rest of the class, she kept slipping, calling me by my old name. *Liz*. Hearing the name brought me back to a place far in my past. This was a place to start from. I was not that old self anymore, but all the potential embodied within her still existed inside me, sheathed by an outer form that had been newly made through years of travel. I was not newly whole, I knew now, but newly flexible, newly at ease in a world of paradoxes. This was a world where you moved halfway around the globe and encountered a mentor as familiar to you as your very hometown. Meeting Karen was completing a circle. I headed back to Pune to collect my things. I was going home.

I had two days in Pune before my flight, and on the first I stopped at the institute to see Iyengar in the library for the last time. I knew what Iyengar thought of Pattabhi. I had to tell him that I'd learned Jois's Astanga Yoga. I was nauseated with fear.

The guru, as always, was pleased to see me. He sat me at his desk, slicked back his hair with both palms, and leaned back, gazing at me with lifted eyebrows. "So, my friend. You have had travels. Tell me."

Telling him required mentioning the name Pattabhi. I muttered a few things about the towns I'd passed through, a few temples I'd visited. Then, in a small voice, I told him what I'd learned from Karen. I identified her as a one-time follower of Pattabhi Jois who no longer had kind things to say about the master.

"And?" His face was open, ready for a punch. "This yoga?"

"I like it," I admitted.

"It makes you feel?"

I paused. "Good."

He kept looking at me. "How?"

"It helps you disengage the mind," I offered. "All the jumping, you're like an animal, in your body." I was careful not to say anything disparaging about Iyengar's system — in truth, if I was frustrated with Iyengar yoga it was only because I felt my teachers led me through it too slowly. But as I heard myself talking, I also noticed I didn't say anything that disparaged the Jois system. The word *focus* came out of my mouth.

"The stable mind you say?" Iyengar began, his eyes wide, his expression patient. "When you are jumping — chaturanga dandasana to urdhva mukha svanasana to adho mukha svanasana to uttanasana — do you find a scattered mind or a stable mind? You think it makes the mind stable, then please do it again. You understand each and every part of the body when you are doing jumpings? Do you remember what happens in chaturanga dandasana? Do you remember what happens in urdhva mukha svanasana? Do you know what actions take place in adho mukha svanasana? Eh?"

Iyengar was ranting. I'd never been the object of his ranting before, but he still seemed affable. He was still smiling, still drinking me in with his eyes.

"My friend, what I have done and left behind don't ask me," he went on. "If you want to substantiate what Pattabhi says, go ahead but don't ask me." His eyes flashed angrily now. *That man.* "I did it like him for years with my guruji. Realizing the ill effect of it, I said good-bye.

"If you do adho mukha svanasana for ten minutes, with me, yes or no do you penetrate, go deep? With jumpings? Can you go deep?"

Now his voice was a shout, and I remembered the strength of the monsoon downpour when it rattled these library windows almost two years back. It occurred to me that his voice, just now, was creating as powerful a rattle as the rain once did. "With me you stay ten minutes in paschimottanasana. You misunderstand what is strength. The mental part is not needed for jumpings. Here mental part is needed. But these things I have to say? Jumping is brainwashing. You move, jump from position to position so it's exhilarating. Why should I culture the mind? The mind has nothing to think of. Are mind and body connected when you jump? Why do you want only physical? Why do you want to walk only in the physical body? Do you think in jumpings they will give you that idea that the energy of each atom is living there?"

I was nodding my head, nervously writing down his words, agreeing, and not agreeing, because to me the practice felt transcendent in its own way, too, if different. Same. Different.

"Why don't you answer me?" he bellowed now. "Why do jumpings, number one? So that the body may become a little more vibrant. But that is not the end. Then the spirit is the end. There is the spirit in all the poses. Our system is twenty minutes, thirty minutes, fifty minutes. Then what path are you to take?"

His eyes bore into mine as I pondered the question, and finally I had to speak: "I don't know, Guruji. I don't know."

The next day, I went to practice for the last time. I knew I'd been reprimanded, knew how easy it would be to hide my face. I had to go back.

Iyengar was there in the studio, alongside Geeta, Prashant, Pandu, the students in their requisite twisting and stretching and bending poses, their strapped-together and hanging permutations.

The day before, Iyengar had challenged me to discover the point of holding poses for long stretches, to reject the easy thrill of the kinetic Jois ones, so I decided to spend the two hours holding six poses for twenty minutes each. I didn't get far though. I rose into a headstand and heard Iyengar lecturing. Those familiar words rang: *Pattabhi. That man.*

Then, though I couldn't see from my headstand position, I heard him beckoning: "You! The jumpings that you like. Do! You!" He tapped me. "Uttanasana, start!"

I came down from the headstand and began a sun salutation, breathing slowly.

"Chaturanga dandasana!" he shouted.

Students gathered around me. Geeta was watching from the ground nearby, holding herself up by elbows that rested on a bolster. "The jumpings Guruji was doing in 1939!" she yelled. "You have seen the video?" She was referring to the film made with funds from the maharaja in Mysore. I had seen it. "He was doing better than anyone! Jumping with both legs to the side, jumping to Vasisthasana! No one did better than Guruji. You have seen?"

Iyengar barked out orders: "Urdhva mukha svanasana! Chaturanga dandasana!"

I followed. *Jump. Jump.*

"You see the collarbones?" he asked the students. "Are they openly across? Tadasana! Are the feet even? Uttanasana!"

Jump. Jump.

"Tell me. The breathing is heavy or the breathing is light?"

Jump. I was winded.

"Why are they doing third-rate yoga when first-rate is available? Tell me. Tell me, why? You like the jumpings? Chaturanga!" Now Iyengar came over to me and peered into my face. His eyes were clear and alive. "Now bakasana," he continued. The test was relentless. This was a difficult balancing posture included in the Jois sequence. I fumbled as I tried to remember its foot arrangement, but he nodded. I'd gotten it right. "You see," he addressed the students, "is she working from the organs? You do like this you will have heavy menstrual bleeding. But still they do. Third-class yoga. Don't come to me when you are paining. Now straighten the arm from the triceps muscles. Yes. Now the organs are they lifting up or falling down? Yes. Up. Good."

In spite of himself, Iyengar was teaching me now, teaching me to do what he objected to, but to do it better. It was strangely kindhearted. Finally he let me go.

I went back to my long headstand, but soon I noticed that

Iyengar had chosen another Westerner on whom to demonstrate. "Headstand!" he commanded.

The Brit took the pose, wobbling slightly under the pressure.

"Every day for six months he comes, has he learned one thing, tell me? One thing. Or does he come for the ego? He is all ego this man," Iyengar began berating him.

I came down to watch along with the rest of the students, and now noticed that throughout the diatribe the guru's eyes kept wandering to mine. When he met them, he lingered, and I let myself get lost there. I still didn't sense his anger. I felt his love.

And then, finally, I took my last pose, forward bend. The studio gossip chattered on as I kept my head buried in my shins.

Soon, I felt the floor vibrate next to me. Suddenly there was something hard on either side of my rib cage. It was Iyengar's shins, bony and dry-skinned. He was straddling me. "Forward!" he shouted, pulling my torso with a strong shove. It carried the heat of his anger. And then he stalked off, his weight in his heels, his steps making the windows vibrate. Then the feet returned. Another shove. "Her name is paschimottanasana," he muttered now.

Pose of the West. *Her name is Pose of the West.* But paschimottanasana was also known as "powerful pose." Formidable. A pose where I once felt spineless.

After, one of Geeta's assistants told me shruggingly that she figured Iyengar's feelings had been hurt. "It's as if you'd told him you danced with another guy, and liked it."

What a silly metaphor, I thought to myself. And yet I knew, somehow, that Iyengar had forgiven me. If I was Pose of the West to him, I'd always been Pose of the West to him. My small betrayal, I suspected, had been excused.

That night, I had another dream about Iyengar. This time, he was a young man. I asked him if he was an impostor. He didn't answer, but repeated his diatribe against Pattabhi Jois. It was a bad system, he said. His own was better.

"See my body; feel my body," he ordered me then. He reached for my hand and pulled it to him, then rested it on his stomach.

I had one more dream about Iyengar when I reached the States. This time, I was on the same bridge that he had led me to in the dream from several months before, on the same open pond. But instead of standing on that bridge immobile, I jumped off. I swam to the bottom of the pond, and there I lay, in savasana. The corpse. And I thought I would like to die. I heard a voice telling me that I would certainly choose to come back up, but I responded to that voice that I wouldn't. Then my body started swimming upward anyway. It lifted up through brilliant blue water. It charged upward. When it pierced the surface, the sky was a shimmering white.

Acknowledgments

This book was an epic undertaking in many senses, and I am indebted to many figures who shepherded it along for brief and extended legs of the journey. I am especially grateful to my agent, Henry Dunow, who saw the potential before there was a plane ticket and held fast to the course through countless drafts and side trips. Thanks also to Melanie Thernstrom, who sat through a deluge of historic proportions one night in Laguna Beach to listen to this story and convince me to write it. I also thank my other co-horts and mentors in the writing program at UC Irvine, especially Michelle Latiolais for her support and J. Brian Schwartz for his boundless brilliance and goodwill. I would never have under-stood the place for a literary treatment of yoga without the en-couragement and wisdom of several writer-yogis who invested their time and attention, including Regan Good, Christopher Beach, Valerie Ross, Valerie Jeremijenko, and Danielle Müller. I am also blessed with a small cabal of coconspirator writers who were unspeakably generous with their editorial attention and direction, among them Dale Maharidge, Wendy Riss, Julian Rubinstein, Jesse Upton, S. Kirk Walsh, and Josh Weil. Thanks go to my editor, Deborah Baker, for her numinous guidance, and to several other mentors who took me to the foot of the path and pointed me forward. These include my yoga teachers Manouso Manos, Gloria Goldberg, Karin O'Bannon, and Lisa Walford, and most especially the inimitable B. K. S. Iyengar. In India, my tutelage with the large-minded, big-hearted Sanskrit scholar S. S. Bahulkar brought unforgettable insight, and I am also grateful to the Fulbright staff in Delhi and Madras and especially Subash Chawla. Along with Fulbright/USEFI, a long list of institutions provided support at many junctures, including Krishnamurti Foundation in India and, in the U.S., Ucross Foundation, Thurber House, Virginia Center for the Creative Arts, Ragdale Foundation, and the Wertheim Study at the New York Public Library. Several authors whose works provided important background are not credited in the text, including Arjun Appadurai, Wendy Doniger, David Gordon White, Christophe Jaffrelot, Lise McKean, and Peter Washington. Most important, there are two people whose creative spirit is too vast to be encompassed in a single explanation for their role in the exploration and discovery that went into this book. They are my mother, Michele McKee; and Paul Weinfield, to whom this book is dedicated.

About the Author

A graduate of the fiction workshop at UC Irvine, Elizabeth Kadetsky has published work in *Gettysburg Review, Santa Monica Review, Natural Bridge, Red Rock Review, Greensboro Review, Cream City Review, Southeast Review, Faultline,* and elsewhere. She has received several literary fellowships and awards, and was a Fulbright grantee to India in creative writing in 1999–2000.

Kadetsky also attended the University of California at Santa Cruz and the Graduate School of Journalism at Columbia University, where she is now an Associate teaching a yearly course on immigration as well as reporting and writing. She previously worked as a correspondent from Mexico and Central America for the *Village Voice, LA Weekly, Ms.,* and *The Nation.* Her reporting on immigration, labor, and women's issues has appeared in *Glamour, Self,* and many other publications.

She lives in the East Village in New York City.